The Muslim Theology of Ḥuzn

Islamic Studies at Gerlach Press

Colin Turner
The Qur'an Revealed: A Critical Analysis of Said Nursi's Epistles of Light. *With a Foreword by Dale F. Eickelman*
ISBN 9783940924285, 2013

Aziz Al-Azmeh
The Arabs and Islam in Late Antiquity: A Critique of Approaches to Arabic Sources [Series: Theories and Paradigms of Islamic Studies]
ISBN 9783940924421, 2014

Sadik J. al-Azm
On Fundamentalisms
ISBN 9783940924223, 2014

Sadik J. al-Azm
Islam – Submission and Disobedience
ISBN 9783940924247, 2014

Sadik J. al-Azm
Is Islam Secularizable? Challenging Political and Religious Taboos
ISBN 9783940924261, 2014

Sadik J. al-Azm
Critique of Religious Thought. First English Translation of Naqd al-fikr ad-dini. With a New Introduction by the Author
ISBN 978394092444, 2014

Carool Kersten (ed.)
The Caliphate and Islamic Statehood – Formation, Fragmentation and Modern Interpretations (3 volumes)
ISBN 9783940924520, 2015

Nasrin Rouzati
Trial and Tribulation in the Qur'an. A Mystical Theodicy.
With a Foreword by Colin Turner
ISBN 9783940924544, 2015

Ester Peskes (ed.)
Wahhabism - Doctrine and Development (Critical Surveys in Islamic Denominations Series (2 volumes)
ISBN 9783940924506, 2016

Muhammad Shahrour
Islam and Humanity: Consequences of a Contemporary Reading. First Authorized English Translation of *Al-Islam wa-l-insan* by George Stergios. *With a Foreword by Dale F. Eickelman*
ISBN 9783959940184, 2017

Seyfeddin Kara
In Search of Ali ibn Abi Talib's Codex: History and Traditions of the Earliest Copy of the Qur'an.
With a Foreword by James Piscatori
ISBN 9783959940542, 2018

Mahshid Turner
The Muslim Theology of Huzn: Sorrow Unravelled
With a Foreword by Alparslan Açıkgenç
ISBN 9783959940405, 2018

Carool Kersten (ed.)
The Fatwa as an Islamic Legal Instrument: Concept, Historical Role, Contemporary Relevance (2 Volumes)
ISBN 9783959940207, 2018

Mohsen Mirmehdi
Systematische Theologie des Korans. Systematic Theology of Qur'an.
(*Text in German with English Summary)*
ISBN 9783959940443, 2018

Nadia Duvall
Islamist Occidentalism: Sayyid Qutb and the Western Other
ISBN 9783959940627, 2018

Sadik J. al-Azm
Occidentalism, Conspiracy and Taboo. Collected Essays 2014-2016
ISBN 9783959940467, 2018

Abdel-Hakim Ourghi
Reform of Islam. Forty Theses
ISBN 9783959940566, 2018

Imène Ajala
European Muslims and their Foreign Policy Interests: Identities and Loyalties (Islam and International Relations Series, Vol. 1)
ISBN 9783959940603, 2018

Mustafa Shah (ed.)
Islamic Theological Discourses and the Legacy of Kalam. Gestation, Movements and Controversies (3 volumes)
ISBN 9783959940481, 2018

www.gerlach-press.de

Mahshid Turner

The Muslim Theology of Ḥuzn

Sorrow Unravelled

With a Foreword by Alparslan Açıkgenç

GerlachPress

First published 2018
by Gerlach Press
Berlin, Germany
www.gerlach-press.de

Cover Design: Frauke Schön, Hamburg
Set by Anne Jeschke, Gerlach Press
Printed and bound in Germany

British Library Cataloguing in Publication Data.
A catalogue record for this book is available from the British Library.

Bibliographic data available from Deutsche Nationalbibliothek
http://d-nb.info/113643531X

ISBN: 978-3-95994-040-5 (hardcover)
ISBN: 978-3-95994-041-2 (eBook)

Contents

Foreword

In a well-known hadith, the Prophet Muhammad is reported to have stated that *"Islam began as a stranger and will return as it began, as a stranger; and blessed are the strangers."* The word for "strange" in Arabic is *gharīb*, a word which connotes a feeling of sorrow in the spiritual sense. It connotes the feeling of loneliness, of being away from ones loved ones, albeit temporarily. The spiritual element of the emotions is largely missing in the psychological literature. In her investigation into *ḥuzn*, an emotion that receives considerable attention in the Islamic sources, Dr Mahshid Turner has produced a work of pioneering status. This work is not concerned only with the nature of this emotion as such; it is concerned also with the significance and ontology of sorrow, a feature which adds to the value of this work, rendering it very useful for the psychology and theology of *ḥuzn*.

Human nature has been defined variously by philosophers and other thinkers, but the most widely circulated definition, if not the most widely accepted one, is based on "rationality", as in the Arabic term "*haywan al-nâtiq*" or 'rational animal'. Since the time of Aristotle this definition has been adopted by many thinkers, but it is also contested by another idea which says that without emotions, the rational man is nothing more than a robot-like animal. Therefore, what makes us human beings is our emotions, and the existential circumstances which render our life meaningful in many instances. By making such a statement, these thinkers, many of whom, such as Kierkegaard, are existentialists, do not mean that all of the emotions are necessarily desired. However, emotions such as anxiety, pathos, pleasure, boredom, ecstasy, grief, empathy and a host of others help us build a passionate relationship with the truth which is in this sense *only* subjective. If we follow the ontology of emotions, and thus of *ḥuzn*, we may express it as the path of "truth". How can we justify the feeling of sadness leading to "truth", or building a passionate relationship with the truth? We need to inquire briefly into the nature of *ḥuzn* in this sense in order to find an answer to this question.

Traditional description of sadness associated with the loss of loved ones or with other painful circumstances can be considered as "material sorrow". This is distinguished from sadness without a cause or, indeed, sorrow whose cause cannot be described. I would say that we may still describe the second category as "psychological sorrow", the causes of which may still be certain physical effects of the body or possibly certain environmental circumstances leading to sadness. We thus distinguish this from what we may call "spiritual sorrow" which cannot be associated with any apparent material cause. This is the one that is to be emphasized in this context and the rest of the categories of sadness are to be avoided.

Mahshid Turner has utilized all of those works in the Islamic literature, such as those of al-Kindi and Ibn Sina, which try to explain how to avoid such sadness. Indeed, as the reader will see in Chapter One, many Quranic verses are cited which refer to the actual reason for sadness and how to avoid it. Most of the verses cited in this work indicate that unbelief leads to a feeling of loneliness because such a wretched person psychologically feels *alone* in this world even though he or she is physically present among so many people. This feeling of loneliness throws him or her into a state which is not easy to explain. The Quran uses the term *ḥuzn* for this kind of state. The concept of (Divine) "ownership" comes into the fore at this point, and this is evaluated by the author in connection with thinkers such as al-Kindi, Miskawayhi, Ṭabāṭabā'ī and Nursi. According to this state of mind a believing person passionately feels that s/he *owns* nothing; all his or her possessions, including the body, the soul and all the worldly properties, actually belong to God. These are all entrusted to the person temporarily to see whether the person will utilize these for good or for evil. In this state what belongs truly to the person is self-consciousness; the feeling that the person is in fact an existing independent individual bestowed with certain responsibilities as a result of accepting this "trust" (*amana*). In the face of these possessions the person is so powerless and impotent that when even the slightest physical inability comes, the person cannot dispel it. If I cannot control my brain, my stomach and any of my organs how can I claim ownership over them? Realising their true owner gets rid of this negative feeling of sadness. It is for this reason that belief is defined by Nursi as "realisation of the true owner" (Nursi, *Mektubat*, "Yirminci Mektup").

I believe that this pioneering work will open a new horizon to research more deeply into the nature of this and similar emotions in order to uncover those spiritual aspects which are positive and beneficial for humanity. This kind of approach to human nature reminds us of our true selves. There is no doubt that Turner's work is a comprehensive examination of only one emotion, but one that is multi-dimensional. She has examined the emotion of *ḥuzn* chiefly from the perspective of the modern Muslim scholar, Said Nursi, but without neglecting a Quranic typology and the study of the interpretations of *ḥuzn* by a number of key Quranic exegetes and Muslim philosophers from the traditions of *kalam* and *tasawwuf*.

There is no study of this concept that approaches the subject as this study does, namely from a multi-disciplinary perspective that spans psychology, philosophy and theology. I think it would not be an exaggeration to state that this work constitutes a major step forward in emotion studies. For Mahshid Turner explores in this work only one emotion in all its details, producing as a result a truly pioneering work in the field of the psychology of emotions.

Alparslan Açıkgenç Istanbul, May 2018

Acknowledgements

I am deeply indebted to the people who have supported me throughout the long but enjoyable study which has culminated in this book. I am grateful for the initial support I received from Professor Chris Cook for his guidance and advice, and to Dr. Abed Al-Zuweiri for helping me with the translation of Avicenna's original manuscript from Arabic into English. Also my appreciation and thanks goes to Professor Faris Kaya, Hakan Gülerce and other members of the Istanbul Foundation for Science and Culture for giving me the opportunity to participate in some of their conferences and workshops.

Special thanks goes to Dr. Susan Frenk, principal of St. Aidan's College, whose support has been invaluable.

I have to thank my dear husband who has not only been very understanding during this busy period of my life but has been extremely helpful in giving me much valuable advice. I also thank my children and family for being so supportive.

However, the greatest debt of thanks and appreciation goes to my supervisor, Professor Robert Song, who patiently supported me through every stage of my research. Without his encouragement and constructive criticisms I would not have been able to complete this work.

The aim of this book is to carry out a critical analysis of the work of the contemporary, twentieth century Muslim thinker Said Nursi (1876-1960). The focus of this book is on his views on the Quranic understanding of the concept of *ḥuzn*. This is the first academic work which uses Nursi's understanding of *ḥuzn* for a greater insight on this concept.

The study begins by carrying out a contextual of analysis of *ḥuzn* by researching Muslim literature on this concept and comparing it with Said Nursi's Quranic interpretation in order to obtain an in-depth understanding of the narrative on *ḥuzn*. It explores the idea that since *ḥuzn* is a universal condition, there must be a reason for its existence.

In order to obtain an in-depth understanding of the narrative on *ḥuzn* the Quran itself is the first point of reference. It begins with examining all the occurrences of the word *ḥuzn* in the Quran so that that a typology can be built for an initial Quranic narrative of this concept. This initial framework is then followed by a brief thematic analysis of this word in order to obtain a more holistic understanding of this word.

Izutsian methodology is also used for a more scientific as opposed to an atomistic or cultural approach to the understanding of this concept.

Quranic exegetes' and Muslim thinkers' understanding of *ḥuzn* from both medieval and modern periods are also compared with Nursi's understanding of this concept in order to throw further light on the reason for the existence of *ḥuzn* and the role it has to play. If indeed it does have a positive role to play then this will impact greatly on how *ḥuzn* should be viewed and treated.

1

Introduction

We created not the heavens, the earth, and all between them, merely in [idle] sport.[1]

The subject of sadness in general is vast and historically there has been no consensus as to how it should be defined and, consequently, how it should be treated. Traditionally, physicians of the classical era drew a clear distinction between sadness that was associated with the loss of loved ones or with other painful circumstances; and sadness without a cause, and consequently offered different treatments for the two categories.[2] Medieval Muslim thinkers such as Al-Kindī (800-870) and Balkhī (849-934) also followed their Greek and Roman predecessors, prescribing certain behavioural techniques to combat sadness that arose from environmental causes.[3]

Contemporary psychiatry has been criticised for largely ignoring the distinction between these two different kinds of sadness, and for focusing more on symptoms than on context. According to some critics, classification according to symptoms can lead to the wrong diagnosis since it is possible on occasion for both categories of sadness to display similar symptoms.[4]

As expressed in the Quranic verse above, nothing is created in futility, and therefore ultimately there must be a purpose for everything in existence. This book examines this idea further, arguing that since sadness is a universal condition, and bearing in mind that nothing exists without a reason, then *ḥuzn* must have a purpose too. The aim therefore is to carry out a contextual analysis of *ḥuzn* by researching Muslim literature on this concept and comparing it with Said Nursi's Quranic interpretation in order to arrive at an in-depth understanding of the narrative on *ḥuzn*, the perceived reasons for its existence and why and how, on a practical level, it is believed that it can be obviated.[5]

The Objective

As early as the ninth century, Muslim thinkers such as Abū Zayd Aḥmad ibn Sahl Balkhī (850-934) made a clear distinction between *ḥuzn* ('sadness or depression') that was due to environmental factors and *ḥuzn* that occurred for no apparent reason. Their differentiation between these two categories bears a remarkable resemblance to modern definitions of reactive depression and endogenous depression.[6] Balkhī's recommendation was that the latter should be treated both physically, with medication, and psycho-spiritually, with methods such as "music" and "pleasant conversation", and that the former, attributable to the loss of loved ones or any possessions that one values, should be addressed not with medication but with strategies of behavioural change. Since the medieval Muslim thinkers believed that the actual events in people's lives were not the real cause of reactive depression, but that the problem was down to how they interpreted their particular experiences, they devised strategies and methods for retraining the mind in order to help individuals to distinguish between what was real and what was imagined. Both medieval and modern critics have pointed to the fact that reactive depression should not be classed under the same category as major depressive disorders.[7] Horwitz and Wakefield criticize the fact that contemporary psychiatry has tended to ignore the distinction that used to be made between the two categories when it is still very much relevant today:

> Normal sadness, or sadness "with cause," was associated with experiences of loss or other painful circumstances that seemed to be the obvious causes of distress. The response to such normal reactions was to offer support, to help the individual cope and move on despite the loss, and to avoid confusing the person's sadness with illness.
>
> The other kind of condition, traditionally known as *melancholia*, or depression "without cause," was a medical disorder distinguished from normal sadness by the fact that the patient's symptoms occurred despite there being no appropriate reason for them in the patient's circumstances.[8]

According to The World Health Organization's (WHO) estimation, depression is the leading cause of disability for 15-44 year olds and is thus a huge cost to the public health budget.[9] Horwitz and Wakefield attribute the increase in depressive disorders to be due primarily to the unclear distinction between reactive and endogenous depression.[10]

Research has shown the importance of the role of faith leaders – imams, for example – as sources of support for mental health sufferers in Muslim communities, while highlighting their general lack of awareness regarding mental health and support services. However, although this research acknowledges the need for cultural and religious input, its emphasis is on raising awareness about the current psychotherapeutic model of practice, which, as discussed above, has been questioned by its critics.[11] Although the recommendation of the aforementioned research that Muslim religious leaders be made more aware of mental health issues and services is helpful, it is not adequate, since it is grounded in the current secular model.[12] Moreover, it fails to take into account the dearth of contemporary discourse on the esoteric[13] aspect of Islam and the fact that the role of imams is confined mainly to support regarding the externals of religion.[14] With the increase in the number of Muslim chaplains, whose role emphasises the importance of pastoral care,[15] there is arguably a greater need for a deeper understanding of the Muslim perspective on *ḥuzn* and how it should be treated.

This book cannot be neatly categorized as theological hermeneutics, for it is based on a study of the Quranic usage of the term *huzn* – an approach which defies disciplinary categorization. Indeed, some of the writings of philosophers such as Avicenna and al-Kindī are, on account of their focus on the nature of the 'self', often described as 'psychological' texts.[16]The eminent Persian philosopher, Mulla Sadra, describes philosophy as the journey of "the perfecting of the human soul"[17], while for al-Kindī, philosophy is merely "the knowledge of reality of things".[18] Contemporary Muslim scholars tend often to conflate theology with jurisprudence, whereas medieval Muslim thinkers recognized, quite rightly, the distinction between theology and jurisprudence, with philosophers and theologians in the classical period focusing primarily on questions such as the difference between essence and existence or issues such as Divine determining and human freewill. This book will therefore tell the story of *ḥuzn* from various disciplinary perspectives, with the primary emphasis on exegetes and philosophers, whose understanding of the topic is clearly inspired by the Islamic revelation. The lion's share of the scholarship studied here belongs to those scholars of the classical period whose approaches were in a sense what we today would describe as multi-disciplinary. Al-Kindī, for instance, is known as the father of Arab philosophy, yet his epistle on *ḥuzn* could be described quite easily as a work of psychology, dealing as it does with behavioural change.

As the concept of mental illness is a very broad one, the aim of this book is to critically examine one particular aspect of 'mental illness', namely 'sadness' (*ḥuzn*), from a Muslim perspective generally and from the perspective of Said Nursi in particular. It endeavours to determine whether sadness has a positive role to play and, if so, whether it should be treated as something that is 'normal'. It tries to understand why sadness is acknowledged as something which is both given to, and taken from, individuals by God, but yet is apparently viewed by the Quran as a negative feeling that is to be obviated whenever possible. It also questions why, if *ḥuzn* is a negative attribute, believers – prophets in particular – were not exempt from it, particularly given its link to unbelief.[19]

To this writer's knowledge, this is the only work to date which analyses the specific concept of *ḥuzn*, and which uses Izutsian methodology for the ontological study of the concept of *ḥuzn* in the Quran. In contrast with philosophical ontology, which is concerned mainly with the understanding of metaphysical concepts at an abstract level, the Izutsian methodological and analytical study of this concept allows a more concrete world view to come into view, thus leaving less potential for bias. The originality of this book also lies in the fact that no one else has written on the specific concept of *ḥuzn* as it pertains to the Quran, to Muslim exegesis, to Muslim scholarly thinking in general, and to the teachings of Said Nursi in particular.

It is hoped that these different perspectives will contribute to a greater understanding of, and research on, the subject of *ḥuzn* in general, and greater awareness of its classification and categorization in particular. It is also hoped that the study will benefit Muslim pastoral care, both conceptually and practically.

It should be noted that this book is not concerned with endogenous depression, since the Quranic meaning of *ḥuzn* connotes degrees of sadness owing to reaction to loss, and is thus linked more with environmental factors. It is hoped that this study will encourage research that is aimed at the development of approaches to the treatment of reactive depression which are based on Islamic principles. Although this book is targeted at academics and interested laypersons who wish to hear the story of *ḥuzn* and obtain a clear understanding of this concept, it will be particularly useful for practitioners and professionals interested in Muslim pastoral and practical theology.

Said Nursi and pastoral theology

While pastoral care in the Christian tradition has its roots in Christian ministry and the work of chaplains stretching back to St. Martin of Tours (316 AD)[20], no actual tradition of institutionalised Muslim chaplaincy has existed to date.[21] However, the concept of pastoral theology itself is central to the Muslim faith and is given prime importance in the Quran. Indeed, the Quran is full of examples of prophets as perfect role models to follow with regard to pastoral care (For example, Quran, 33:21; 21:107-108 and 4:36). However, true pastoral care can take place, as these verses exemplify, only if the focus on Divine unity and not ascribing partners to the one God does not become blurred. In other words, submission has to follow belief, and belief has to encompass every aspect of people's lives. Said Nursi's work mirrors this Quranic message as he attempts to look beyond the apparent in search for meaning for every encounter or event in his life. His teachings therefore fit in well into the category of practical theology and consequently he is considered by the author to serve as an excellent example of a contemporary Muslim pastoral theologian.

Forrester defines practical theology as "the theological discipline which is primarily concerned with the interaction of belief and behaviour"[22]," While Woodward and Pattison describe it as a "transformational activity" and "a kind of conversation between theory, theology and practice."[23] As I attempt to demonstrate, Said Nursi shows through his work how his initially negative views of creation were transformed by reflecting upon his own experiences and by asking questions about the nature of reality and then seeking answers from revelation. Nursi therefore did not start out with his own theories and principles; rather, these emerged from his reflections on his own life events from a Quranic perspective.

Nursi's method can therefore be described as inductive, since he looks first at the reality of things in creation and then derives general truths and principles from his observations. His approach can also be described as deductive, since his conclusions are always deducible from revelation.

Although Said Nursi's *Rīsale-ī Nur* is not, strictly speaking, a work of systematic exegesis, it is nevertheless a modern commentary and an interpretation of Quranic concepts. Turner summarises Nursi's work as:

> a sort of hermeneutical prism, catching what its author considers to be the effulgence of divine light from the Quran and refracting it as colours visible to, and understandable by, the eye of the human heart.[24]

His work therefore mirrors the major themes in the Quran, namely Divine Unity, revelation, prophethood, the hereafter, and the relationship between God and man.

Although Nursi's work is influenced by classical mystical thinkers,[25] he has his own particular didactic and literary style, and by taking the reader along with him through the journey of his personal life experiences, the reader is able to engage more with his analytic discussions on Quranic concepts such as *ḥuzn*.

Nursi's highly idiosyncratic style of writing is characterised by, *inter alia*, his extensive use of persuasive arguments and allegories and a view of the world which always proceeds from the 'self'. He does not provide *a priori* proofs as such but points to God as being both transcendent and immanent. He points to God's immanence by stressing the point that one is able to know God only through His creation. For Nursi therefore, creation is nothing more than a gallery of signs pointing to God, or a house of mirrors reflecting all of His attributes through their very being. He explains that the wretchedness of human beings and the existence of all ills in society are attributable to a misconceived interpretation of the creation – an interpretation that effectively disconnects the created realm from its Maker. Nursi encourages his readers to read the 'great book of creation' in the correct way, namely as signs which are 'Other-indicative' (*ma'nā-i ḥarfī*) rather than as things which are 'self-referential' (*ma'nā-i ismī*) and point to themselves alone[26] His use of Quranic concept pairs such as light and darkness, belief and unbelief and so on helps the reader to move beyond the surface to an understanding of transcendence, that is, by taking the reader with him through the journey of creation and pointing to the true nature of created beings as transient, ephemeral and contingent, Nursi is able to conclude that the Creator of all beings must be absolute. Nursi's work centres on the concept of Divine Unity, which is the central ontological focus of all the concepts in the Quran, including the narrative on *ḥuzn*.

Scope and Structure

Although the general concept of sadness has been discussed by certain Muslim philosophers and thinkers, there is no substantive work dedicated solely to the narrative of *ḥuzn* in the Muslim theological literature; where *ḥuzn* has been discussed, it appears only incidentally.

Mystics, in particular the Persian poet Mawlānā Jalāl al-Dīn Balkhī (1207-1273), known in the West as Rumi, have written much about the general concept of sadness, expressing this through music and poetry. Rumi was not simply a poet; nor was he in the technical sense of the word an exegete of the Quran. Nevertheless his work, especially his *Mathnawī*, is considered to be a significant literary representation of important themes in the Quran.[27] In Rumi's poetry, sadness generally, which includes the concept of *ḥuzn* as well as *balā* (divine tribulation), is considered to be a positive notion and therefore rather than be obviated, he urges that it be welcomed.[28]

Echoing the Sufi path, Nasrin Rouzati's recent *Trial and Tribulation in the Qur'an: A Mystical Theology*, a study of the notion of *bala* in the Quran, aims to dispel the popular understanding of the notion of *bala* by presenting positive aspects of Divine tribulation.[29]

Also, Abu Ḥāmid al-Ghazālī's (1058-1111 AD) book *Mīzān al-ʿAmal* (Criterion of Action) contains a short chapter entitled *Mudāwāt al-ghamm* (Remedy for Sorrow) in which he argues that sadness is due to lack of understanding and the inability to reason; he also argues that it stems from our deep attachment to the things we have become accustomed to.[30] He explains that an intelligent person would be able to realise the pointlessness of being sad about something that has happened in the past and which is no longer relevant, and as for the present, if sadness is due to jealousy such as being envious of other people's wealth and high position in life, then again this shows the person's ignorance of the fact that actually God has favoured them by not putting the heavy burden of the world on their shoulders; if only they were aware of this, he says, they would be grateful. When he relates sadness to the future, he gives the examples of old age and death, reiterating that this sadness is due to lack of understanding and the absence of trust in God's Divine decree and Determining.[31]

Ghazali's arguments regarding the futility of sadness are based for the most part on the idea that this is 'the best of all possible worlds',[32] where apparent imperfections are necessary:

> If the imperfect is not created, the perfect will not be known. If beasts had not been created, the dignity of human beings would not be evident, for the perfect and the imperfect are manifested in relation to one another. Therefore, Divine generosity and wisdom require that Creation includes both perfect and imperfect.[33]

It is not deemed necessary to provide a separate account of Sufi ideas of this concept, firstly because there is very little literature on their specific understanding of *ḥuzn*, and secondly, Nursi's work is inspired by the same classical Sufi ideas such as those of Ghazali and Rumi and therefore can be described as a Sufi path that obviates the need for a *murshid-murīd* relationship. Nursi's work can be described as a modern manifestation of classical Sufism, offering not only a 'safer' route[34] but also a more detailed and practical methodology, with the *Risale* itself taking the place of the *murshid* and leading the reader safely and securely towards the gnosis of God.

This book will therefore concentrate mainly on works which have been dedicated specifically to the concept of *ḥuzn*. The problem of defining and categorizing sadness has been mainly due to the inability or unwillingness to disambiguate the different degrees, states and kinds of 'sadness' and it is therefore hoped that by narrowing down the general concept of sadness to the specific meaning of *ḥuzn*, a clearer understanding of this concept will reveal itself.

The book comprises seven chapters. Chapter One is the introduction to the whole thesis. Chapter Two is divided into two parts. The first part builds a typology of some of the occurrences of the word *ḥuzn* in the Quran in order to examine the notion of sadness and its cognate concepts from a purely scriptural perspective. The verses which relate directly to the kind of people who will not have *ḥuzn* are grouped together in order to produce a picture of the 'type' of people who are able to avoid *ḥuzn*. The rest of the verses which mention the word *ḥuzn* are then classified thematically. A thematic analysis enables an holistic approach rather than a narrow or literal understanding of the concept by considering the meaning of other verses in which the word *ḥuzn* is used, thus allowing the Quran to interpret itself (*tafsīr al-Quran bīl-Quran*). The typology and thematic analysis provide an appropriate background for a comparison of the notion of *ḥuzn* with the interpretation of the concept as formulated by Muslim exegetes, philosophers and speculative theologians.

The second part of Chapter Two focuses on the semantic field of the word *ḥuzn*. To this end, the method pioneered by Toshihiko Izutsu has been used to consider terms which are closely linked to this concept in order to obtain a contextual meaning of *ḥuzn* rather than an atomistic one. [35] The Izutsian semantic analysis is arguably conducive to a more scientific approach to the meaning of concepts such as *ḥuzn* in the Quran. Izutsu's method purports to decrease the possibility of the analyst's imposition of his or her own historical, cultural or political consciousness on the text, thus allowing the story of *ḥuzn* to unfold more organically in accordance to the general *Weltanschauung* of the Quranic text. The analysis has been carried out by gathering together all the verses where this concept is mentioned in order to compare them with each other as well as with other synonyms and antonyms of the word, in order to better understand this concept beyond its basic meaning. A detailed description and discussion of the Izutsian method and analysis has been given in Chapter Two.

Chapter Three focuses on a selection of Shiite and Sunni works of exegesis from the classical and modern periods in an attempt to explore how exegetes have understood the Quranic approach to *ḥuzn*. Some of the verses which relate to the obviation of *ḥuzn* have been grouped together while others have been categorized thematically. Although most exegetes tend to be cautious with regard to the interpretation of the Quran and thus deal mainly with its exoteric meanings, focusing on a detailed explanation of the text rather than delving deeply into the esoteric dimension,[36] it is envisaged that their interpretation will serve, to an extent, as supporting information for the general study of the concept of *ḥuzn*. As well as original sources, on-line sources and DVDs have been used to achieve more rapid access to the works of the exegetes in question. The dates of access to these are mentioned only in the first reference in order to avoid repetition.

The focus of Chapter Four is on Muslim thinkers who have written about the concept of *ḥuzn*. Abū Yūsuf Ya'qūb b.Ishāq al-Kindī is the main thinker analysed, and his work, 'On the Device for Dispelling Sorrows' (*Risāla Ya'qūb b. Isḥāq al-Kindī fī al-ḥīla lī-daf' al-aḥzān*) has been compared with works of a selection of other Muslim thinkers who have written specifically on the subject of *ḥuzn*. Al-Kindī's notion of *ḥuzn* is then compared with the Quranic narrative discussed in the typology in Chapter Two; with the exegetes' interpretation of *ḥuzn* in Chapter Three; and later with Said Nursi's definition and understanding of this concept in Chapter Six. This epistle is al-Kīndī's only extant work on ethics. It is written in the form of a letter of response to a request from a friend on how to dispel sorrow. The reason al-Kindī has been chosen for this study is that he is the first Muslim philosopher to write a comprehensive treatise specifically on the subject of *ḥuzn*. In this treatise he defines the meaning of *ḥuzn*; explains why it is totally negative and must be eliminated; and then offers important precepts, principles and practical devices – ten in all – for its obviation. This epistle is considered to be one of the earliest contributions to psychotherapy as it focuses specifically on the nature of *ḥuzn*, which it defines as:

> "Psychological pain [*alam nafsānī*] [literally meaning sickness of the soul], occurring due to the loss of an object of love or the missing of things desired."[37]

Al-Kindī's solution for the obviation of *ḥuzn* is not to be sought in medical treatment; rather, he recommends a more practical approach through self-training and change of habitual behaviour.

Chapter Five serves as a bridging chapter to Chapter Six and consists of a brief account of Said Nursi's life and works. The *Risāle-ī Nur*, apart from being an interpretation of the Quran, doubles in a sense as a spiritual biography in which Nursi reflects on his life experiences, many of which were tinged with *ḥuzn*. It is important to present a brief historical background to Nursi's life and works in order to provide a contextual backdrop for Chapter Six, which examines in greater depth the narrative of Nursi's life and how his own experience of *ḥuzn* may have influenced his writings.

Chapter Six examines Nursi's methods and approach in his understanding of *ḥuzn*. In this chapter, instances of the use of the word *ḥuzn* in various parts of the *Risāle* is subjected to the same kind of Izutsian analysis that was used in the chapter on the Quran. The aim is to move beyond the basic meaning of the word by examining its relationship with other concepts such as happiness. Since the concept of *ḥuzn* is closely related to *balā* (Divine tribulation) the question of theodicy will also be discussed in this chapter in order to examine how hardships experienced in life are viewed from a Nursian perspective.

According to Rumi, since suffering is inflicted by God, it must be positive; one should not attempt to flee from it since it offers the potential for one to abandon the 'self' and find union with God.[38] Sufi understanding of *ḥuzn* therefore is expressed only in positive terms and emphasizes the fact that sorrow is a mercy from God and should therefore be welcomed:

> There is an animal called the porcupine that becomes large and fat if you beat it with a stick. The more you beat it, the more it thrives, growing fat on the blows of the stick. The believer's spirit is in truth a porcupine, for the blows of suffering make it large and fat. That is why the suffering and tribulation inflicted upon the prophets is greater than that inflicted upon all the world's creatures.[39]

Nursi adopts the use of Quranic concept pairs such as belief (*īmān*) and unbelief (*kufr*) in his work. However, although in the Quran the concept of *ḥuzn* is not defined explicitly in binary terms, Nursi starts out by offering two definitions for *ḥuzn*, one apparently positive and the other apparently negative:

> And sadness is of two sorts. It is either a dark sorrow arising from the lack of friends, that is, having no friends or owner,[40] which is the sorrow produced by the literature of civilization, which is stained by misguidance, enamoured of nature, tainted by heedlessness…

Or it is the second sorrow. This arises from the separation of friends, that is, the friends exist, but their absence causes a yearning sorrow. This is the guidance-giving, light-scattering sorrow which the Quran produces.[41]

Nursi's binary definition of both *ḥuzn* and happiness has a whole series of ramifications which also accord with his use of other concept pairs in his writings.

The final Chapter summarizes the findings and then suggests how it can contribute to a greater understanding of Muslim perspectives on this most important phenomenon, *ḥuzn*.

2

Quranic Narratives on *ḥuzn*

Part One: A typology and thematic analysis of *ḥuzn*

This chapter looks at the Quran in an attempt to explore its approach to *ḥuzn* (sadness) and how it posits its obviation. The Quranic understanding of the word *ḥuzn* will serve as a valuable comparison with Said Nursi's understanding of the term in Chapter Six.

According to Nursi, the most appropriate cure for the problems of the age is to be found in belief, and the only way to progress, felicity and salvation, he claims, lies in following the criteria of the Quran.[1] In fact the whole of Nursi's *Risale-i Nur* mirrors the five major themes in the Quran, namely, Divine unity, revelation, prophethood, the hereafter, and the relationship between God and man.[2] This Chapter focuses on Nursi's source of inspiration, the Quran.

A typology of some of the occurrences of the word *ḥuzn* in the Quran is constructed in order to explore the notion of 'sadness' and its cognate concepts from a scriptural perspective. [3] The typology is followed by a brief thematic categorization of the rest of the verses containing the word *ḥuzn*. More detail of what a thematic categorization entails is given in the introduction. The Izutsian approach is not used in Part One of this chapter; reference is made only to the narrative in the Quran in order to provide a general, scripturally-mediated understanding of the term.

It is in Part Two of this chapter that a detailed explanation of the Izutsian approach and the rationale behind its use is given.

As the aim of this chapter is to obtain insights into the Quranic approach to *ḥuzn*, the main references are from the Quran itself. The on-line Quran translations of Yusuf Ali, Pickthall, Sahih International, Shakir, Muhammed Sarwar and Mohsin Khan are used for easy reference.[4] While all translations apply the necessary techniques to reach as wide an audience as possible, they cannot convey the full understanding of the Arabic, or, to put it more precisely, the Quranic meaning. That is because Quranic discourse has its own complex and unique features with regard to syntax, semantics, phonetics and so on; it is totally distinct from other types of Arabic prose and cannot be replicated adequately in any language other than Arabic. Therefore, for the purposes of this chapter the Arabic text itself is the first subject of analysis.

There are forty-two verses in the Quran in which the word *ḥuzn* and its derivatives are mentioned. Of these, twenty-six were revealed in Mecca and sixteen in Medina. The significance of the Mecca-Medina split with regard to verses containing the term *ḥuzn* is also explored.

All of the verses which relate directly to the kind of people who will not be visited with *ḥuzn* (sadness) have been grouped together in order for us to obtain a picture of the 'type' of people who are able to avoid such suffering. A table is also provided for easy reference. The rest of the verses are grouped according to themes. The typology and the Izutsian semantic analysis is examined in accordance with these two categories. It must be stressed, however, that these verses do not fall neatly into any particular theme, as there is considerable thematic overlap between them. Nevertheless, a thematic analysis provides another useful tool for a broader understanding of the concept of *ḥuzn.*

The Quran is the criterion against which all sources are ultimately judged; consequently, as Mutahhari opines, any sayings of the Prophet or exegetical findings that go blatantly against the teachings of the Quran should not be accepted.[5] Thus the main source for obtaining an interpretation of the Quran is the Quran itself. But in order to get closer to understanding the full meaning of a verse or concept it is important that the verses should not be taken out of context; rather, they are to be studied as part of an integrated and unified whole, owing to the fact that certain verses explain other verses, or, to put it in another way, every verse at the microcosmic level is linked to the macrocosm of the whole Quran.

A thematic approach not only enables a verse to be examined but also allows its relationship with other verses sharing similar themes to be taken into consideration. In other words, the Quran is explained by the Quran itself (*tafsir al-Quran bi'l-Quran*). The aim is to try to obtain a Quranic understanding of any issue related to human life or the workings of the cosmos by identifying all the verses related to the topic or theme in question in order to capture a fuller picture of the overall meaning. There are many verses in the Quran which, when studied in isolation, give a totally different meaning, or even appear to contradict one another, if not seen in the light of other verses which deal with the same subject or theme.[6] The advantage of applying the process of thematic interpretation or, as Wadud terms it, 'a holistic intra-Quranic interpretation', is that the interpreter is required to prioritise 'universals' rather than 'particulars', with the result that she/he is less likely to run the risk of ending up with 'narrow and inflexible laws' as can often be found in the methodology of jurisprudence.[7] However, although the advantage of this method is that the aim of the exegete is to understand a particular verse without any preconceived ideas in order to find the answers in the

Quran itself, whether the method is conducive to yielding totally neutral or passive stance is clearly open to question.

The Izutsian and thematic methods adopted for this chapter provide a useful tool for understanding concepts such as *ḥuzn* in the Quran. This synthetic approach reduces the risk of imposing human experience on the Quran by synthesising verses and their meanings into a composite view, with the aim of achieving the unification of the human experiential aspect with the Quran.

Typology of the word ḥuzn

In Part One of this chapter a typology of *ḥuzn* is constructed in order to obtain a general understanding of the concept. The Izutsian method is not used here as the aim is to uncover the overarching 'story' of *ḥuzn* in the Quran. All of the verses which explain how *ḥuzn* can be obviated are classified together and the rest of the verses are grouped together in accordance with their themes.

Criteria for the obviation of ḥuzn

According to the Quran, the key to avoiding *ḥuzn* is accepting that there is only one God and not associating any partners with Him. The emphasis is on believers who turn in worship to one Lord only and, by remaining firmly on that path, link all events, whether desirable or undesirable, to the Creator of the Universe. Verse 46:13 stresses the importance of accepting only one Lord (*rabb*) and not straying from that path, thus indicating that it is deviation from belief in one God which results in dependence on other things or people, with the resultant effect of causing *ḥuzn*.

> *Verily those who say, "Our Lord is God," and remain firm (on that path), – on them shall be no fear, nor shall they grieve [yaḥzanūna].*[8]

The fact that belief in one God is followed by belief in the Last Day suggests that belief in the Last Day is a necessary corollary of true belief (*īmān*). Verse 29:64 explains the reality of life on earth, which is in fact a temporary abode and hence only a period of preparation for the next world, which is the 'real' home. This indicates that unlike this world, which is a transient realm of trials and tests, the next world is everlasting.

> *What is the life of this world but amusement and play? But verily the Home in the Hereafter, that is life indeed, if they but knew.*[9]

But in order not to have *ḥuzn*, it appears that merely belief in one God and the Last Day is not enough. Submission (*īslām*), which is also seen as a necessary corollary of true belief, must follow. This submission means following Divine guidance in order to carry out one's responsibilities. And the means of this guidance are the signs in creation (*āyāt takwīnī*) as well as the Quran and the Prophets.[10] According to the verse below, submission includes carrying out 'acts of righteousness', 'regular prayers' and 'giving charity'. But just as faith alone is not deemed to be true faith if it comes without righteous deeds, submission without faith is also not acceptable. Therefore belief (*īmān*) and submission (*islām*) cannot be separated.[11]

> *Those who believe, and do deeds of righteousness, and establish regular prayers and regular charity, will have their reward with their Lord: on them shall be no fear, nor shall they grieve [yaḥzanūn].*[12]

The emphasis is on fulfilling the above criteria of belief completely and with total sincerity. Therefore not just Muslims, but Christians, Jews and Sabians – indeed, anyone who follows the above criteria – will also not have cause for fear or grief:

> *Nay-whoever submits His whole self to God and is a doer of good-He will get his reward with his Lord; on such shall be no fear, nor shall they grieve [yaḥzanūn].*[13]

> *Those who believe (in the Qur'an), and those who follow the Jewish (scriptures), and the Christians and the Sabians,- any who believe in Allah and the Last Day, and work righteousness, shall have their reward with their Lord; on them shall be no fear, nor shall they grieve [yaḥzanūn].*[14]

Believing in one God also means focusing on the 'Other' rather than the 'self' through total trust and submission. For belief and righteous acts can be sincere only if they are carried out for, and in the name of, God, rather than for one's own material or worldly benefit. Among those who reach this self-less state and who will not be affected by fear or grief (*ḥuzn*) are: 'the friends (*awlīyā*) of God'[15]; the 'companions of the Garden' (*ashāb al-janna*)[16]; God's 'devotees'[17] (*'ibād*, meaning servants of God, that is those who worship only one Lord)[18]; the 'righteous' (those who have *taqwā*); those who are slain in God's way (*qutilū fī sabīlīllāh*)[19]; and those who spend their substance/wealth (*amwāl*) in the cause of Allah.[20]

In Quran 8:29 it is clarified that without belief it is impossible to judge between right and wrong since if the criterion is not based on the Divine it will be based on one's own desires and fancies, which will ultimately lead to one's destruction. Therefore, in order to be given a criterion by which to judge between right and wrong, firstly one must have belief and secondly one must have *taqwā* (translated here as having 'fear of God').[21] Therefore belief (*īmān*) and being in a state of righteousness – that is, having *taqwā* – come as a result of following the right criterion, namely the Quran and the

Prophet's *sunna*. This criterion is seen as a gift from God and an opportunity for self-reform, and those who take heed will not experience *ḥuzn*.

> *O ye Children of Adam! Whenever there come to you Apostles from amongst you, rehearsing My signs unto you – those who are righteous ['ataqa – from taqwā] and mend [aṣlaḥa] their lives on them shall be no fear [khawf] nor shall they grieve [yaḥzanūn].*[22]

> *We send the apostles only to give good news and to warn: so those who believe [āmana] and mend [aṣlaḥa] their lives, upon them shall be no fear [khawf], nor shall they grieve [yahzanūn].*[23]

The criterion for the obviation of sadness is summarized in Table 1 below.

Table 1: People who will not have *ḥuzn*

No.	People who will not have *ḥuzn* ('sadness')	No. of chapter and verse in the Quran	The derivative of *ḥ-z-n*
1	Those who follow guidance	2:38 Med.	*lā hum* ***yaḥzanūn*** – nor shall they grieve
2	Those who are true in faith	3:139 Med.	*lā* ***taḥzanū*** – nor fall into despair
3	Those who believe in God, the Last Day and who do acts of righteousness	2:62 Med.	*lā hum* ***yaḥzanūn*** – nor shall they grieve
4	God's 'devotees'	43:68 Mec.	*lā antum* ***taḥzanūn*** – nor shall ye grieve
5	Those who believe and do deeds of righteousness, establish regular prayer and give regular charity	2:277 & 21:94-103 Med. & Mec.	*lā hum* ***yaḥzanūn*** – nor shall they grieve and *lā* ***yaḥzunuhum*** – will bring them no grief
6	The righteous	39:61 Mec.	*lā hum* ***yaḥzanūn*** – nor shall they grieve
7	Those who are martyred in battle	3:169-170 Med.	*lā hum* ***yaḥzanūn*** – nor have they (cause to) grieve
8	Muslims, Christians, Jews & Sabeans who believe in God, the Last Day and do acts of righteousness.	2:62 Med. 5:72 – Mec.	*lā hum* ***yaḥzanūn*** – nor shall they grieve
9	Those who believe, and mend their lives (reform themselves)	6:48 Mec.	*lā hum* ***yaḥzanūn*** – nor shall they grieve
10	Those who are righteous and mend (their lives)	7:35 Mec.	*lā hum* ***yaḥzanūn*** – nor shall they grieve
11	The companions of the Garden (heaven)	7:44-49 Mec.	*lā antum* ***taḥzanūn*** – nor shall ye grieve
12	'Friends' (*awliya*) of God	10:62 Mec.	*lā hum* ***yaḥzanūn*** – nor shall they grieve
13	Those who say, "Our Lord is God," and remain firmly (on that path)	46:13 & 41:30 Mec.	*lā hum* ***yaḥzanūn*** – nor shall they grieve *lā* ***taḥzanū*** – do not grieve
14	Whoever submits His whole self to God and is a doer of good.	2:112 Med.	*lā hum* ***yaḥzanūn*** – nor shall they grieve
15	Those who spend their belongings (*amwāl*) in the cause of God	2:262 & 2:274 Med.	*la hum* ***yaḥzanūn*** – nor shall they grieve

* 'Mec'= revealed in Mecca; 'Med'= revealed in Medina.

Therefore, according to the above table, in order not to experience *ḥuzn* one must believe in one God and the hereafter, and one must follow God's guidance and submit one's whole self to God through belief and submission. The question as to whether any human being has the potential to retain this level of belief at all times and whether *ḥuzn* is a totally negative concept which must be obviated will be discussed in detail in Chapters Six.

Thematic categorization of the word ḥuzn

Other instances where the word *ḥuzn* and its derivatives have been used have been categorized here into three groups in accordance with the contextual structure of the Quran:

1. *ḥuzn* as a test or trial
1. *ḥuzn* as a reminder as well as a source of comfort and reassurance to Prophets and believers
2. *ḥuzn* due to separation and/or loss

Ḥuzn as a test or trial

In the previous section we saw that being in a state of 'righteousness' (*taqwā*) required following guidance which comes through God's signs (*āyāt*) manifested in creation and elucidated or interpreted by God's Messengers. These 'signs' are posited as the means or the opportunity for all individuals to take heed and reform their lives. In this way they serve as a test for individuals to choose either to ignore the signs and fall to the lowest level (*asfal al-sāfilīn*)[24] or to rise to the highest point in creation (*aḥsan-i taqwīm*)[25] as vicegerents of God. God states that the whole creation was created for humankind and jinn in order that they serve and worship Him[26] and thus all will have the potential to rise to the highest level of manifesting the Divine attributes.

In 2:153 and 2:155 it is made clear to believers that everyone will be tested in one form or another:

> *O ye who believe! [āmanū from the root āmana] seek help with patient perseverance [ṣabr] and prayer [salāt]: for God is with those who patiently persevere.*[27]

> *Be sure we shall test [balā] you with something of fear and hunger, some loss in goods, lives and the Fruits (of your toil), but give glad tidings to those who patiently persevere.*[28]

Stress given as a lesson not to grieve

Chapter Three, called Āl-i 'Imrān ('the family of 'Imrān) and revealed in Medina, tells *inter alia*, the story of the battles of Badr and Uhud. The moral of the battle narratives is that patience and perseverance will have its own rewards while lack of trust will result not only in physical defeat but also in moral defeat. Verse 3:153 describes the state of confusion among the Muslims fighting against the Quraysh[29] and the series of stresses (*ghamm*) given one after another as a lesson to not grieve over small mistakes and to have more trust in God:

> *Behold! ye were climbing up the high ground, without even casting a side glance at any one, and the Apostle in your rear was calling you back. There did God give you one distress [ghamm] after another by way of requital, to teach you not to grieve [taḥzanū – from root ḥazana] for (the booty) that had escaped you and for (the ill) that had befallen you. For God is well aware of all that ye do.*[30]

Distress (*ghamm*) therefore on this occasion had an important role to play and was given as a test. It is followed by the words 'to teach not to grieve (*ḥuzn*)', thus indicating that distress (*ghamm*) can be changed by not grieving (*ḥuzn*) over loss. In this verse, reference is made to the loss of booty and health as an example. There is an indication here that grief (*ḥuzn*) can have a positive and guidance-giving outcome if there is submission to apparent loss rather than the desire for retaliation or the falling into despair. The test is to not attribute things to causes and to accept God's Divine Determining. In other words, if one trusts God totally and perseveres patiently, then one can learn to stop worrying/grieving (*ḥuzn*) over any kind of change or loss.

Stress given as a lesson that one should not 'own' good deeds

Verse 9:92, quoted below, tells the story of the people who wanted to be part of the Prophet's army but who were turned away, possibly on account of their lack of armour and other equipment needed for fighting the enemy. These people were filled with *ḥuzn* because they could not find anything to spend in the way of God. The emphasis here is on the test: it is not *what* is done but the intention with which it is done. They intended to spend in the way of God and were not able to do so. In the verse below, reassurance is given that if barriers are encountered in an attempt to carry out good deeds, those intending such deeds will still be rewarded if there is sincerity and total trust in their Lord.

> *Nor (is there blame) on those who came to thee to be provided with mounts, and when thou sayest, "I can find no mounts for you", they turned back, their eyes*

streaming with tears of grief [ḥazanan] that they had no resources wherewith to provide the expenses.[31]

Satan used as a means of testing mankind

58:10 suggests that Satan has no real power and that he is merely a means by which believers are tested.[32] His job is to encourage believers to grieve (*ḥuzn*) and, ultimately, to make them deviate from the right path; however, as long as they have trust in God, no harm will come to them unless God wishes it. And if God were to allow it, then it would be for the good of the believer, as it would be an opportunity to be tested and reach a higher rank in belief by showing trust (*tawakkul*) and submission to God through the non-attribution of power to anything or anyone except their Lord.

> *Secret counsels are only (inspired) by the Evil One, in order that he may cause grief [ḥuzn] to the Believers; but he cannot harm them in the least, except as God permits; and on God let the Believers [mu'mīnūn] put their trust [tawakkul].*[33]

God gives ḥuzn and also takes it away

In 35:34 below again there is the notion of the positive aspect of *ḥuzn*, as believers recognise that it is God who gives it and it is also He who removes it, hence the recognition that they are being both guided and tested by God to see beyond apparent causes, and also that they have been given the opportunity to show total trust in His decree.

> *And they will say: "Praise be to God, Who has removed from us (all) sorrow: for our Lord is indeed Oft-Forgiving Ready to appreciate (service).*[34]

28:8, quoted below, states that the reason Moses was destined to be with Pharaoh was to cause him and his followers sorrow (*ḥuzn*). If within the meaning of *ḥuzn* there is the potential for guidance, then it shows that this would be a test for them, and an opportunity to either be guided or to refuse and opt instead for a short life of purely material riches. Sorrow (*ḥuzn*) then has the potential to have a positive or negative outcome, depending on whether one chooses to persist in unbelief or to take heed of the 'signs' (*āyāt*) of God, which have the potential to save people from their own 'selves' and their egoistic desires.

> *Then the people of Pharaoh picked him up (from the river): (It was intended) that (Moses) should be to them an adversary and a cause of sorrow [ḥazanan]: for Pharaoh and Haman and (all) their hosts were men of sin.*[35]

The testing of Prophetic judgment

In 33:51, quoted below, Muhammad receives a special dispensation with regard to marital duties which is different to the precepts pertaining to other Muslims. This is a test not only for the Prophet but also for his wives, giving them the opportunity to have total trust in his judgment.

> *Thou mayest defer (the turn of) any of them that thou pleasest, and thou mayest receive any thou pleasest: and there is no blame on thee if thou invite one whose (turn) thou hadst set aside. This were nigher to the cooling of their eyes, the prevention of their grief [ḥuzn], and their satisfaction – that of all of them – with that which thou hast to give them: and God knows (all) that is in your hearts: and God is All-Knowing, Most Forbearing.*[36]

Reminders, reassurance and comfort given to Prophets and believers so that they may avoid ḥuzn

The reassurance and comforting of Prophets

In 36:76 and 10:65, Muhammad is reminded not to be saddened by what people say as ultimately they have no power. Furthermore, he is pained by the people rushing headlong into unbelief, and he is reminded not to grieve (*ḥuzn*) on this account. Here God is guiding, comforting and reminding the Prophet that there is no need to grieve, and that the ultimate responsibility for the fate of unbelievers is with Him.[37] After all, He is the Lord (*rabb*) and unbelievers will not be able to cause any harm without His permission; furthermore, they will get their just punishment in the hereafter. Again, here is a reminder that secondary causes have no actual effect. The actions of these people are brought into effect not by them, but directly by God, and it is on account of their bad intentions that they are punished. The apparent creation of evil generally, and in this case the example of people rushing into unbelief, serves as a guide and a test for individuals to carry out their duty without expectation of results by submitting to the All-Knowing and All-Powerful Lord of creation.

> *Let not their speech, then, grieve thee. Verily We know what they hide as well as what they disclose.*[38]

> *Let not their speech grieve thee: for all power and honour belong to God: It is He Who heareth and knoweth* (all things).[39]

Let not those grieve thee who rush headlong into Unbelief: Not the least harm will they do to God: God's Plan is that He will give them no portion in the Hereafter, but a severe punishment.[40]

In 5:41, quoted below, once again Muhammad is comforted and reminded not to grieve over the loss of people who have chosen unbelief (*kufr*). *Kufr* comes from the verbal root *kafara* which means "to cover, deny, hide, renounce, reject, disbelieve, be negligent, expiate, darken".[41] It is stated clearly in this verse that no one, including Muhammad, can do anything for those who intend to cause *fītna*, and thus there is no point in grieving over them. The outcome of their actions will be justly recompensed. *Fītna,* translated below as 'trial', has the underlying meaning of 'punishment' or a 'test'.[42] In other words, God is comforting the Prophet and reminding him that he has done his duty and that no more is expected of him; if unbelievers choose to deny themselves the opportunity to repent then it is their choice. Furthermore, God will permit this and no one can do anything for them.

O Apostle! Let not those grieve thee [ḥuzn], who race each other into unbelief [kufr]: [Whether it be] among those who say, "We believe [āmannā] with their lips but whose hearts have no faith; Or it be among the Jews, men who will listen to any lie, will listen even to others who have never so much as come to thee. They change the words from their [right] times and places: they say, "If ye are given this, take it, but if not, beware!" If any one's trial [fītna] is intended by God, thou hast no authority in the least for him against God. For such – it is not God's will to purify their hearts. For them there is disgrace in this world, and in the Hereafter a heavy punishment.[43]

In 6:33, quoted below, Muhammad is being comforted as he may be blaming himself for the apparent failures he is experiencing, and he is being reminded that God knows well what he is going through and that it is not him that people are rejecting, but it is the signs (*āyāt*) of God which they refuse to accept, and it is on account of this that they will receive their due punishment. In 6:34, Muhammad is reminded that previous messengers were also persecuted and rejected, accepting their lot patiently until God came to their aid.[44] And in 6:35 it states clearly that nothing could convince the believers because they do not want to be convinced; furthermore, because they choose to ignore God's signs, then God will not guide them.[45] Therefore ultimately they have no power apart from the choice to take heed or to ignore God's signs. It is a reminder that Muhammad should not feel responsible for their choice of action, and also that God is aware of their actions, and will deal with them justly and in due course.

> *We know indeed the grief [ḥuzn] which their words do cause thee: It is not thee they reject [kadhaba]: it is the signs [āyāt] of God, which the wicked [ẓālimīn] condemn/deny [jahada].*[46]

In 16:127, Muhammad is again reminded to be patient, as patience is an attribute of God which should always be manifested, especially in difficult times and situations. He is also being reminded not to grieve (*ḥuzn*) if people refuse to believe and not to feel helpless or troubled (*ḍayq*) [47] by the schemes and plots of the unbelievers as ultimately God has power over all things.

> *And do thou be patient [ṣabr], for thy patience is but from God; nor grieve [ḥuzn] over them: And distress [ḍāqa] not thyself because of their plots [makr].*[48]

Many of the verses in sura 15 are about reminders, comforting and consolation, including 15:97, where Mohammad is being consoled: "*We do indeed know how thy heart is distressed* (*yaḍiqū*)[49] *at what they say*"[50] and in 15:92, where he is reassured: "....*We will of a surety, call them to account*". In 15:95 further reassurance is given when God states that "...*sufficient are We unto thee against those who scoff*", thus again reminding Muhammad that he is not responsible for those who refuse to take heed, and that his responsibility is simply to give the message, since all human beings have their own trial and it is up to them to accept or reject.[51]

In 15:88, quoted below, Muhammad is being consoled and comforted about the unequal distribution of wealth, the consequences of which lead to poverty for some and a life of luxury for others. This verse came during the period when he and his companions were undergoing many difficulties and restrictions, resulting in unfair treatment and poverty. The Prophet's trading activities had come to an end; his wife's wealth had been used up; and the economic boycott by the Quraysh had resulted in the homelessness and poverty of the Companions.[52] It was a difficult time for Muhammad and it pained him to see how his Companions were being persecuted by their opponents, reduced as they were to poverty while their adversaries enjoyed a life of luxury. At this point Muhammad is reminded that what his enemies have is not really 'true' wealth; he is instructed to reassure the Companions that this so called 'wealth' will not be of any real value to their opponents either in this world or in the next.[53]

> *Strain not thine eyes (wistfully) at what We have bestowed on certain classes of them, nor grieve [lā taḥzan] over them: but lower thy wing (in gentleness) to the believers.*[54]

Verse 29:33, quoted below, pertains to the concerns of Lot when he was visited by some handsome young men, and to his helplessness to protect them against certain sexual predators in their midst. He was not aware that they were messengers sent by God to save him and his followers until he was comforted and reassured by them that he need not fear or worry as to what might happen to them in the future; his followers, they reassured him, would be saved, while those who had strayed, including his wife, would be punished justly for the outcome of their illicit actions.

> *And when Our Messengers came to Lūt, he was grieved on their account, and felt himself powerless (to protect) them: but they said: "Fear thou not, nor grieve: we are (here) to save thee and thy following, except thy wife: she is of those who lag behind.*[55]

The reassuring and comforting of the faithful

In 70:27, God instructs the Prophet to reassure the faithful that those who are guilty of transgression are ultimately powerless, and therefore as long as they remain in a 'righteous' state, they need not be anxious about the transgressors' plots and schemes. The unbelievers' devious plans (*makr*) will not come to fruition if God so wishes, since as stated in 3:54, they may scheme and plot (*makr*) but "God is the best of planners".[56]

> *But grieve [ḥuzn] not over them, nor distress [ḍayq] thyself because of their plots [makr].*[57]

Verse 9:40 gives the example of Muhammad's comforting and reassuring one of his companions. It tells the story of the time when the two were trapped in a cave with a huge army outside looking for them. At that point, Muhammad's companion felt a sense of isolation, fear and *ḥuzn* about their plight. Had Muhammad not reminded him not to have *ḥuzn* and that God was their guardian, his sadness might have led easily to despair. This verse shows that if God wills, even a huge army cannot conquer two people; it also shows that feelings of comfort and ease (*sakīna*) can be obtained if there is trust in God rather than attributing power to secondary causes.

> *If ye help not (your leader), (it is no matter): for God did indeed help him, when the Unbelievers [those who cover 'kafara'] drove him out: he had no more than one companion: they two were in the cave, and he said to his companion, "Have no fear [ḥuzn], for God is with us": then God sent down His peace [sakīna] upon him, and strengthened him with forces which ye saw not, and humbled to the depths the word of the Unbelievers. But the word of God is exalted to the heights: for God is Exalted in might, Wise.*[58]

In 19:24, Mary, who is about to give birth to Jesus, is told not to be saddened (i.e. not to have *ḥuzn*), and she is comforted and reminded that she is not alone since God is watching over her. She is also instructed to drink from a rivulet beneath her and eat a date from the palm tree in front of her. The water and the date serve as nourishment and comfort and also as a reminder to Mary that God does not need secondary causes to bring things into being. If He can bring water from no source and bring a dead palm tree to life again, He can surely bring a human being to life without apparent secondary causes, to which human beings have become normalised. God comforts Mary, who at this critical time of giving birth is frightened of what may happen. God's comforting is manifested through the provision of water that is provided for her specifically by her Lord (*Rabb*). This is also a sign that God is the only protector and therefore the Only One to whom she needs to turn. He is the One who has willed this to happen and she will need to trust that He will take care of the consequences.

> *But (a voice) cried to her from beneath the (palm tree): "Grieve not! [ḥuzn] For thy Lord hath provided a rivulet beneath thee."*[59]

In 20:39, Moses's mother is being inspired by God to put her baby in a basket and to place the basket in the river.[60] Moses's mother knew that she could not hide her baby for very long from Pharaoh's soldiers, who had been instructed to kill all new-born males, and so she trusted in God and His promise and reassurance that Moses would be safe and secure and would one day be restored to her. Verse 28:7 is also linked to the theme of separation.

> *So We sent this inspiration to the mother of Moses: "Suckle (thy child), but when thou hast fears about him, cast him into the river, but fear not nor grieve: [lā taḥzani] For We shall restore him to thee, and We shall make him one of Our apostles."*[61]

Sura 41 of the Quran focuses on the fruits of belief and the demerits of unbelief. Unbelievers are warned about the consequences of their opposition to the truth and in 41:30 believers are reassured and consoled so as not to fear the threats of the unbelievers or be distressed (*taḥzanū*) by anything, for they have their Lord, Who is their constant protector in this world as well as the next. They should therefore bear the temporary deprivations of this transient world since very soon they will be rewarded with everything they ask for.

> *In the case of those who say, "Our Lord is God", and, further, stand straight and steadfast, the angels descend on them (from time to time): "Fear ye not!" (they suggest), "Nor grieve! but receive the Glad Tidings of the Garden (of Bliss), the which ye were promised!*[62]

In Sura 31, Luqmān is advising his son about matters of faith. In 31:23, quoted below, reassurance is given that men of God need not be distressed about those who obstinately refuse to believe, since ultimately they will be answerable to God. They will be allowed to pursue their amusement in this life for a short time but in the next world they will be held accountable for all their deeds.

> *But if any reject Faith, let not his rejection grieve [yaḥzunak] thee: to Us is their return, and We shall tell them the truth of their deeds: for God knows well all that is in (men's) hearts.*[63]

Ḥuzn due to separation and loss

According to the Quran, the only people who are exempt from being in total confusion and loss are those who possess the following four qualities: faith; righteous deeds; inviting one another to the truth; and exhorting one another to exercise patience:

> *By (the token of) time (through the Ages), Verily Man is in loss, Except such as have faith, and do righteous deeds, and (join together) in the Mutual teaching of Truth, and of patience and constancy.*[64]

Therefore, whoever does not at all times demonstrate the above qualities will be in a state of loss (*khusr* – from the verbal root *khasira,* meaning 'to wander from the right path'). The criterion for belief is to believe sincerely in one God[65] and to be steadfast in this belief.[66] Only by remaining at this level of faith is one able to submit with total trust to all of the trials and tests sent by God. The story of Joseph,[67] described below in brief, shows how even Jacob found God's trial of separating him from his son Joseph not just difficult but almost unbearable.

Jacob had twelve sons from different wives. Ten of these brothers were extremely jealous of what they believed to be excess attention to Joseph by their father and so one day they planned to take Joseph to the hills with them for the usual grazing of the sheep, but with the real intention of getting rid of him. They believed that once Joseph was out of the way, they would have their father's full attention and affection all to themselves. 12:13 is about Jacob's mixed feelings. He expresses his feelings openly to his sons saying that he is frightened and sad (*ḥuzn*) that his brothers will neglect Joseph and leave him open to an attack by wolves. Eventually, however, he gives in and allows the brothers to take Joseph with them. It is a possibility that he suspected that something would happen to Joseph, but was it actually desert wolves that he feared, or the jealousy of Yusuf's brothers and, consequently, what they might do to him? What is sure is that not seeing Joseph again would be a separation and a loss which he would not be able to bear, even though he knew that ultimately he should place his trust in God.

> *(Jacob) said: "Really it saddens me [yaḥzunī] that ye should take him away: I fear [akhāfū] lest the wolf should devour him while ye attend not to him."*[68]

In verse eighty-four of the same chapter, we see that Jacob's fears were not unfounded. After throwing Joseph down into an empty well, the brothers returned home pretending that a wolf had eaten him. This loss was too much for Jacob to bear, but he bore it in silence. The severity of his grief was such that he lost his faculty of sight, his eyes becoming 'white with sorrow' (*ḥuzn*).

> *And he turned away from them, and said: "How great is my grief for Joseph!" And his eyes became white with sorrow, and he fell into silent melancholy.*[69]

> *He (Jacob) said: "I only complain of my distraction and anguish to God, and I know from God that which ye know not..."*[70]

In 12:86, Jacob makes it clear that he is not attributing the loss of Joseph to secondary causes, in this case his sons; he is well aware that ultimately it is God Who had taken Joseph away from him and that He was also the only One Who was able to give him the ability to bear the loss of Joseph. If sadness (*ḥuzn*) is to be understood as guidance, then this separation was a test for Jacob and an opportunity for him to question his attachment to Joseph.

28:13 tells the story of Moses's being restored to his mother, so that she might be comforted and not grieve (*ḥuzn*) for her loss and so that she might realise that God keeps his promise. Here, the mother of Moses has to let go of her child and entrust him to God before being rewarded by being reunited with him. Like Abraham, who had to be ready to sacrifice Ismail before his son could be returned to him, [71] and like Jacob, who had to let go of Joseph before he could have his son back again, the mother of Moses had to have complete trust (*tawakkul*) in God who would reunite her with the baby she had been separated from.

> *Thus did We restore him to his mother, that her eye might be comforted, that she might not grieve, and that she might know that the promise of God is true: but most of them do not understand.*[72]

In 20:40 we are told about the trials and tests Moses has to undergo. The test of trust begins with his mother, who has to leave the fate of her child in God's hands. In order to decrease her worries (*ḥuzn*), God ensures that as his wet nurse she will be able to keep close to her son. Moses is saved from *ghamm* after having killed a man, hence indicating that *ghamm* potentially occurs after an action that has taken place, while the word *ḥuzn* is used for worry or distress about what might happen in the future as a result of an incident in the past, such as the anxiety Moses's mother might have had if she had not been able to be with her child.

> *"Behold! thy sister goeth forth and saith, 'shall I show you one who will nurse and rear the (child)?' So We brought thee back to thy mother, that her eye might be cooled and she should not grieve (taḥzan). Then thou didst slay a man, but We saved thee from trouble (ghamm), and We tried thee in various ways. Then didst thou tarry a number of years with the people of Midian. Then didst thou come hither as ordained, O Moses!'*[73]

The typology and the thematic analysis of *ḥuzn* based on Quranic narratives have yielded a general understanding of this concept. In the next section, the Izutsian analytical method is applied to the *ḥuzn* narrative in the Quran. The semantic structures of the main concepts related to this word is analysed in order to obtain a contextual understanding rather than, as Izutsu puts it, a word for word interpretation.[74] The analysis of this word begins with the gathering of the main words which, as shown below, appear to be synonymous with, or have a similar meaning to, *ḥuzn*.

Part Two: Izutsu's method

Izutsu's method has been chosen because it is an excellent tool for understanding words and concepts in the Quran. It is a method of analysis which enables the Quran to 'interpret its own concepts and speak for itself'.[75] According to Izutsu, translated words tend to give literal meanings and hence give only a partial understanding, which is inadequate and can sometimes even be misleading.[76] He gives the example of the word 'weed' and how in one dictionary this word is defined as 'a wild herb springing where it is not wanted', giving the impression that it is an 'undesired' or 'unwanted' herb. But in reality, one cannot objectively label any herb as 'undesirable'[77] outside of the context of one's personal needs and purposes. The subjective way of meaning-making is also influenced to a large extent by our social surroundings. Izutsu gives the example of a round table and a square table, explaining that for the English native, the word table could be applied to both objects, but according to Benjamin Whorf, in non-Indo-European parts of the world, people categorise things in accordance with their form and shape because their view of the world is focused more on shape than on purpose and hence according to their world view in no way can a round table and a square table be categorized in the same group: they are considered to be totally different things and hence must have different names.[78]

These examples can be extended to all the words that are in usage and one therefore has to consider that all words are largely culturally and historically polluted. In other words, what we describe as reality is inextricably permeated with culturally inherited symbols.

Semantic analysis

In order to move away as much as possible from subjective, historical, cultural or political influences, I attempt to use Izutsu's method which is more scientific since it is an inductive approach and an analytical means of understanding the meaning of concepts such as *ḥuzn* in the Quran. This method of linguistic analysis, that is, describing the semantic categories of a word in accordance with the conditions in which it is used, enables the Quran to speak for itself, hence resulting in arguably a less biased interpretation. Izutsu defines semantics as:

> ...an analytic study of the key-terms of a language with a view to arriving eventually at a conceptual grasp of the *Weltanschauung* or world-view of the people who use that language as a tool not only of speaking and thinking, but, more important still, of conceptualizing and interpreting the world that surrounds them.[79]

In practice, then, this would mean finding out what *ḥuzn* means from the Quranic *Weltanschauung*. To do this I have firstly gathered together all the verses where the word is mentioned, and then compared them and checked them against each other, as well as with other synonyms and antonyms of the word, hopefully in order to obtain what Izutsu describes as a 'word-thing' interpretation as opposed to a word-to-word interpretation.[80] This is not an easy task. As Izutsu himself admits, it is a process of 'trial and error'[81] and can be quite arduous; however, it is absolutely necessary here if we are to attempt to obtain the Quranic 'worldview'. This does not mean that philological work on, and exegesis of, the Quran are not valuable resources – in fact I use these in this and following chapter – but these serve more as secondary resources.

The idea that language conveys a 'worldview' is not new. Izutsu's theory of meaning is based largely on the work of Ferdinand de Saussure and also Leo Weisgerber's type of semantics called *sprachliche Weltanschauungslehre*, which is the study of the interrelations between cultural as well as linguistic patterns, the origin of which can be traced back to Edward Sapir and what would be referred to today as 'ethnolinguistics'. What Izutsu has contributed is the unification of these theories and its application to the Quranic hermeneutics.[82]

Quranic key terms in history

Izutsu himself talks about Quranic key terms in history, but only to show how concepts can change over time. His reference to *jāhilī* or pre-Islamic vocabulary therefore is to show that although many of the words in the Quran existed before the revelation, the Quranic theocentric *Weltanschauung*, despite its origins, has its own semantic field which means that it requires a totally new system of interpretation. He gives the example of the word *Allāh*, which was widely used by the pre-Islamic Arabs, but with the difference that conceptually, it had a totally different meaning. All semantic fields in the Quran are connected directly to the concept of *Allāh*; in other words, ontologically, *Allāh* is the central focus of all the concepts in the Quran, whereas with regard to the pre-Islamic era, *Allāh* was, as a concept, on par with other 'gods'.[83]

Another example of the total change in meaning of concepts is the word *karīm*. This word used by the pre-Islamic Arabs connoted the notion of 'noble birth', as well as carrying the meaning of extravagance in generosity to the point of squandering. However, in the Quranic context the meaning changed completely and becomes linked closely to the word *taqwā*, which means 'God-awareness'This represents a total change in how the previous notion of one who is *karīm* is viewed, namely that a noble person is not one who is rich by birth and who flaunts that wealth by squandering it, but, rather, one who uses it in the way of God.[84]

The difference between 'basic' and 'relational' meanings

Izutsu points out that each word in the Quran has its own basic or core meaning, even if taken out of the Quranic context, thus:

> ...while the 'basic' meaning of the word is something inherent in the word itself, which it carries with it wherever it goes, the 'relational' meaning is something connotative that comes to be attached and added to the former by the word's having taken a particular position in a particular field, standing in diverse relations to all other important words in that system.[85]

As an example, he points to the word *kītāb*, which at its basic level means 'book' in all contexts. In the Quranic context, however, this word is placed in a new system whereby it acquires new semantic elements which have the tendency to change the original meaning. Thus, in the context of the Quran, the word *kītāb*, because of its close connection with the words *Allāh*, *waḥy* ('revelation'), *tanzīl* ('the sending down of Divine words'), *nabī* ('Prophet') and *ahl* ('people'), has to be understood in connection with these words. Izutsu calls this the 'relational' meaning, which is much more important than the 'basic' meaning, since without this semantic structure, the Quranic concept of the word cannot be comprehended. As Izutsu reiterates, the basic meaning is purely a methodological concept which is useful for scientific analyses, since it always carries its 'conceptual core' in all contexts. Therefore although it is useful to use the basic meaning as a 'working hypothesis', one should bear in mind that in fact all words are tainted by the cultural milieu in which they are embedded.[86] As *ḥuzn* is the central subject for analysis in this study, the main concepts which have a strong relation with the *term* will be identified in order to explore why people become sad and what is its cure from the perspective of the Quranic *Weltanschauung* – the world-view upon which the whole of Nursi's work is based.

Primary and secondary level ethical terms

Izutsu makes a distinction between primary and secondary level ethical terms, despite the fact that all words originate at the primary level, that is, from a purely descriptive aspect. Therefore, secondary level words such as 'good' still have a descriptive aspect with an evaluative charge which belongs to the ethical metalanguage.[87] For example, the sentence 'Cecil never forgets my birthday and is therefore a good friend' belongs to the ethical metalanguage as it has both a descriptive as well as an evaluative aspect.

Primary-level ethical terms are therefore descriptive words that are charged with an evaluative force, while secondary-level terms have more of a classificatory function, used to classify descriptive properties such as 'humility' or 'generosity' into a category of moral values. The Quran itself consists mainly of primary ethical terms. The classificatory terms, such as the five categories of acts below, and referred to as the *aḥkām* ('rulings'), are more representative of secondary ethical terms related to jurisprudence:[88]

1. *wājib* – obligatory duties
2. *mandūb* – recommended but not obligatory
3. *jā'iz/mubāḥ* – may or may not be done/permissible
4. *makrūḥ* – discouraged
5. *ḥarām* – forbidden

The above are classic secondary level terms which, as Izutsu describes, are 'an elaborate system of metalanguage'[89] in which all deeds are classified in accordance with the above classifications. The moral values in the Quran, however, belong in the main to the primary ethical structure, which, while adopting many of the pre-Islamic words, uses them with often totally different meanings. For example, the word 'humility' in pre-Islamic discourse signified a trait that was looked down upon by people, while its opposite, 'haughtiness', was a sign of noble character. In the new monotheistic setting, however, both words acquire completely opposite meanings.[90]

The limitations of the Izutsian method

According to Montgomery Watt, Izutsu's analyses are based on logic to the neglect of the consideration of the politico-religious context. Watt opines that the verses in the Quran were revealed over a period of more than twenty years and that those verses revealed earlier on may have different meanings from those revealed later on. For Watt, then, Izutsu's method does not take the historical context into account.[91] Fazlur Rahman is also in agreement with Watt with regard to the importance of the historical context. His criticism is that while Izutsu's methodology is not just a mechanical analysis of the terms in the Quran in isolation, but one which takes the Quranic context into account, it lacks the kind of historical approach conducive to a better understanding of the evolution of concepts.[92] According to Norman Calder, there are verses in the Quran which, without reference to their historical context, or what is referred to as *sha'n-i nuzūl*, cannot be fully comprehended. He goes as far as to say that to look at a text in isolation of its *sha'n-i nuzūl* is not only unproblematic, 'it is meaningless'.[93]

Rahman also says that Izutsu makes no distinction between the Meccan social order and that of the Bedouin Arabs. He argues that a semantic analysis is not adequate to understand fully the historical distinction between the Meccan socio-economic situation and the socio-economic situation of the Bedouin Arabs. He points to Izutsu's contradictory claim that his analytical methodology is centred on a scientific study that excludes all preconceptions, when in fact he is referring to a specific time when the Meccan Arabs were receiving warnings regarding heaven and hell. But Rahman points out that in fact, when seen in its correct historical context, these doctrines came much later, only after the rich Meccans had rejected the reasoning for God's existence and were too proud to deny the fact that they were not 'self-sufficient' or had 'natural rights'.[94]

Izutsu also talks about 'key terms' in the Quran such as *islām*, īmān (belief), *kufr* (unbelief), *nabī* (prophet).[95] Although in principle there would be little disagreement with regard to the importance of these concepts, one may question why or how Izutsu came to the conclusion that they are key, and whether in fact he relies on the kind of preconceived understanding against which he himself cautions.

Although with the Izutsian method there is indeed a lack of reliance on secondary sources, which may have the disadvantage of not capturing adequately the socio-political and historic context, nevertheless it is considered to be a relatively good method to use for this study as its 'scientific' or non-biased approach seeks to reduce the influence of any pre-set understanding such as those encouraged by engagement with jurisprudence, theology, philosophy, and so on.

Application of the Izutsian method

The application of the Izutsian method begins with gathering, comparing and putting in relation to each other all the terms which correspond, resemble and also oppose the word *ḥuzn* and its derivatives in the Quran. That is, the Izutsian analysis is conducted by looking at the semantic category of each word that relates to 'neighbouring words belonging to the same meaning field'[96] in order to obtain a contextual rather than a basic meaning. However, as stated earlier, this process is not only an extremely 'arduous task', as Izutsu himself admits,[97] but can easily lead to volumes of work. Therefore, for the purposes of this chapter an analysis of semantic categories of only a selection of key words is carried out.

As Izutsu suggests, verses which give little value in terms of semantic analysis may be left out.[98] He proposes seven cases in which passages become useful for semantic analysis:[99]

1. When the meaning of a word is explained in its context by means of verbal description.
2. When a synonym is used in the same passage, it can be very useful to investigate the semantic category of the synonym as well.
3. The semantic structure of terms may be elucidated by their opposite meaning, especially cases where there is more than one word which conveys the same meaning, such as the words *ḥasana* and *khayr* which both mean 'good' in Arabic. Therefore, examining the antonyms of these words, such as *sharr*, which is the opposite of *khayr*, and *sayyi'a* which is the opposite of *ḥasana*, will help considerably in shedding more light on the meaning of these two concepts.
4. The semantic structure of an obscure word can often be better understood through its negative form. In other words, learning how people behave who do not possess trait X, for example, can often tell us more about those who do possess it, and can be a useful way of determining the semantic category to which the word describing trait X belongs.
5. Words which have a patterned semantic relationship, such as the English words 'wind' and 'to blow'. Although these are two different words, they are related together in meaning.
6. Rhetorical parallelism is also another useful device for revealing the existence of a semantic relationship between two or more words. Izutsu gives verse 26:46-49 as an example:

   And none denies Our signs save the kāfir.

   And none denies Our signs save the ẓālim.

   The example above demonstrates that *kāfir* and ẓālim are semantically related due to their connection with regard to the refusal to believe in Divine signs.
7. Use of 'secular' words in the Quran, that is, words used in a non-religious context, can be helpful in understanding the structure of the word. For

example, when Pharaoh accuses Moses of being one of the *kāfirīn*, the context makes it evident that *kāfirīn* means 'the ungrateful' rather than the usual translation of 'unbelievers'.

The concept of ḥuzn ('sadness') in the Quran

As mentioned earlier there are forty-two verses in the Quran in which the word *ḥuzn* and its derivatives appear; twenty-six were revealed in Mecca and sixteen in Medina. A brief outline of the difference between Meccan and Medinan verses will be given before moving on to give the lexical meaning of *ḥuzn* and its derivatives. The aim of looking at the differences is to understand later on in the chapter whether, if at all, the place of revelation has any bearing on how the word *ḥuzn* is used and understood.

The difference between the Meccan and Medinan verses

Against the background of polytheism, the main message of Islam was focused on the concept of the oneness of God. At Mecca, therefore, Islam was mainly concerned with the propagation of fundamental principles related to the concept of Divine absoluteness. However, after Muhammad's migration to Medina, where Muslims from all over Arabia had also gathered to form a community, and where a small 'city-state' was established, although its focus was still on Divine unity (*tawḥīd*), the Quran had to turn its attention to practical issues as well by including the social, economic, political and legal rulings to facilitate the harmonious working of the new community. This is generally the difference between the themes of the verses revealed in Mecca and those revealed in Medina.[100] It must be stressed, however, that Muhammad did not make a distinction himself between the Meccan or Medinan verses; this categorisation was made later by his companions. It should also be added that the distinction between the Meccan and Medinan verses is not clear cut and some ambiguities exist.[101] For some the distinction is purely temporal rather than geographical. For others, categorisation of revelations is divided into 'early', 'middle' and 'late', be it in Mecca or Medina.[102] Another way of making a differentiation is based on content. The Meccan verses are shorter and there is a tendency to address Muhammad or 'men' generally, while the Medinan verses tend to be longer and address 'the believers'. There is, however, a general agreement that the verses revealed after the migration of Muhammad to Medina are Medinan and are mainly legislative in nature, while the verses revealed prior to his migration are Meccan and are more prophetic and metaphysical in tone and tenor.[103]

Since theologians and grammarians have distinguished a difference between not only the circumstances of Muslims at the time of revelation and the language used, but also between the style and themes of the Medinan and Meccan verses,[104] this study hopes to be able to discover whether this distinction is of any relevance to the topic of *ḥuzn*.

Derivatives of ḥ-z-n in the Medinan verses

2:38 (*yaḥzanūn*); 2:62 (*yaḥzanūn*); 2:112 (*yaḥzanūn*); 2:262 (*yaḥzanūn*); 2:274 (*yaḥzanūn*); 2:277 (*yaḥzanūn*); 3:170 (*yaḥzanūn*); 5:69 (*yaḥzanūn*); 3:139 (*taḥzanū*); 3:153 (*taḥzanū*); 3:176 (*yaḥzūnka*); 5:41 (*yaḥzūnka*); 9:40 (*taḥzan*); 9:92 (*ḥazanan*); 33:51 (*yaḥzanna*); 58:10 (*yaḥzun*).

Derivatives of ḥ-z-n in the Meccan verses

6:33 (*yaḥzunuka*); 10:65 (*yaḥzunka*); 31:23 (*yaḥzunka*); 36:76 (*yaḥzunka*); 6:48 (*yaḥzanūn*); 7:35 (*yaḥzanūn*); 10:62 (*yaḥzanūn*); 39:61 (*yaḥzanūn*); 46:13 (*yaḥzanūn*); 7:49 (*taḥzanūn*); 43:68 (*taḥzanūn*); 12:13 (*yaḥzununī*); 12:84 (*al-ḥuzn*); 12:86 (*ḥuznī*); 15:88 (*taḥzan*); 16:127 (*taḥzan*); 19:24 (*taḥzanī*); 28:7 (*taḥzanī*); 20:40 (*taḥzana*); 28:13 (*taḥzana*); 21:103 (*yaḥzunuhumu*); 27:70 (*taḥzan*); 29:33 (*taḥzan*); 28:8 (*ḥazanan*); 35:34 (*al-ḥazan*); 41:30 (*taḥzanū*).

The lexical meaning of ḥuzn

The triliteral root of the word *ḥuzn* (*ḥā zāy nūn* or *ḥ-z-n*) occurs forty-two times in the Quran in three derived forms: thirty-seven times as various declensions of the first form verb *ḥazina*; twice as the noun *ḥuzn*; and three times as the noun *ḥazan*. The basic meaning of *ḥuzn* is: grief, mourning, lamentation, sorrow, sadness and unhappiness. *ḥuzn*, a simple substantive, is used when the nominative or genitive case is employed and *ḥazan*, an infinitive noun, is used when the accusative is employed.

Derivatives of ḥ-z-n in the Quran

As discussed in 2.6.2, in order to obtain a clearer meaning of *ḥuzn*, its derived forms will be given below:

- *ḥuzn* – grief
- *ḥuznī* – my grief
- *al-ḥazana* – the sorrow
- *ḥazanan* – grief
- *li-yaḥzuna* – that he may grieve
- *yaḥzanūna* – they will grieve
- *yahzanna* – they grieve

- *la-yaḥzununī* – it surely saddens me
- *taḥzanūna* – you will grieve
- *taḥzana* – she may grieve
- *taḥzan* – he was or became affected with *ḥuzn*
- *taḥzanī* – grieve
- *yaḥzunuka* – grieve you
- *yaḥzunuhumu* – will grieve them
- *lā yaḥzunka* – (let) not grieve thee
- *lā taḥzan* – thou grieve not
- *lā taḥzana* – she should not grieve
- *lā taḥzanū* – you grieve not

The Izutsian analayis of the semantic field of ḥuzn

Words which appear to be synonymous with the word ḥuzn: their basic and relational meanings

There are a number of words in the Quran which have been translated variously into English as 'sadness', 'distress', 'grief' or 'wretchedness'. Sometimes one can find a number of these different words in the same verse. It is important to explore how they differ in meaning from *ḥuzn* and in what context they are used. In this section I aim to look at the semantic fields of some of these words in order to be able to differentiate their 'basic meaning' from the 'real meaning' as used in the Quranic context. The words are listed below:

- *shaqīya* (to be miserable or unhappy)
- *ḍanaka* (wretched; straitened)
- *sīa* (distress; grief)
- *ḍāqa* (to become distressed; to become narrow or tight)
- *'asībūn* (distressful)
- *ghamm* (distress ; anguish)
- *hamm* (worry; anxiety)
- *asaf* (grief; sorrow)
- *bakha'a* (to worry; to grieve to death)
- *kaẓama* (to restrain one's grief and anger)

The generic verb for describing general misery and suffering is *shaqīya*. The dictionary translation of this word is: to be miserable; to be wretched and in distress; to be unhappy.[105] The Quranic meaning for this word and its various derivatives refers to those who turn away from God and reject His guidance. For example, in verses 11:105 and 20:2 respectively we read:

"The day it arrives, no soul shall speak, except by his leave: Of those [gathered] some will be wretched [shaqī] and some will be blessed."

"We have not sent down the Quran to thee to be [an occasion] for thy distress [tashqi]. But as an admonition from those who fear [yakhshā] [Allah]".

Although other terms form a constituent element of *shaqiya*, they are more specific in relation to the context in which they are applied. These include the word *ḥuzn* itself as well as the following words:

- *ḍanaka*, from which we get the idea of 'narrowness' or 'straitened and wretched'. It occurs only once in the Quran as the adjective *ḍankan*.
- *sī'a*, meaning 'he was distressed or grieved'. The triliteral root *sīn wāw hamza* occurs 167 times in the Quran in twelve derived forms. Its main meaning verb (form 1) is 'to be evil', although in verses 3:120, 5:101, 9:50, 11:77, 17:7, 29:33 and 67:27 it is translated in ways that connote grief, distress and sadness. Its meaning is linked to anything that makes a person sad or sorrowful.
- *ḍāqa*, meaning 'to become narrow or tight', 'to become distressed'. In the Quranic context, it is used to express a sense of being powerless under certain circumstances. The use of this word in the verse below demonstrates Lot's powerlessness in the face of the impending evil that he thought to be imminent.
- *aṣaba* is a triliteral root which occurs five times in the Quran in two derived forms: four times as the noun *uṣ'bat*, meaning 'group' or 'company'; and once as the adjective *'aṣībūn* (cited below) meaning 'distressful' in the sense of being difficult to deal with.

The difference in meaning between the words *ḥuzn*, *ḍayq*, *sī'a*, and *ḍank* is exemplified in the verses below. In the first and third verses, *ḥuzn* is used in the sense of the comforting linked to a sense of loss, the giving of hope, the giving of guidance and the reminders given that one ought not to be anxious about the future. *Ḍayq* is used almost exclusively to express the state of hopelessness brought about by difficult circumstances. The word *sī'a* in the second verse is linked to Lot's anguish with regard to the evil that he thought was bound to come about as a result of the presence of the handsome young men who had come to visit him. Unaware that they were messengers of God, Lot felt powerless to protect them against the sodomitic practices of many in his community. In the fourth verse, the word *ḍank* is used to point out that a world that does not encompass remembrance of God is a dark world of unhappiness and wretchedness.

"And be patient, (O Mohammad), and your patience is not but through Allah. And do not grieve [lā taḥzan] over them and do not be in distress [ḍayqīn] Over what they conspire."[106]

"And when Our messengers (the angels), came to Lot, he was anguished for them [sīa] and felt for them great discomfort [ḍāqa] and said, 'this is a trying day' ['āṣībūn]."[107]

"And when Our messenger came to Lot, he was distressed [sīa] for them and felt for them great discomfort [ḍaqa]. They said, 'Fear not, [lā takhaf] nor grieve [lā tahzan]. Indeed we will save you and your family...."[108]

And whoever turns away from My remembrance, indeed, he will have a Depressed [ḍankan] life, and We will gather him on the day of resurrection blind.[109]

- *ghamm*, from the triliteral root *gh-m-m*. It occurs eleven times in the Quran in three derived forms: once as the noun *ghumma* meaning 'doubt'; four times as the noun *ghamām*, meaning 'clouds'; and six times as the noun *ghamm,* meaning 'distress' or 'anguish'. The verse below makes it clear that *ghamm* is given by God purposefully in order that individuals may come to the realisation that everyone's fate is in accordance with Divine determining and decree. It is with such realisation that there exists the potential for believers to avoid *ḥuzn* (sadness) and *khawf* (fear).

(Remember) when you (fled and) climbed (the mountain) without looking aside at anyone while the Messenger was calling you from behind. So Allah repaid you with distress [ghamman] upon distress [ghammin] so you would not grieve [lā taḥzanū] for that which had escaped you (of victory and spoils of war) or (for) that which had befallen you (of injury and death). And Allah is (fully) acquainted with what you do.[110]

The *ghamm* or distress that is given may come in the form of *balā*, which connotes a trial, a tribulation or any kind of temporary suffering imposed on believers as a test of faith. It is usually linked to objects of attachment such as goods, health, power, wealth, and so on.

Be sure we shall test [balā] you with something of fear and hunger, some loss in goods or lives or the fruits (of your toil), but give glad tidings to those who patiently persevere. Who say, when afflicted with calamity: "To Allah we belong, and to Him is our return".[111]

- *hamm* is a word which occurs nine times in the Quran in two derived forms: eight times as the form I verb *hamma*, meaning 'inclined', 'determined', 'resolved', 'planned', 'plotted' or 'desired'; and once as the form IV verb *ahamma*, meaning 'to worry' or 'to be in an anxious state due to impending harm'. The word *ḥamm* is therefore linked to anxiety about what one is expecting to happen, while *ghamm* is linked to what has already happened. In the verse below, *hamm* is associated with the negative kind of anxiety which stems from one's own imagination.

After (the excitement) of the distress [ghamm], He sent down calm on a band of you overcome with slumber, while another band was stirred to anxiety [ahammathum] by their own feelings, Moved by wrong suspicions of Allah – suspicions due to ignorance. They said: "What affair is this of ours?" Say thou: "Indeed, this affair is wholly Allah's." They hide in their minds what they dare not reveal to thee. They say (to themselves): "If we had had anything to do with this affair, we should not have been in the slaughter here." Say: "Even if you had remained in your homes, those for whom death was decreed would certainly have gone forth to the place of their death"; but (all this was) that Allah might test [lī-yabtalīa – from balā] what is in your breasts and purge what is in your hearts. For Allah knoweth well the secrets of your hearts.[112]

- *asaf* occurs five times in the Quran, in three derived forms. It appears once as the form IV verb *āsafu*, meaning 'they angered', and four times as the nouns *asif* and *asaf* with the basic meaning of 'grief' or 'sorrow'. However, again as is demonstrated in the verse below, the relational meaning of *asaf* is linked to anger, disappointment and hurt at what has actually taken place rather than what might happen in the future.

When Moses came back to his people, angry [ghaḍbāna] and grieved ['asīfan], he said: "Evil it is that ye have done in my place in my absence: did ye make haste to bring on the judgment of your Lord?" He put down the tablets, seized his brother by (the hair of) his head, and dragged him to him. Aaron said: "Son of my mother! The people did indeed reckon me as naught, and went near to slaying me! Make not the enemies rejoice over my misfortune, nor count thou me amongst the people of sin.[113]

- *bakha'a*, means 'to slaughter'. The verb is also used to denote 'anything to a great extent....'[114] The triliteral root *b-kh-'ayn* occurs twice in the Quran as the active participle *bākhī'*, meaning 'the one who kills'[115] or 'would kill'[116] However, in the Quranic context, used with the word *nafs* (self), it is translated as: 'to worry or grieve to death'.[117]

Thou wouldst only, perchance, fret thyself to death [bākhī'un], following after them, in grief ['asafan], if they believe not in this Message.[118]

It may be thou frettest thy soul with grief [bākhī'un] that they do not become Believers.[119]

Compared to verse 16:127, where the word *ḥuzn* is used to comfort and gently remind Muhammad not to be anxious about the plots of the unbelievers, the use of the verb *bakha'a* with *nafs* shows the extremity of his sadness on account of not having been able to achieve his aim of changing people's attitudes. The extent of his sadness shows the human side of the Prophet, together with the high expectation he had of himself, as well as the importance – as he was reminded – to carry out his duty without expectation of positive results.

- *kaẓama* means 'to shut', 'to stop', 'to abstract', 'to choke', 'to suppress' or 'to restrain one's anger'.[120] The triliteral root occurs six times in the Quran in three derived forms. It appears three times as the noun *kaẓīm* ('a suppressor of grief'); twice as the active participle *kaẓīmīn* ('those who restrain'); and once as the passive participle *makẓūm* ('was distressed').[121] Verse 12:84 below discusses three psychological states linked with sadness. Firstly, there is *asaf*, which, as already discussed, means 'sorrow', and is linked in this verse to the profound sorrow Jacob felt as a result of the loss of Joseph. Indeed, his anxiety and worry (*ḥuzn*) was such that he was in danger of completely losing his eyesight. However, he did not show the extent of his sorrow openly, with the result that his heavily suppressed grief (*kaẓīmūn*) became a real cause for concern among his family members.[122]

And he turned away from them, and said: "How great is my grief [asafā] for Joseph!" And his eyes became white with sorrow [ḥuzn], and he fell into silent melancholy [kaẓīmūn].

They (Jacob's sons) said: "By Allah! [never] wilt thou cease to remember Joseph until thou reach the last extremity of illness [ḥaraḍan], or until thou die [hālīkīn]

The relational meaning of khawf with ḥuzn

The word *ḥuzn* is paired with the word *khawf* seventeen times in the Quran, thus indicating that they enjoy a strong relational meaning with one another. In order to get closer to the meaning of *ḥuzn* it will be useful to analyse the word *khawf* along with other words which are similar or which appear to have the same meaning as *khawf*.

Words which appear to be synonymous with khawf

- *rahiba* ('to fear'; 'to dread'; 'to be in awe')
- *ḥadhira* ('to fear'; 'to be forewarned')
- *taqwā* ('fear'; 'piety'; 'protection')
- *khashīya* ('awe with reverence and fear')

The triliteral root *kh-w-f* occurs 124 times in the Quran, in seven derived forms: eighty-three times as the form I verb *khāfa*. meaning 'to fear' or 'to be afraid'; four times as the form II verb *khawwafa*, meaning 'to frighten' or 'to threaten'; twenty six times as the noun *khawf*, meaning 'fear'; six times as the noun *khīfat* meaning 'in fear' or 'a fear'; six times as the active participle *khā'if*, meaning 'fearful' or 'fearing'; once as the form II verbal noun *takhwīf*, meaning 'a warning'; and once as the form V verbal noun *takhawwuf* meaning 'a gradual wasting'.[123]

The word *khawf* and its derivatives are paired at least seventeen times with the word *ḥuzn* and its derivatives. In verses 2:38, 2:62, 2:112, 2:262, 2:74, 2:77, 3:170, 5:69, 6:48, 7:35, 7:49, 10:62, 43:68 and 46:13, the root *kh-w-f* appears as the noun *khawf*, meaning 'fear' and in verses 28:7, 29:33 and 41:30 it appears as declensions of the form I verb *khawifa*, namely as *khīf'tī*, *takhaf* and *takhāfū* respectively, all of which mean 'you fear'. Eight of these verses were revealed in Medina and nine were revealed in Mecca. As was discussed earlier, the Meccan verses deal primarily with the foundational issues of Islam such as monotheism, revelation and the hereafter. The audience targeted are believers, and this is inclusive of Christians, Jews, Sabeans and all others who believe in one God and the Hereafter. The Medinan verses are characterised by their inclusion of verses which are legislative and jurisprudential in nature, and which are relatively conspicuous by their absence in the Meccan narratives.

In analysing these seventeen verses in which the words *ḥuzn* and *khawf* appear together, I have identified a clear difference between the Meccan and Medinan verses. The nine verses revealed in Mecca (46:13, 43:68, 41:30, 29:33, 6:48, 7:35, 7:49, 10:62, and 28:7) are linked mainly to the issue of belief, e.g. 'those who say Our Lord is God and remain firm on that path' (46:13) and 'Those who say our Lord is God' (41:30) will not have cause for *khawf* or *ḥuzn*. The Medinan verses (2:38, 2:62, 2:112, 2:262, 2:274, 2:77, 3:170 and 5:69) however, are linked to both belief and submission, clarifying that in order not to have *khawf* or *ḥuzn* it is necessary to move to the next stage, that is, to add to ones belief in good acts of submission such as regular prayers, giving charity and performing other righteous deeds.

There are other words in the Quran which approximate to 'fear', such as *rahība*, *khashīya*, *hadhīra*. These words take on different meanings depending on the context. It is outside the scope of this study to examine all the words which have a semantic link with the word *khawf*. However, a brief reference to some of these words will demonstrate the importance of grammar and syntax and how words can have a totally different meaning depending on their grammatical form. For example, the 1st form verb *rahiba* means 'to fear', 'to dread' or 'to be in awe', but in its 4th and 10th forms it means 'to terrify'. Similarly, although the nouns *rahb* and *rahab* mean 'fear', the derivative *ruhbān*, however, means 'monks', while *rahbānīyyatan* means 'monasticism'.[124] The 1st form verb meaning 'fear' is closely connected with the word *taqwa* as it is used mainly in the context of not fearing or taking guidance from anyone except God, such as in 16:51 below:

> *And Allah said, 'Do not take for your selves two deities. He is but One God, so fear only Me'.*

The verb *ḥadhīra*, as it appears in verses 2:235, 5:41, 9:64 and 2:19 also means 'to fear', but in the sense of being aware, taking precautions and being forewarned. Another key word usually translated as fear is *taqwā*. The word *taqwā* comes from the verb *waqaya* which has the basic meanings 'to protect'; 'to save'; 'to preserve'; 'to ward off'; 'to be secure'; 'to be shielded' and 'to guard against evil and calamity'.[125] In the Quranic context it takes the meaning of being dutiful and guarding against sin. However, this concept does not lend itself easily to a word-for-word translation as it is linked closely to the attributes of a believer and is connected eschatologically with the fear of the hereafter. For example, in the following verse there are slightly different translations of the same word *'attaqā*. Variations of translation include: 'whosoever refraineth from evil'; 'those who are righteous'; 'whoever fears Allah'; 'whoever shall guard [against evil]'; 'those who choose piety'; 'whosoever becomes pious and righteous'; and 'whosoever is god-fearing'.[126]

> *O children of Adam, if there come to you messengers from among you relating to you My verses, then whoever fears [attaqā] Allah and reforms – there will be no fear concerning them, nor will they grieve.*[127]

A person who has *taqwā* attains a state of righteousness by worshipping only one Lord (*rabb*).[128] Moreover, it also requires a state of submission to the one God. The verse below describes the characteristics of the 'righteous' (*al-muttaqūn*).

> *Righteousness is not that you turn your faces toward the east or the west, but [true] righteousness is [in] one who believes in Allah , the Last Day, the angels, the Book, and the prophets and gives wealth, in spite of love for it, to relatives, orphans, the needy, the traveller, those who ask [for help], and for freeing slaves; [and who] establishes prayer and gives zakah; [those who] fulfil their promise when they promise; and [those who] are patient in poverty and hardship and during battle. Those are the ones who have been true, and it is those who are the righteous.*[129]

Therefore, some of the key words in the semantic category of *taqwā* are 'true belief', or 'righteousness', which means not only belief in God, the hereafter and the angels, and following God's guidance through revelation and the prophets, but also submitting actively through prayer, charitable giving, and through manifesting God's attribute of patience through difficult times. In this sense, the word *taqwā* is also linked closely to the heart and the concept of justice,[130] and connotes reaching a level where one fears nothing and no-one other than God.[131] This state of *taqwā* is posited as being the ultimate goal, with total submission resulting hopefully in the obviation of *ḥuzn* and *khawf*.

The word *khashīya* means 'awe', but awe that is mixed with reverence and fear; as such it is associated closely with the word *taqwa*. Again, the meaning of this word is linked to the notion of not being frightened, primarily in the sense of not being accountable to anyone else except God.

> *[It is in the practice of those] who preach the messages of Allah, and fear Him, and fear none but Allah. And enough is Allah to call [men] to account.*[132]

Although the basic meaning of *khawf* is 'fear', used together with *ḥuzn* it becomes almost synonymous with it, acquiring a new meaning of 'fear and apprehension' related to anxiety in relation to the future or to the unknown. As Table 1 in this chapter demonstrates, the key to the obviation of anxiety linked to loss is the promise of the hereafter, a place of eternal happiness for those who have belief (*īmān*) and who demonstrate their belief through sincere submission (*islām*).

Another example of people who will not have to suffer *ḥuzn,* are those who follow guidance (*hudā*).[133] The word 'guidance', then, has a close relationship with the word *khawf* and *ḥuzn* through its opposite meaning, in the sense that those who follow God's guidance will not experience sadness or fear. It is therefore useful to analyse the semantic category of the word 'guidance' in order to explore the nature of guidance and the essential quality of those who follow God's guidance.

Those who follow guidance (hudā)

In 2:2-5 it is made clear that guidance should be sought in 'the Book' (*al-kītāb*). It is a mercy from God and the only route to prosperity (*falaḥ*). The means that one is to attain guidance is through belief in the revelation, the hereafter and the world of the unseen, and in submission to God through prayer and through charitable giving out of what God has provided.[134] In other words, 'the Book' will be a source of guidance only for those who obey God and have God-awareness (*taqwā*).[135]

There is much emphasis on the oneness of God and no one – not even the prophets – can give guidance, as it can originate from God alone. Therefore, God is the only One who guides and He has no partners to share in this task. And there is no one and nothing in the world able to shield or protect anyone against God, since He is the only Protector (*walī*) and helper (*naṣīr*).[136] The role of the prophets is essentially to direct and support people towards understanding and submitting to the message and guidance of God.[137] God usually speaks of Himself in the first person plural form – 'We' – but although the verse below starts with the plural form it changes to the singular 'Me' in order to emphasise that guidance is solely from Him.[138]

> *'We said: "Get ye down all from here; and if, as is sure, there comes to you Guidance/ hudā from Me, whosoever follows My guidance [hudāya], on them shall be no fear [khawf], nor shall they grieve [yaḥzanūna].'*[139]

Verse 2:97 clarifies the role of the Angel Gabriel as the 'carrier' of both guidance and revelation for those who have belief (*īmān*). However, as regards those who reject the manifest signs (*kāfir*), that is, those who do not believe in God, His apostles and His angels, they will not be guided as they are of 'the perverse kind' (*fāsiqūn*).[140]

Therefore, God as the only Protector (*walī*) and Helper (*naṣīr*) guides only those who are believers (*mu'min*). And true believers are: those who believe in the Book (*kitāb*); in the Unseen (*ghayb*) and in the Hereafter (*ākhira*); and those who are righteous (*muttaqīn*) ; that is, the ones who are steadfast in prayer (*ṣalāt*) and who carry out good actions (*khayr*) purely 'for the sake of God' (lit. 'seeking the 'face' (*wajh*) of Allah)[141] and not for expectations of favours in return. They also spend (*infāq*) of their wealth, both in a financial and a spiritual or metaphorical sense, and they perform acts of righteousness (*khayr*) for the sake of God.[142] This is the state of total sincerity which in fact is the ideal or innate state for human beings to be in: a state which ensures true prosperity (*mufliḥūn*).[143] These actions of the believers would not only be justly rewarded but would also benefit their own souls (*nafs*).[144]

The word *kāfirūn* ('those who reject faith') comes in direct opposition to those who believe (*mu'minūn*). The *kāfirūn* are people who do not have faith in God, His messengers and His angels; they are referred to as 'the perverse kind' (*fāsiqūn*)[145] as opposed to the believers (*mu'minūn*), who are referred to as the *muttaqīn* ('those who are God-aware').[146] Therefore the path to the obviation of sadness lies in following guidance in order to reach a state of *taqwā* in belief as opposed to unbelief, which is the state of the perverse (*fāsiqūn*).

The important twin concepts of belief and unbelief is discussed below and a table is provided later in this Chapter for easy reference to show some of the words which belong in the semantic category of this key binary pair.

> *Those who are true in faith (mu'minūn) 'So lose not heart [tahinū], nor fall into despair [taḥzanū]: For ye must gain mastery if ye are true in Faith [mu'minīn].'*[147]

The above verse implies that there is no reason for those who have true faith (*īmān*) to have *ḥuzn*, as long as they believe in the truth (*haqq*) - that is, by following God's guidance through revelation – and as long as they trust and fear (*taqwā*) their Lord (*rabb*) by submitting to Him through engaging in good works (*aḥsana*) and carrying out acts of righteousness (*'amilū al-sālīḥāt*). Through belief, trust, submission and perseverance in patience (*ṣabr*), they will be able to avoid anxiety about the future since they will be guided towards the right path and are promised a permanent life in paradise.[148]

However, there are those who choose not to believe (*kāfir*), and refuse stubbornly to heed the Messenger's warnings. These people are referred to as the *fāsīqūn,* and are 'led astray' because they have chosen to block guidance and forsake the path.[149] As the verses below demonstrate, the words *fāsīqūn* (those who rebel) and *ẓālimūn* (wrong-doers) have a very strong connection with the semantic field of *kāfīrūn* (unbelievers), since all of these terms describe those who do not judge by what God has revealed – in other words, those who refuse to follow guidance.

> *And whoever does not judge by what Allah has revealed – then it is those who are the disbelievers [kāfīrūn].*[150]

> *And whoever does not judge by what Allah has revealed – then it is those who are the wrongdoers [ẓālīmūn].*[151]

> *And whoever does not judge by what Allah has revealed – then it is those who are the defiantly disobedient [fāsīqūn].*[152]

The analysis of the words 'are led astray'[153] is very important here, for one may question why an all-compassionate and all-merciful God would want to misguide people. The answer lies in the fact that everything in the Quran points to God's Unity and the refutation of polytheism, in the sense that no one has the power to do anything. But although there is nothing else in creation which can have any influence, and it is solely God Himself Who guides the believers and misleads those who reject faith, there is in fact no compulsion: the choice actually lies with the individual as to whether they want to be guided or not.

It also becomes clear that 'not believing' is not actually an action; rather, it is in fact 'a denial' or 'a covering of the truth'. In the Quran, the analogy of light and darkness is used to describe belief and unbelief.[154] The state of denial therefore is like darkness, which does not have an external existence, since it is in fact merely a lack of light. The key to salvation from this 'darkness' then – or one might say this state of pretention – into 'light', is belief. To choose unbelief, on the other hand, is to choose to remain in darkness, or in other words in a state of total loss.

According to Izutsu, the basic meaning of the word *kafara* is 'to be ungrateful' or 'to show ingratitude', as opposed to *shakara,* which means 'to be thankful'. But, when contrasted with 'belief' in the Quranic context, *kafara* underwent a 'semantic transformation' and acquired a new meaning of 'unbelief'. That is, *kafara* became the antonym of āmana ('to believe') rather than *shakara* ('to be grateful').[155] However, although the main meaning of *kufr* is 'unbelief', as it is devoid of all the qualities of belief, one may argue that it still retains its original meaning of ingratitude, that is, ingratitude to God in the Quranic context. The reason is that, as explained below, *shakara* ('to be thankful') is itself almost synonymous with the word āmana ('to believe'). Therefore, as shown in the following verses, it appears that as well as being the antonym of āmana, the verb *kafara* is also inevitably the antonym of *shakara.* Therefore, it has not undergone a total transformation as such but has acquired, in the Quranic context, a much broader meaning within the semantic field of 'belief'.

> *And remember! Your Lord caused to be declared {publicly}: "If you are grateful [shakartum], I will add more {favours} unto you; but if you show ingratitude [kafartum], truly my punishment is terrible indeed."*[156]

> *This is from the favour of my Lord to test me [bala] whether I will be grateful [ashkuru] or ungrateful [akfuru].*[157]

> *And We had certainly given Luqman wisdom {and said} "Be grateful to Allah." And whoever is grateful [yashkuru] is grateful for {the benefit of} himself. And whoever denies {His favour} [kafara] – then indeed, Allah is free of need and praiseworthy.*[158]

> *If you disbelieve [takfuru] – indeed, Allah is free from need of you. And He does not approve for His servants disbelief [kufr]. And if you are grateful [tashkuru], He approves it for you.*[159]

The following verses show that thankfulness is a necessary corollary of belief. In fact, as Izutsu himself opines, in the Quranic context, some verses show that "*shakara* becomes almost synonymous with āmana".[160]

In the last verse, the analogy of darkness and light is used, which, as discussed previously, describes the state of belief and unbelief.[161] This verse links the bringing of people out of darkness into light with being grateful (*shakūr*).

> *Rather, worship {only} Allah and be among the grateful.*[162]

> *What would Allah do with your punishment if you are grateful [shakartum] and believe [āmantum]? And ever is Allah Appreciative and Knowing.*[163]

> *And We certainly sent Moses with Our signs, {saying}, "Bring out your people from darkness into the light and remind them of the days of Allah." Indeed in that are signs for everyone patient and grateful [shakūr].*[164]

The semantic structures of belief and unbelief can be found in Table 2 below, where some of the key concepts concerning belief, together with the characteristics and qualities of believers as opposed to those of people who choose to reject faith, are summarized.

Table 2: Semantic categories of Belief & Unbelief

Qualities of a those who believe (*āmana*)	**Qualities of those who reject faith (*kafara*)**
Will not have sadness or fear 2:38	Will be at a loss 103:1-3
Shows gratitude 39:66	Ingratitude 14:7 and 31:12
Follows guidance 2:38	Does not judge by what God has revealed 5:44
Work righteousness (*amilū sāliḥāt*) 103:2 and 2:25	Perverse (*fāsiq*) 2:26
Will be guided to the right path (*hudā*) 6:154 and 2:26	Strays from the right path (*dhila*) and (*fāsiq*) 2:26
Spends (*yunfiqūna*) of what God has provided for them 2:3, 2:254	Stinginess (*bukhl*) 4:37
Believes in the Unseen (*ghayb*) 2:3	Rejects the manifest signs *(āyāt)* 2:99
Will have patience (*ṣabr*) 3:200	
Will fear God/be righteous (*taqwa*) 3:200	The worst of creatures 98:6
Will worship God alone and not associate partners with Him (*shirk*) 12:38	Association of partners with God (3:151)
Will do good (*ahsana*) 6:154	
Carries out good actions (*khayr*) 2:272	Allured to the life of this world (*al-hayāt-al-dunyā*) 2:212
Will receive God's Mercy (*raḥma*) 33:43	
Join together mutual teachings of truth (*ḥaqq*) 103:3 and 2:26	
Believes in The Book/Revelation (*al-kitab*) 6:154	Will not believe (*la yu'minūna*) 2:98
Submits to God (*Islam*) 10:84; 4:59; 8:1; 33:36; 4:103	Wrongdoing themselves (*ẓālimī 'anfusihim*) 16:28
Belief linked to light (*nūr*) 33:43	Unbelief linked to darkness (*ẓulumāt*) 33:43
Steadfast in prayer (*salāt*) 2:3	
Believes in the hereafter (*ākhira*) 2:8 and 2:4	Denies the hereafter 41:7
Will prosper (*mufliḥūna*) 2:5	Will be in a wretched state (*bi'sa*) 3:151

Will not be dealt with unjustly (*lā tuẓlamūna*) 2:272	Wrong-doers (*ẓālimūn*) 5:45
Their portion is Gardens (*jannat*) 2:25	Their abode is the fire 24:57
Will be in a state of security and peace (*amīn*) 6:82	Will be at a loss (*khusr*) 103:1
Seek God as their only Protector (*walī*) and helper (*naṣīr*) 2:120	Allah is an enemy (*'aduww*) to those who reject faith 2:98

* It should be noted that the right-hand column, namely the qualities of those who reject belief, is a separate list, and so the meanings are not necessarily in direct opposition to those in the left-hand column, i.e. qualities of those who believe.

The semantic structure of antonyms of ḥuzn

As Izutsu recommends, in order to go beyond the basic meaning and get closer to the 'real meaning' of a word, it may be helpful to look at the opposites of the concepts in question. In this case the opposite of *ḥuzn* would be 'happiness'/and its cognates. Some of the Quranic terms which convey the meaning of happiness are studied briefly here:

- *fariḥa* ('to be glad or happy')
- *sa'ada* ('to be prosperous, happy')
- *sarra* ('to be glad; 'to rejoice')

The basic meaning of the verb *fariḥa* is: 'to be glad, happy, delighted'; 'to rejoice'; 'to be cheerful or pleased'; 'to exult'.[165] The triliteral *f-r-ḥ* occurs twenty-two times in the Quran in two derived forms: sixteen times as the form I verb *fariḥa* and six times as the noun *fariḥ*, meaning 'one who rejoices'. Within the Quranic context, most of the verses point to human beings' being immersed in the rejoicing in this worldly life and forgetting the source of the bounties given to them.[166]

> *It is He who enables you to travel on land and sea until, when you are in ships and they sail with them by a good wind and they rejoice therein, there comes a storm wind and the waves come upon them from everywhere and they assume that they are surrounded, supplicating Allah, sincere to Him in religion, "If You should save us from this, we will surely be among the thankful."*[167]

> *But when He saves them, at once they commit injustice upon the earth without right. O mankind, your injustice is only against yourselves, [being merely] the enjoyment of worldly life. Then to Us is your return, and We will inform you of what you used to do.*[168]

In the first verse above, the word 'thankful' (*shukr*) is used. As discussed previously,[169] thankfulness is a characteristic of a believer, as opposed to ingratitude, which is a characteristic of an unbeliever, that is, someone who covers the truth. It is interesting here that the Quran talks about those who, while all is well at sea, sail along happily with no thought of God, and who are thus immersed in ingratitude; it is only when a storm brews, and they are threatened with immersion in the raging sea that promises of gratitude are made. The second verse goes on to explain that neglecting to give thanks is an injustice, particularly to one's own soul. Therefore, there is a link here between the concepts of belief, gratitude, balance and equilibrium with ever-lasting happiness, as opposed to the link between unbelief with injustice, imbalance and the transient enjoyment of worldly life.

The basic meanings of the verb *sa'ida* are 'to be prosperous, blessed, happy, auspicious' and 'to thrive'.[170] The triliteral root occurs twice in the Quran in two derived forms: once as the third person plural form of the form I verb, i.e. *su'īdu* 'they were glad'; and once as the noun *sa'īd* meaning 'those who are glad', translated below as 'the prosperous'.

> *The Day it comes no soul will speak except by His permission. And among them will be the wretched [shaqī] and the prosperous [sa'īd].* (11:105)

> *As for those who were [destined to be] wretched, they will be in the Fire. For them therein is [violent] exhaling and inhaling.* (11:106)

> *And as for those who were [destined to be] prosperous [su'īdu], they will be in Paradise, abiding therein as long as the heavens and the earth endure, except what your Lord should will – a bestowal uninterrupted.* (11:108)

As discussed previously[171] the Quranic meaning of *shaqīya* is linked to the notion of 'those who turn away from God and reject His guidance'. Hence the wretched are the unbelievers whose abode is the fire, as opposed to believers who will be in a state of bliss, dwelling in paradise. Therefore *shaqīya* has a semantic link with unbelief, while *sa'ida* has a strong semantic link with belief.

The basic meanings of the verb *sarra* are 'to make glad'; 'to rejoice'; and 'to be glad'.[172] The root *s-r-r* occurs forty-four times in the Quran, in nine derived forms: once as the form I verb *tasurru* meaning 'pleasing', eighteen times as the form IV verb *asarra* meaning 'to conceal', eleven times as the noun *sirr* meaning 'secretly', once as the noun *sarā'ir* meaning 'the secrets', twice as the noun *sarrā* meaning 'ease', six times as the noun *surur* meaning 'thrones', once as the noun *surūr* meaning 'happiness', twice as the passive participle *masrūr* meaning 'happy' and twice as the form IV verbal noun *as'rār* meaning 'secrets'.[173]

> *When the sky is rent asunder, And hearkens to (the Command of) its Lord, and it must needs (do so); – And when the earth is flattened out, And casts forth what is within it and becomes (clean) empty, And hearkens to (the Command of) its Lord, – and it must needs (do so); – (then will come Home the full reality). O thou man! Verily thou art ever toiling on towards thy Lord – painfully toiling – but thou shalt meet Him. Then he who is given his Record in his right hand, soon will his account be taken by an easy reckoning, and he will turn to his people, rejoicing! [masrūran] But he who is given his Record behind his back, – Soon will he cry for perdition, And he will enter a Blazing Fire. Truly, did he go about among his people, rejoicing! [masrūran] Truly, did he think that he would not have to return (to Us)! Nay, nay! for his Lord was (ever) watchful of him! What then is the matter with them, that they believe not? - And when the Qur'an is read to them, they fall not prostrate, but on the contrary the Unbelievers reject (it). But Allah has full knowledge of what they secrete (in their breasts). So announce to them a Penalty Grievous, except to those who believe and work righteous deeds: For them is a Reward that will never fail.*

Chapter eighty-four of the Quran above concerns, among other things, the link between happiness (*surūr*) and belief. It states that true happiness in the hereafter awaits only those who heed God's guidance, as opposed to the unbelievers who reject the Quran and amuse themselves in the worldly life; their reward will be a blazing fire. Therefore, it becomes clear that the concepts of belief and guidance have a strong relational connection with the concept of happiness, as opposed to the concept of unbelief, which has a strong semantic link with ultimate perdition in the hereafter.

Conclusion

The forty-two verses in the Quran which contain the word *ḥuzn* were collated and those from among them which were related to the obviation of *ḥuzn* were grouped together in order to obtain a picture of the type of people who are in theory able to avoid *ḥuzn*. The rest of the words– namely those which are not related directly to the obviation of *ḥuzn* – were grouped according to themes. The typology and the thematic analysis showed that there are many words in the Quran which are similar in meaning to *ḥuzn* and although it often happens that they are all treated in translation as though they were identical, these concepts when examined in their Quranic context have different nuances of meaning. The concept of *ḥuzn* itself appears to mean 'grief which occurs as a result of loss', for example the loss of a loved one such as was experienced by the mother of Moses mother (28:13), or by Abraham having to let go of his son Ismail (37:99-110); or by Jacob in his attachment to Joseph (12:84). *Ḥuzn* is a feeling that is given by God, and thus its existence is necessary as it contains the positive component of guidance.

The sadness which is prohibited is the extreme kind of sadness that comes from the refusal to accept events decreed by Divine Determining. The kind of *ḥuzn* experienced by the prophets falls mainly in the first category since it appears to serve them as a means of guidance. *Ḥuzn* as discussed in the typology demonstrates the human aspect of the prophets. For example, Jacob was reluctant initially to send Joseph out to the pastures with his brothers because he feared that some harm would come to him, but nevertheless in the end he accepted, possibly due to the realisation that ultimately Joseph's safety was in God's hands. Hence as a prophet, Jacob did not want to attribute power to secondary causes. But when the brothers returned without Joseph, Jacob was unable to bear the separation. His extreme compassion for Joseph resulted in unbearable grief (*asaf*), to the extent that he lost his sight and fell into a silent melancholy (*kaẓīm*).

The term *kiẓm* denotes the psychological state of suppressed grief, which in the case of Jacob's extreme sadness may have contributed to his loss of sight and the consequent concerns that his sons had with regard to his health. Jacob's sons begged him to let go of his attachment to Joseph as it was making him extremely ill (*haraḍan*) and might, if unchecked, have even caused him to possibly even die of grief (*hālīkīn*). But Jacob knew that ultimately his unbearable situation was part of the Divine Determining (*qadar*), and so he kept his sorrow (*ḥuzn*) to himself while admitting his weakness directly to his Lord. This seems to be an admission of weakness on the part of Jacob. At the same time, however, it demonstrated Jacob's recognition that it was God who had given him this sadness in order to submit to his total state of impotence, and that it was only through God's grace and mercy that the sadness would be lifted from him. For Jacob, then, even though *ḥuzn* was at times excessive, it served as a test and a form of guidance.

In the case of Muhammad, as discussed previously, his deep pain on account of the indifference shown by his community to the warnings he was giving them was that Quranic verses were revealed which admonished him and cautioned him to stop blaming himself for his people's choice of action.[174] The verses were revealed to remind and guide him, as messengers before him were guided, that ultimately everything that was taking place would be in accordance with Divine decree and determining. He was told that there should therefore be no sadness or regret (*hasrat*) about the past, nor any sadness or worry (*ḥuzn*) with regard to the effect of loss or the non-attainment of goals. This non-attribution to secondary causes is akin to being in a state of total submission (*tawakkul*).

The Izutsian methodology and the analysis of the concept of *ḥuzn* began by comparing and contrasting some of the terms which were both similar and opposite to *ḥuzn* in order to obtain a contextual rather than an atomistic meaning of the concept.

Two of the words which had a strong semantic relation with the word *ḥuzn* were 'belief' and its opposite, 'unbelief'. The Izutsian analysis showed that the key to the obviation of *ḥuzn* is to have belief. It showed that sincere belief translated is belief in only one God, which in turn means fearing and trusting Him only by not ascribing partners to Him; by following the guidance included in the precepts of the Quran; by carrying out acts of righteousness purely for His sake; and by showing patience and perseverance at the time of hardship. As shown in Table 2,[175] belief is also linked to the notion of gratitude, while unbelief is linked to the concept of ingratitude.

The Izutsian analysis shows that sincere believers are the ones who are able to avoid *ḥuzn* by submitting totally to God, whereas the *kāfirūn* and the *fāsiqūn* are the ones who cover the truth and rebel against it, becoming *ẓālimūn* (wrong-doers) in the process, since through their own choice and their attachment to the transient world, they remain in darkness by blocking out the light of belief.

It has also been demonstrated that the word *khawf* also has a strong relational meaning with *ḥuzn*, as they are paired seventeen times in the Quran. The analysis of the word *khawf* showed that with belief, this negative concept can be changed to *taqwā*, which also means 'fear', but in a positive sense, since it also means trust in, and submission to, the one God. The analysis of the word *khawf* with *ḥuzn* revealed that the state of non-attribution of effects to secondary causes, fearing God alone, and believing in the hereafter constitute the key to the obviation of both sorrow that comes from loss and fear pertaining to possible calamities and death in the future.

The analysis of these seventeen verses also showed that nine of the verses which were revealed in Mecca were linked mainly to the principles of belief such as monotheism, revelation and the hereafter, while the Medinan verses were linked to both belief and submission, thus clarifying the point that for the obviation of *ḥuzn* and *khawf* to obtain, the next stage, namely submission as well as belief, is necessary.

The next chapter looks at key textual sources in order to gain insights into the concept of *ḥuzn* as understood by Quranic exegetes from both classical and modern periods.

3

The Concept of *ḥuzn* in Quranic Exegesis

Introduction

After a general discussion about the interpretation of the Quran, followed by a brief look at the historical background of Quranic exegesis, this chapter will introduce a number of classical and modern exegetes with the aim of exploring their interpretation of the concept of *ḥuzn*.

The interpretation of the Quran by the Quran itself is considered to be the most reliable and authentic method of exegesis.[1] Given that the tenets of faith are formulated in the Quran itself, providing all that is needed for moral regeneration in both one's social and personal life, it is clear why, as revelation itself argues, the Quran would be seen as the criterion upon which everything should be based.[2] Although the Quran invites all individuals to use their intellect to understand the purpose of their existence, it states that God alone has knowledge of its true meanings:

> *It is He who has sent down to you, [O Muhammad], the Book; in it are verses [that are] precise – they are the foundation of the Book – and others unspecific. As for those in whose hearts is deviation [from truth], they will follow that of it which is unspecific, seeking discord and seeking an interpretation [suitable to them]. And no one knows its [true] interpretation except Allah. But those firm in knowledge say, "We believe in it. All [of it] is from our Lord. "And no one will be reminded except those of understanding.*[3]

Moral guidance, however, is only one dimension – the exoteric or *ẓāhirī* dimension – of the Quran; the overwhelming majority of Quranic verses are more ethico-theologically oriented, and have an esoteric dimension or *batin* which is considered to be timeless and not limited to a specific historical period or event.[4] There are also verses in the Quran which are described as being 'clear in meaning' (*muḥkam*), as opposed to verses which are more ambiguous or allegorical (*mutashābih*). Differences of interpretation and disagreement among exegetes concern in the main these *mutashābih* verses and how they are understood.[5] The principle of 'abrogation' (*naskh*), where certain Quranic verses are considered to be supersedable by others revealed later, further complicates matters, particularly it concerns verses which are considered to have been abrogated textually but not conceptually. While some scholars link the abrogating verses with the *muḥkam* verses and the abrogated verses with the *mutashābih* verses, there is no actual consensus among the exegetes as to which verses abrogate and which verses are abrogated.[6]

Furthermore, most classical exegetes have exercised great caution in their interpretation of the Quran, aware as they no doubt were of the warnings included in 3:7, cited earlier. The tradition-oriented exegetes believed that personal opinion should not be used and that the criterion for acceptance of any interpretation should be the supporting evidence of the Quran itself or, in the absence of such support, the Traditions.[7] Thus it is a reality that most works of exegesis are detailed explanations of the exoteric dimension of the Quranic verses, with analysis of its esoteric dimensions for the most part avoided. Nevertheless, it is envisaged that the examples of exegetical work used in this chapter will serve at least to some extent as sources of supporting information for the study of the concept of *ḥuzn*. It must also be added that the omission of comments by some of the exegetes on some of the verses is down to the simple fact that not all of the exegetes comment on every verse in the Quran. Furthermore, Tustarī's exegesis, for example, is only a partial commentary, covering around one sixth of the total verses in the Quran.[8]

Before exploring what the exegetes have to say about the concept of *ḥuzn* in the Quran, a brief historical background of the selected sources now follows.

Quranic exegesis (tafsīr)

The word *tafsīr* occurs only once in the Quran.[9] It is derived from the root *f-s-r*, meaning 'explanation' or 'commentary'.[10] *Tafsīr* was based initially mainly on Prophetic traditions (*ḥadīth*); the first works of exegesis were little more than reiterations of those Traditions in which the meanings of various verses had been given by Muhammad himself. However, the 'exegetical Traditions' ascribed to Muhammad and his companions are few in number and represent for the most part answers given by the Prophet to questions asked by his followers about the meaning of certain Quranic verses. Initially, these interpretations were passed on orally, and it was only with the emergence of different schools of exegetical thought that written *tafsīr* came into existence. In these early stages, when *tafsīr* was mainly the domain of *ḥadīth* scholars, *tafsīr* and *ḥadīth* were not easily distinguishable, and the exegesis which took place was dedicated almost exclusively to the explanation of ambiguous or abstruse words and phrases in the Quran.[11] However, these brief explanations were not enough to address the new problems facing the growing community of Muslims, who understandably looked to the Quran for answers. The need for Quranic commentary that would be able to help people understand new and changing situations eventually gave rise to the emergence of independent exegetes.

This chapter will focus on the works of a selection of both Shiite and Sunni exegetes from the classical and modern periods in an attempt to discover their understanding of how the Quran uses the word *ḥuzn*.

Exegetes from the classical period

The first selected work of exegesis from the classical period is *Jāmi' al-bayān 'an ta'wīl āy al-Qur'ān* by Muḥammad ibn Jarīr al-Ṭabarī (840-923). Ṭabarī was born in Amol, in the Mazandaran region of modern Iran. He was well versed in most of the Sunni schools of jurisprudence and although he initially followed the Shafi'ite school, he later formed his own independent school – the Jarīriyya – which eventually became extinct. The exegetes he quotes from are mainly from among the companions of the Prophet, in particular Ibn 'Abbās, traditionally known as the founder of the Meccan school of *tafsīr*.[12]

Tabarī used the terms *tafsīr* and *ta'wīl* interchangeably, unlike the Shi'ites, who made a marked distinction between these two approaches to interpretation. According to Shi'ites, *ta'wīl* could be performed only by the Imams whereas *tafsīr* could be carried out by anyone qualified in the field of exegesis, as it concerns only the outward (*zāhir*) meaning of the Quran. But *ta'wīl* was the exclusive domain of the Imams from the family of the Prophet, since it was believed that they were endowed with the ability to interpret the ambiguous or inner meanings (*bāṭin*) of the Quran. These interpretations from the Imams were transmitted in the form of narrations through the first generation of Shi'ites, more or less in the same way as the narrations were transmitted from Ibn 'Abbās and other companions of the Prophet for the Sunnis.

Ṭabarī's interpretation falls in the category of exegesis known as '*tafsīr* by tradition', since it is based heavily on narrations (*ḥadīth*) and linguistic analysis for its interpretation of the Quran. It is, as Saeed argues, a textualist rather than a contextualist approach.[13] Ṭabari describes his own work thus:

> It is a book containing all that people needs {that is, concerning the interpretation of the Quran}. It is so comprehensive that with it there is no need to have recourse to other books. We shall relate in it arguments wherein agreement was achieved and where disagreement persisted. We shall present the reasons for every school of thought or opinion and elucidate what we consider to be the right view with utmost brevity.[14]

Ṭabarī's work on the Quran has been chosen primarily because it represents a major contribution to the development of exegesis, and one which has been widely used by other commentators;[15] as such it will provide a useful contrast with the works of modern exegetes such as Ṭabāṭabā'ī who are more analytical in their approach.

The second exegete included from the classical period whose work is included here is Ismā'īl 'Imād al-Dīn Abū al-Fidā' ibn Kathīr (1300-1373). Ibn Kathīr was a famous Sunni jurist from the Shaf'ite school of law. He was a historian and compiler of narrations whose main scholarly focus was on Traditions (*ḥadīth*). As a supporter and follower of Ibn Taymiyya, he is considered to have a more conservative approach to exegesis.[16] Although he has been criticised as being dogmatic, with little respect for the intellectual tradition,[17] his interpretation of the Quran has been chosen for analysis since he is still considered to be a prominent figure by many modern Sunnni Muslim scholars, especially for his work *The Interpretation of the Mighty Quran (Tafsīr al-Qur'ān al-'aẓīm)*.[18]

The third exegete chosen from the classical period is Sahl al-Tustarī (818-896).[19] Tustarī was originally from Tustar in the Persian province of Khuzestan, but eventually moved to Iraq. Among his disciples were Dhū'l Nūn al-Miṣrī (796-859); 'Abdullāh Muḥammad b. Aḥmad b. Sālīm al-Baṣrī (d. 279/909) and al-Ḥallāj (d. 309/922). Tustarī is known for the spiritual and ascetic practices which shaped his intellectual development and attracted many people to both him and his teachings. As none of the works ascribed to Tustarī is extant, he is not considered to be primarily a scholar. However, there are collections of his work composed by his followers which convey his teachings. Among these is Tustarī's partial commentary on the Quran. It is partial in that it covers only one sixth of the verses in the Quran.[20] Tustarī has been chosen here because of his prominence as an important figure from a sub-group of Quranic exegetes who represents an approach to the Quran that is more 'mystical' than Tradition-based. His work has also had considerable influence on the development of *Sūfī* thought and practices.[21]

Contemporary exegesis

The first Quranic exegesis selected from the modern period is *Tafhīm al-Quran* by Sayyīd 'Abd al-A'la Mawdūdī (1903-1979). He was born in Aurangabad (now Maharashhra) and traced his lineage back to the great Chīshtī Sūfī saints. However, having served as the founder of the 'Islamic Movement' (Jamā'at-ī-Islāmī) in India, his interpretation of the Quran is grounded more in revivalist and revolutionary ideas. Although he endeavours to interpret the Quran in a holistic way, he relies heavily on Traditions to express the importance of practice as carried out by Muhammad and his followers. Mawdūdī has been selected here as a representative of modern Sunni exegesis whose clear interpretation of the Quran is accessible not only to the educated classes but also to the wider audience.[22]

The second work of Quranic exegesis chosen from the modern period is *al-Mīzān fī al-tafsīr al-Qur'ān* by the Shi'ite scholar Muḥammad Ḥusayn Ṭabāṭabā'ī (1904-1981).[23] Ṭabāṭabā'ī was born in Tabriz, in north-western Iran, but spent much of his life studying in the shrine cities of Najaf and Qumm. The method used by Ṭabāṭabā'ī in his commentary is both descriptive and analytical. As well as using standard exegetical tools such as lexicography and grammar, he attempts to carry out a thematic interpretation of the Quran. Ṭabāṭabā'ī's rational and philosophical approach has gained him recognition as one of the greatest Shi'ite scholars of the twentieth century.[24]

Selected Quranic narratives

In this chapter I will examine the aforementioned exegetical works and discuss their perspective with regard to the concept of *ḥuzn*. As discussed previously, the Quranic 'story' of *ḥuzn* is told through forty-two narratives. As before, they have been grouped into two categories: verses which relate directly to the kind of people who will not have sadness and fear; and verses grouped together according to the different themes of test and trial, separation and loss, and the giving of reminders, reassurance and comfort to the Prophets and to the faithful. In order to provide an in-depth understanding of the concept of *ḥuzn*, twenty-five key verses have been selected; an analysis of all forty-two verses would have been beyond the scope of the study. However, the verses selected constitute an adequate and meaningful representation of their group, exploring the wider context yet avoiding too much repetition of the same themes.

Characteristics of those who will not experience sadness (ḥuzn) and fear (khawf)

Those who follow God's guidance

> *We said, "Go down from it, all of you. And when guidance comes to you from Me, whoever follows My guidance – there will be no fear concerning them, nor will they grieve.*[25]

According to Ibn Kathīr, guidance in this verse refers to "the prophets, Messengers, the clear signs and plain explanation." Consequently, "*whoever follows My Guidance*" therefore refers to those who accept what is contained in God's Books and what is sent with the Messengers. Ibn Kathīr interprets "*there shall be no fear on them*" as being related to the hereafter, meaning that those in question will have no worries or concerns with regard to the life to come. He links the sentence *"nor shall they grieve"* to this world, indicating that they shall have no sadness with regard to their present life. Thus, those who follow God's guidance *'will not be misguided in this life or miserable in the hereafter'*.[26]

Tabarī concurs with Ibn Kathīr, stating that guidance is directly from God, but is channelled through the prophets. He points out that *'go down...'* was addressed not just to Adam and his offspring and Iblīs ('Satan'), but to all of humankind, and that those who have fallen have the opportunity to repent. But one can receive guidance only if repentance is followed by acceptance of the 'clear exposition' which is conveyed through the 'tongue of His Messenger, Muhammad'.[27] And those who follow this guidance need not fear God's punishment or the terrors of resurrection; nor will they grieve for what they have left behind in this world. Therefore, according to Ṭabarī also, the word fear (*khawf*) in this verse is related to the fears of the future with regard to the hereafter, while and sadness (*ḥuzn*) is linked to the idea of loss, that is, what has been left behind in this world.[28]

Ṭabāṭabā'ī relates the above verse to the covenant made by Adam, that is, his promise of total submission to his Lord. But since Adam forgot about the covenant and tasted the fruit of the forbidden tree, it resulted in his fall into a world full of test and trials. However, just as Adam was saved by repenting to God, so too do all human beings have the potential to be saved. The key, according to Ṭabāṭabā'ī, is to accept "the Mastership of Allah" and one's own servitude.[29]

Ṭabāṭabā'ī goes on to explain that accepting God's Mastership means the realisation that one owns nothing and has no authority over anything, including one's own life. With the knowledge that everything belongs to God, one realises that one has no ownership over anything and that nothing can sustain itself independently from Him. Furthermore, if one comes to understand that everything that emanates is good because it is ultimately from Him, one will see that whoever submits to this truth will be open to guidance and thus will neither dislike nor fear anything apart from those things disapproved by the Creator. As Ṭabāṭabā'ī states, with the knowledge that everything belongs to God, "why should he worry how the Master manages His own property?" He goes on to say:

> This submission to Allah creates a perfect tranquillity, a truly happy life, untarnished by unhappiness; a light without darkness, a joy without sorrow, a benefit without harm, and a richness without want. It all happens because he believes in Allah and His Mastership.[30]

In contrast, the unbeliever, cut off from the Master, imagines that he or she is independent, with complete ownership of his or her own power. Ṭabāṭabā'ī describes this as a self-destructive position in which one is in constant fear of what may happen and is always sad about the loss of opportunities and loved ones in the past. To be lured by the attractions of this world and to rely on one's own ability to obtain them leads, he says, to a state of despair when obstacles get in the way of aspiration.[31]

Those who believe

In verse 2:62, those who, it is claimed, will not experience fear and grief are defined as those who believe; this includes Christians, Jews, Sabians and anyone else who believes in God and the Last Day, and who carries out good deeds. Ibn Kathīr refers to 3:85 below, and also to Alī b. Abī Ṭalḥa, who narrated from Ibn Abbās, to argue that 'Allah does not accept any deed or work from anyone unless it conforms to the law of Muḥammad',[32] and that this verse only applied only to the Jews, Christians and Sabians who followed the guidance of their own prophets before the appearance of the Prophet Muhammad. Thus it seems that even though he does not use the word *naskh* (abrogation), Ibn Kathīr may be implying that verse 2:62 is no longer applicable to people today, and that it is abrogated by 3:85, quoted below.

> *And whoever desires other than Islam as religion – never will it be accepted from him, and he, in the Hereafter, will be among the losers.*[33]

Ṭabāṭabā'ī, however, does not mention that this verse is no longer applicable to the Jews or Christians of today. His emphasis is on the phrase 'whoever believes in God…', hence pointing to the importance of sincere belief in God, resurrection and righteous deeds, which applies to all human beings, regardless of their title or their rank.[34]

As far as abrogation is concerned, there is no general agreement among Muslim scholars as to which verses abrogate other verses or, indeed, whether the concept of abrogation itself is a valid one.[35] Most of the discussions about abrogation in the Quran are related to legal issues, with emphasis on the fact that although a few general rulings may be amended, the objective of those rulings can never be abrogated.[36]

Mawdūdī's interpretation of this verse is similar to that of Ṭabāṭabā'ī, and stresses that there is no special religious group which God favours over others; rather, salvation depends on the extent of one's belief and good deeds rather than on connection with a particular group.[37]

Ṭabarī also has views similar to those of Ṭabāṭabā'ī. He states that there is no distinction being made in this verse between the religions mentioned, asserting that the words '*whoever believes in Allah and the last day*' apply equally to all those people mentioned at the beginning of the verse. He also links fear with 'the terrors of the Resurrection' and sorrow with the loss of what has been left behind in this world.[38]

Avoidance of sadness and fear through total submission and being a 'doer of good'

The criteria for the avoidance of sadness or fear in verse 2:112, which is quoted below, is total submission and being a 'doer of good'. Ibn Kathīr interprets this verse as saying that 'whoever performs deeds in sincerity, for Allah alone, and without partners.'

> *Yes [on the contrary], whoever submits his face in Islam to Allah while being a doer of good will have his reward with his Lord. And no fear will there be concerning them, nor will they grieve.*[39]

He refers to Sa'īd bīn Jubayr, who is reported to have said that *'whoever submits'* is linked to sincerity, while *'his face'* means in 'his religion' and *'he is a muḥsīn'* ('doer of good') means 'he follows the Messenger'. Ibn Kathīr refers to the Prophetic Traditions as recorded by Muslim to substantiate his argument that for deeds to be accepted, two conditions must be met: firstly, the deeds must be done solely for God's sake; and secondly, the deeds must be in conformity with the dictates of jurisprudence. He therefore concludes that the good deeds of priests and rabbis will not be accepted, even if they performed them in total sincerity and for the sake of God alone, because they were not in accordance with the method of Muhammad or with the accepted laws of jurisprudence.[40]

Tustarī does not discuss this verse in detail, but he also emphasises the importance of total sincerity and complete submission to God. He interprets 'face' as 'purpose', and appears to be in agreement with Ibn Kathīr to some extent. For although he does not spell out that the good deeds of Christians and Jews are not accepted, he does aver, however, that the one who submits his purpose to God is one "who dedicates his religion purely to God", which is inclusive of "Islam and its laws".[41]

Ṭabāṭabā'ī, however, stresses that spiritual felicity does not depend on 'name or nomenclature'. He states that the requirement in this verse is total submission and doing good (*al-iḥsān*), which he interprets as being synonymous with good deeds.[42]

Avoidance of sadness and fear through spending of wealth for the sake of God

Verse 2:262 below is about carrying out deeds for the sake of God; in this particular case, it is the giving of charity, which should also be solely for God's sake.

> *Those who spend their wealth in the way of Allah and then do not follow up what they have spent with reminders [of it] or [other] injury will have their reward with their Lord, and there will be no fear concerning them, nor will they grieve.*[43]

Ibn Kathīr states that the words *'or with injury'* means harming or hurting anyone while giving charity, which will result inevitably in the cancellation of the charitable act. Also, one should not remind people of their charity or expect anything in return, as it is God Himself who rewards those who carry out this righteous action. As before, Ibn Kathīr relates the words *'on them shall be no fear'* to the hereafter and *'nor shall they grieve'* to loved ones and worldly possessions left behind in this world. He is thus alluding to the fact that those who give charity with total sincerity and purely for the sake of God will obtain their reward from God and consequently they will neither have fear of punishment in the hereafter, nor will they be sad about leaving the life of this world.[44]

Ṭabāṭabā'ī explains that the phrase *'the way of Allah'* relates to 'anything which leads to the pleasure of Allah', while the word *al-itbā,* means both 'to follow' and 'to attach one thing to other'. It appears that Ṭabāṭabā'ī is putting forward this second meaning possibly because it connotes a disconnection of any causal relationship, hence reinforcing the importance of charitable giving that is done in total sincerity and purely for the sake of God. He further explains that the root meaning of *al-mann/mannan* ('with reminders of generosity') is 'to cut'; the meaning of *al-adha* is 'immediate injury'; *khawf* (fear) is the expectation of harm linked to the future; and *ḥuzn* (grief; sadness) is 'the kind of sorrow which greatly disturbs the soul, and which is caused by real or almost real misfortune'. He goes on to explain the importance and wisdom of spending purely for the pleasure of God:

> When that spending is done in the way of Allah, seeking His pleasure, the increase is sure to occur without fail. If wealth is spent, but not for the pleasure of Allah, then it is done for selfish aims – the rich man spends on a poor man to avert his evils from himself. Or he thinks that if the poor man becomes self-supporting, the whole society will become a better place to live in, and in this way the benefactor will live in it more happily. This type of spending is a sort of subjugation of the poor who is exploited by the rich for selfish purposes. Such a charity creates bad effects in the poor. Sometimes these hard feelings accumulate and then burst out in riots and revolutions. But the spending which is done only for the pleasure of Allah is free from these defects; it creates only good, and only bliss and blessings result from it.[45]

Avoidance of sadness and fear through belief, righteous deeds and charitable giving

Ibn Kathīr does not give a detailed interpretation of verse 2:277, seen below; rather, he notes rather briefly that believers who are thankful and appreciative, and who obey God's commands through submission, will be safe from negative repercussions when the Day of Resurrection arrives.[46]

> *Indeed, those who believe and do righteous deeds and establish prayer and give zakah will have their reward with their Lord, and there will be no fear concerning them, nor will they grieve.*[47]

According to Ṭabāṭabā'ī, the law against usury was forbidden in Judaism and this law was not abrogated: there are verses in the Quran which forbade usury even before these seven verses (2: 275-281) were revealed. He states that these usury verses are linked to previous verses about 'spending in the way of Allah', and he points to the contrast between interest and charity: "Interest is taking without giving anything in exchange; charity is giving without taking anything in exchange". He adds that interest has received harsh condemnation by God in these verses, stressing that interest, along with another vice, namely 'befriending the enemies of religion', are worse than sins such as gambling, fornication or even murder, since these crimes are in the main confined to the individual whereas usury affects the social order in society, dividing humankind into two different unequal groups:

> The wealthy who enjoy all the blessings of life, and the poor who find it difficult to meet their barest necessities.[48]

Ṭabāṭabā'ī explains that while trade has been allowed (2:275), interest has been forbidden, as it is a deviation from the straight path, and an injustice that is not in conformity with belief in God. Therefore, those believers who refrain from taking interest and give charity will be on the straight path and '*shall have no fear; nor shall they grieve*'.[49]

Avoidance of sadness and fear by those who are killed 'in the cause' of God

Verse 3:170, quoted below, is linked to the subject 3:169, namely '*those who have been killed in the cause of Allah*', stating clearly that they are not dead, but very much alive and enjoying the sustenance given by God.

> *Rejoicing in what Allah has bestowed upon them of His bounty, and they receive good tidings about those [to be martyred] after them who have not yet joined them – that there will be no fear concerning them, nor will they grieve.*[50]

Ibn Kathīr once again links fear (*khawf*) in this verse to the future, and sorrow (*ḥuzn*) to the past, that is, what has been left behind in this world. He thus indicates that by living for the present, the martyrs do not have any fears regarding the future or any grief on account of that which they have left behind.[51]

Ṭabāṭabā'ī interprets 3:170 as saying that those killed in the way of God are not cut off from this world; rather, they continue to receive news about believers who are still in this realm. The good news that they receive is that these believers '*shall have no fear or grief*'. He explains that rejoicing (*al-faraḥ*) is the opposite of sorrow (*ḥuzn*) and that it is a comprehensive rejoicing, covering not just their own joy but the joy of other believers as well. He states that the intention of the verse is to describe the reward of the believers, which consists of their sustenance – a favour and grace from their Lord. He gives a further explanation of the meaning of fear and sadness in this verse:

> The thing that comes before the eyes is that the fear and sorrow are removed from the martyrs. Fear takes shape when there is possibility of something occurring which would nullify an existing happiness of man; sorrow appears when that thing has already happened. Misfortune – or any undesirable phenomenon – is feared as long as it has not befallen; but once it has begun, the fear gives way to sorrow. There is no fear after a misfortune has taken shape, and no sorrow before that.
>
> Fear, with all its aspects, may be removed from man only when there is no chance of deterioration or extinction for any bounty that he enjoys and possesses. Sorrow, with all its aspects, may be removed from him only when he is not deprived of any such bounty to begin with, nor has he lost it after finding it. When the Qur'an says that Allah has removed general fear and general sorrow from a man, it means that He has given him all possible bounties and favors for his enjoyment; and those bounties and favors will never deteriorate or be taken away from him. In other words, man will remain alive forever enjoying the everlasting happiness.[52]

The above interpretation supports the notion that fear is linked to something which has not yet happened, namely the concerns that one has about possible unhappy events in the future, while sorrow occurs when that unhappy event has already taken place. Therefore, there is no cause for fear or sorrow within the concept of 'everlasting happiness', as God's bounties will not be removed.

Mawdūdī's explanation of verse 3:170 is totally different to that of Ṭabāṭabā'ī. While Ṭabāṭabā'ī explains the link between the concept of 'everlasting happiness' promised to a true believer and the obviation of fear and sadness, Mawdūdī explains that those believers who are blessed by God for their good deeds in this world will be in such a cheerful state that they will never wish to return to this earthly realm. However, he states that the case of martyrs is different as they do wish to be sent back to this world to enjoy the pleasures they missed here.[53] This interpretation raises the question, of course, why such pious people, who had devoted their life for the way of

God, and have been promised everlasting happiness, should want to return to a world full of trials and tribulations.

Avoidance of sadness and fear by those who believe in God, the Last Day and carry out righteous deeds

Verse 5:69 below is very similar to verse 2:62:

> Indeed, those who have believed [in Prophet Muhammad] and those [before Him] who were Jews or Sabeans or Christians – those [among them] who believed in Allah and the Last Day and did righteousness – no fear will there be concerning them, nor will they grieve.[54]

As mentioned previously, Ibn Kathīr in his interpretation of 2:62 reiterates that belief in God and the hereafter and the performance of good deeds are not adequate for the salvation of these groups: each group must also conform to Muhammad's law in order not to have fear of what will happen in the future or be saddened by what has been lost in this world.[55]

Ṭabāṭabā'ī also repeats the explanation he gave for verse 2:62, emphasizing that the only quality needed for the obviation of fear and sadness is belief in God, the Last Day and the performance of righteous deeds:

> A group is called believers, another is named Jews, a third is labeled Sabaeans, and a fourth is branded Christians. But none of the titles will be of any benefit before Allah; the only quality needed is the belief in Allah, the Last Day and good deeds.[56]

Avoidance of sadness and fear by those who believe and reform

In verse 6:48, quoted below, the words '*does righteous good deeds*' is the translation of the word *aṣlaha*.[57] The 1st form verb *ṣalaha* does mean 'righteous', but the form of the verb used in this verse is the 4th form, which actually means 'to reform' or 'to correct oneself'.[58] However, Ibn Kathīr also interprets *aṣlaha* as ' doing righteous good deeds' and states that 'whoever believes and does righteous deeds' refers to those who have sincere, heartfelt belief in the message of the prophets and who carry out works of righteousness by emulating them. These people, he says, will not have any fear or anxiety about the future; nor will they grieve about what they have lost in this world, since God will be the protector of all that they have left behind. Once again Ibn Kathīr stresses the importance of belief in all Messengers and of emulation of their way of life as a means of obviating fear of the future and eliminating sadness over what has been lost in the past.[59]

> *And We send not the Messengers but as givers of glad tidings and as warners. So whosoever believes and does righteous good deeds, upon such shall come no fear, nor shall they grieve.*[60]

Ṭabāṭabā'ī explains that the above verse is addressed to Muhammad, who is being told that the duty of a prophet is merely to bring glad tidings and act as warner. Prophets cannot make people follow the truth, as it is up to them which tribe they choose to follow. They have the choice to follow believers, who carry out good deeds; or deniers of the truth, who transgress all bounds.[61]

Avoidance of sadness and fear by those who fear God and reform

Another condition for the obviation of fear and sadness is *taqwā*,[62] translated in 7:35 as 'fear of Allah'.[63]

> *O children of Adam, if there come to you messengers from among you relating to you My verses, then whoever fears Allah and reforms – there will be no fear concerning them, nor will they grieve.*

Ibn Kathīr explains the word *taqwā* in terms of 'abandoning prohibitions and performing acts of obedience'. Hence, he is again stressing the importance of total submission for the obviation of fear and sadness.[64]

Avoidance of sadness and fear by those who are 'the friends of Allah'

Verse 10:62, quoted below, states that 'the friends of Allah' will also have no cause to experience fear or grief:

> *Behold! verily on the friends of Allah there is no fear, nor shall they grieve;* [65]

Ibn Kathīr relates the meaning of 'the friends of God' to the word *taqwā*.[66] These pious and God-fearing people will not have cause to fear any punishment in the hereafter, nor will they be grieved about what they have left behind in this world. He refers in this regard to the Prophetic Tradition, recorded by Abu Jarīr, which has it that the 'friends of God' are those

> ...who loved one another for the sake of Allah without any other interest like money or kinship. Their faces will be light, upon platforms of light. They shall have no fear (on that Day) when fear shall come upon people. Nor shall they grieve when others grieve.[67]

Tustarī describes 'the friends of God' as:[68]

> ...those who strive in God's cause, who outstrip others in their [journeying] towards Him, and whose actions are constantly in conformity [*muwāfaqa*].[69]

According to Ṭabāṭabā'ī, the emphasis of this verse is on belief in the oneness of God. He states that a 'friend' (*walī*) of God is one who has reached a high station of belief, to the extent that s/he no longer sees any partners in God's works and sees everything emanating from Him. Thus with this state of belief, the *walī* has no cause to fear death or be sad about the loss of his or her life.

He explains that fear and sadness are the outcome of ownership, but for the *walī* who does not associate any partners with God, and who believes that everything, including his own life, belongs to God, there is no reason to have fear or sadness. Ṭabāṭabā'ī states that this position or station of the *walī* is linked not just to the hereafter, as some exegetes believe, but also to this world. That is, the 'friends of Allah', because of their submission and trust (*taqwā*) in God, do not have any fear or sadness in this world or the next.[70]

Ṭabāṭabā'ī also disagrees with the exegetes who state that to have fear and sadness is a normal condition for everyone, including all believers, as fear and sadness is part of a believer's education and perfection, and the tests and difficulties given by God serve as a means to strengthen their patience and belief. Ṭabāṭabā'ī states that a differentiation should be made here between ordinary people and those who have reached high spiritual stations (*maqāmāt ma'nawī*). The *awliyā* (pl. of *walī*) are *muwaḥḥid*, that is, they attribute all secondary causes to God and have thus reached the station of *taqwā*, and so for them there is no cause to fear or be sad about anything except those things God wants them to avoid or be sad about.[71]

It is not clear here whether Ṭabāṭabā'ī understands the concept of *walī* as a state that may not be permanent, that is, a position which is ideal to reach but which can fluctuate, or whether he considers it a permanent state for the *walī*, in which case he or she would never have cause to fear or be saddened. The argument for the state of the *walī* being a fixed state is difficult to square with the verses in the Quran where even Prophets are told not to be sad.[72]

Avoidance of sadness and fear by those who recognise God as their Lord and remain on the straight path

Verse 41:30, below, shows that the obviation of fear and sadness is dependent on belief in God as the only Lord, together with the need to remain on that straight path:

Indeed, those who have said, "Our Lord is Allah" and then remained on a right course – the angels will descend upon them, [saying], "Do not fear and do not grieve but receive good tidings of Paradise, which you were promised.

Ibn Kathīr interprets this verse as a call to do good deeds with sincerity and purely for the sake of God. He refers to Traditions traceable to Abu Bakr[73] which have it that those who say 'Our Lord is Allah, and then stand firm' means 'those who do not associate anything with Allah' and also 'those who shun sin'. These people will not have any fears with regard to the hereafter or sadness with regard to what they have left behind in the life of this world.[74]

Tustarī also interprets those who say '*Our Lord is Allah*' in the above verse as those who do not associate any partners with God. These people will be greeted by angels and reassured that they will have no cause to fear for their souls or any cause to grieve with regard to the Day of Judgement.[75]

Mawdūdī states that this verse addresses those with sincere belief in God, namely those who practice their belief in accordance with 'the doctrine of *tawhīd*' (Divine oneness). He adds that the descending of angels is not limited to the time of death and resurrection but also applies to this world, where believers are reassured by angels during difficult times. Therefore, the angels are a source of comfort and a reminder to the believers that there is no cause for them to be afraid with regard to the future or to grieve because of the hardships and falsities they have had to confront in this world, since they will be justly rewarded in the next world.[76]

Obviation of fear and sadness by 'God's devotees'

Verse 43:68, quoted below, refers to the Day of Resurrection, and the affirmation that God's 'devotees' or 'servants' (*'ībād*) shall not have any cause to grieve or be fearful.

My devotees! no fear shall be on you that Day, nor shall ye grieve

Ibn Kathīr explains that on the Day of Resurrection everyone will be filled with terror except those who have believed in God's *āyāt* (signs) and were Muslims.[77]

Tustarī refers to God's devotees (*'ibād*) as 'friends of God', that is, those who fully comprehend God's Oneness (*tawḥīd*) and are totally submitted to Him.[78]

Ṭabāṭabā'ī explains that God's servants (*'ibād*) are differentiated from others by the phrase 'those who believe in Our Signs' in verse 43:69, namely the believers who confirm the Prophets and their miracles and have submitted to God with total sincerity and humility.[79]

Avoidance of sadness and fear by those who have confirmed their belief in God and remained on that path

In verse 46:13, quoted below, those who will not have cause to fear or grieve are those who have confirmed their belief in God and have not deviated from the straight path.

> Indeed, those who have said, "Our Lord is Allah," and then remained on a right course – there will be no fear concerning them, nor will they grieve.

In his interpretation of this verse, Ibn Kathīr refers to his explanation given for verse 41:30 where he states that '*those who say Our Lord is Allah, and then they stand firm*' are those who avoid sin and do not associate partners with God. He states that '*on them shall be no fear*' relates to fear concerning the future, while '*nor shall they grieve*' relates to sadness over what is left behind in this world.[80] Ṭabāṭabā'ī states that '*those who have no fear or sadness*' refers to those who believe in One God, confirm verbally their belief in the Prophet, and admit that their Creator is One, without associating any partners with Him.[81]

This brings us to the end of the selected exegetes' interpretations of the verses which relate directly to the kind of people who will not have sadness and fear.

Thematic categorization of the concept of *ḥuzn*

In this section the selected exegetes' interpretations of the remaining verses which directly refer to obviation of sadness and fear have been grouped in accordance with the following themes:

- Fear and sadness given as a test
- Fear and sadness due to loss and separation
- The comforting, consoling and reassuring of the Prophets and the faithful in the time of *ḥuzn*

Fear and sadness given as a test

Verse 3:153, quoted below, follows on from verses about the battle of Uhud[82]:

> *[Remember] when you [fled and] climbed [the mountain] without looking aside at anyone while the Messenger was calling you from behind. So Allah repaid you with distress upon distress so you would not grieve for that which had escaped you [of victory and spoils of war] or [for] that which had befallen you [of injury and death]. And Allah is [fully] acquainted with what you do.*

Ibn Kathīr offers different interpretations of the nature of '*grief after grief*' given by God. One interpretation, which he attributes to Ibn Abbās, is that the first grief was due to the rumour that Muhammad was dead and the defeat of the battle of Uhud, while the second grief was due to the idolaters' presence on the mount. Another interpretation, attributed to 'Abd al-Rahmān b. 'Awf, is that the first grief was due to losing the battle and the second grief due to the rumour that Muhammad had been killed. Ibn Kathīr interprets '*so you would not grieve for that which had escaped you*' as a return or compensation from God for those who fled from the enemy, which consequently led to the loss of the battle and war booty.[83]

Ṭabāṭabā'ī links the loss of battle to the fact that some had transgressed the limits God had set for them. He explains that the Prophet's followers were disputing amongst themselves. While some of them stayed fighting alongside of the Prophet, others, dazzled by the booty, left their positions and ran up the mount to collect the war booty that had been left behind, which consequently led to the loss of the battle. Ṭabāṭabā'ī states that this was a test from God, where the distinction between the hypocrites and the believers, and between believers who were steadfast and those who were not so firm in belief, became apparent. He examines the grammatical structure of the sentence '*so Allah repaid you with distress upon distress so you would not grieve*' and offers different suggestions with regard to its meaning. One of the suggestions includes the possibility that the first sorrow is the remorse and guilt the companions felt for having fled from the scene, while the second sorrow was the loss of victory. Ṭabāṭabā'ī explains that the second sorrow was in fact a grace and bounty from God because it served as a diversion from the first sorrow. Ṭabāṭabā'ī's interpretation tends to suggest that this second sorrow was ultimately a test and a form of guidance for those who had repented and were sorry for their actions. Thus, the second sorrow served as a distraction from the first sorrow, which might have led to despair. He concludes that the words '*what had escaped you*' refer to victory and war booty and '*what befell you*' to their slaughter and injuries.[84]

Mawdūdī offers only a brief and very general interpretation for this verse. He relates that while some of the soldiers fled from their positions, the Prophet and his few companions stood firm in the face of the enemy. He does not offer alternative meanings for the words '*sorrow after sorrow*' but gives a general picture that grief was the outcome of all that which took place, namely the fleeing of some of the fighters; the rumour that the Prophet had been killed; injuries and loss of life of the companions who had stayed to fight; and the ultimate loss of the battle itself.[85]

Verse 9:92, quoted below, is about the volunteers who were discluded from fighting on account of lack of mounts:

> Nor [is there blame] upon those who, when they came to you that you might give them mounts, you said, "I can find nothing for you to ride upon." They

> turned back while their eyes overflowed with tears out of grief that they could not find something to spend [for the cause of Allah].

Mawdūdī and Ṭabarī both stress the importance of sincerity as expressed in the above verse. Ṭabarī opines that if the volunteers were unable to join the battle through no fault of their own, then they will be forgiven for not having taken part.[86] Mawdūdī adds that although these people who offered to join the battle were not accepted due to lack of mounts, they were, because of their determination and sincerity, still part of the troop, since even though they were not able to be there physically, their spirits were with those who went to battle.[87]

Ṭabāṭabā'ī does not pass much comment on this verse but interprets *ḥuzn* in this context as "pain in the heart which arises due to not benefitting from an opportunity".[88] This then can be seen as a test or a form of guidance, for those involved can either remain sorrowful for not having been able to accompany the Prophet, or they can see their situation as a trial or test by accepting God's Decree and Determining.

35:34 is linked to the previous verses 35:32-33, quoted below, where belief is classified into three different categories:

> *Then we caused to inherit the Book those We have chosen of Our servants; and among them is he who wrongs himself, and among them is he who is moderate, and among them is he who is foremost in good deeds by permission of Allah. That [inheritance] is what is the great bounty.*[89]

> *[For them are] gardens of perpetual residence which they will enter. They will be adorned therein with bracelets of gold and pearls, and their garments therein will be silk.*[90]

> *And they will say, "Praise to Allah, who has removed from us [all] sorrow. Indeed, our Lord is Forgiving and Appreciative.*[91]

Mawdūdī opines that the first category, namely those 'who wrong themselves', is mentioned first because it accounts for most of the Muslims. These people are differentiated from the hypocrites and those who are 'unbelieving' at heart' since they do believe in 'the Book' but are weak in practice and hence liable to carry out sinful actions. As for the second category of people, who follow the middle course, although they are less in number than the first category they are more numerous than the third category, and this is why they are mentioned second. These people are described as the ones who fulfil their obligations but not fully, having not completely submitted 'themselves' (*nafs*) to God, and hence they are liable to succumb to the occasional sin.

The third category, those 'foremost in good deeds', are the fewest in number and are the ones who fulfil their obligations in full. They would not commit a sin knowingly and would follow the Book and the way of the Prophet completely.

Mawdūdī explains that exegetes have different views as to who will enter 'the gardens of perpetual residence'. He states that according to Zamakhsharī and Imām Rāzī,[92] only those who are 'foremost in good deeds', that is, the third category, will enter paradise. The reason for not including the other two categories is, he says, to make them anxious about their present state of belief so that they have the opportunity to ameliorate it. Mawdūdī states, however, that the majority of commentators disagree with Zamakhsharī and Rāzī, believing that eventually all these three categories of believers will enter paradise, since they are all believers 'of the Book'.

He adds that for those who are in the 'gardens of perpetual residence' there will be no concept of sorrow (*ḥuzn*), since they will no longer be afflicted by it as they were in their 'worldly life'.[93]

Tustarī refers to the Tradition narrated by 'Umar b. Wāṣil that the one who has 'wronged himself' (*ẓālim*) is the one who is ignorant (*jāhil*) and preoccupied only with this world. The one who is 'in the middle position' (*muqtaṣid*) is the one who is 'learning' (*muta'allim*) and who is preoccupied with both the life of this world and the Hereafter. The one who is 'foremost' (*sābiq*) is the one who is learned and is preoccupied only with the Hereafter.

Tustarī also quotes Ḥasan al-Baṣrī as saying that the good deeds of 'the foremost' outweigh their misdeeds; the good deeds and the misdeeds of those in the middle position balance each other; and the misdeeds of the wrong doers outweigh their good deeds.

Tustarī interprets sorrow in 35:34 – *praise be to God, who has removed from us {all} sorrow* – as being cut off (*ḥuzn al-qaṭī'a*) from God.[94]

Ibn Kathīr explains the first category of believers, 'those who wrong themselves', as believers who, through negligence, omit some obligatory duties and occasionally commit actions which are forbidden. He adds that those who follow 'the middle course' are those who carry out their obligations fully and avoid things which are forbidden, but occasionally carry out actions which are disliked or neglect some opportunities to carry out good deeds. And he interprets those who are 'foremost in good deeds' as those who carry out both obligatory and non-obligatory duties, while avoiding both unlawful and dislikeable actions.

In his interpretation, Ibn Kathīr refers to Ibn Abbas, who comments on this verse that

> 'those who wrong themselves' will be forgiven; 'those who follow a middle course' will have an easy accounting; and 'those who are foremost in good deeds' will enter paradise without being brought into account.[95]

Ibn Kathīr disagrees with those exegetes who believe that 'those who wrong themselves' are not among the *umma* (those whom God has chosen/those who have inherited the Book), and stresses that even though the believers in this category manifest some imperfections in their actions, they are still included among the *umma*. He adds that the believers who have entered the Gardens of Paradise are relieved of all the anxiety they used to experience during their lives on earth, for now their test has come to an end and all obligations have been taken away from them, leaving them to enjoy eternal repose in Paradise.[96]

Ṭabāṭabā'ī also states that there are differences of opinion with regard to the three categories of belief. He says that those who 'wrong their own soul' are those who have committed sin, and that this can include any Muslims who follows the Quran, since as followers of the Book they are also from among the chosen. The word 'moderate', he says, means the 'middle way', while those who are 'foremost in good deeds' means those who are closer to God than the people mentioned under the first two categories.

Ṭabāṭabā'ī states that according to some exegetes, the sorrow referred to in 35:34 is the sorrow of worldly life, from which the people in the verse have been saved, and on account of which they are now praising their Lord. Others, he says, describe it as a sorrow that encapsulates them after departure from the world and before entering paradise; the source of this is fear of sin. He concludes that this verse relates to the first category of believers, or to the first and second categories, since the third category, that is, 'those foremost in good deeds' do not have any sins in their book of deeds about which they need to be concerned.[97]

Fear and sadness stemming from loss and separation

Verses 12:84-86, quoted below, concern the news received by Jacob that his sons, Benjamin and Reuben, were left behind in Egypt – news which brought about Jacob's profound sadness and the consequent loss of his eyesight.

> *And he turned away from them and said, "Oh, my sorrow over Joseph," and his eyes became white from grief, for he was [of that] a suppressor.*[98]

> *They said, "By Allah, you will not cease remembering Joseph until you become fatally ill or become of those who perish."*[99]

> *He said, "I only complain of my suffering and my grief to Allah, and I know from Allah that which you do not know.*[100]

Tabarī's explanation of above verses is very brief. He states that when Jacob heard that Benjamin had been left behind in Egypt, his sorrow doubled and he lost his sight. But in his sleep he had a vision of the angel of death, who told him not to be sad as Joseph was alive and would be returned to him.[101]

Ibn Kathīr states that the news that Benjamin and Reuben had not returned with the brothers rekindled Jacob's sadness, which he had silently kept to himself, adding that it was this suppression of his sadness and his refusal to complain to anyone except God that caused his loss of sight.[102] He adds that Jacob's sons were concerned about their father's health and warned him that if Jacob continued like this, he might die of grief.[103] Jacob's response to them was that he complained of his grief to God alone and that he had knowledge from God which they did not have.[104] Ibn Kathīr is of the opinion that this last statement is related to the inspiration that Jacob received from God which confirmed that Joseph was alive and would accomplish his mission as prophet.[105]

Tustarī's explanation of Jacob's anxiety (*hamm*) and sorrow (*ḥuzn*) [106] is that it was not Joseph himself that he missed: what he could not bear was the separation from the perfect way in which Joseph manifested God's attributes; it was not Joseph per se that he yearned for, but rather the mirror of his son's being which reflected God's names and attributes. This is why, Tustarī adds, he kept his anguish to himself and complained of this separation to God alone. Tustarī goes on to explain that the word *ḥaraḍ* ('severe sickness in the heart'), used by Jacob's sons who were worried that he would end up killing himself because of his intense sadness, was felt not on account of the loss of Joseph himself, but in fear for the potential loss of his faith. Therefore, if he knew for certain that Joseph had not lost his faith then he would have been happy because he would have known that they would be united in the hereafter. But it was this uncertainty that caused him so much grief.[107]

Tustarī brings little evidence to justify that Jacob's grief was due to fear of Joseph's loss of faith rather than the loss of Joseph himself. Therefore, it can be questioned whether Tustarī is taking an apologetic stance in order to justify Jacob's intense grief. Mystics such as Abū Sa'īd al-Kharrāz, Abū Sa'īd al Qursī and Ibn 'Aṭā were not as reluctant or cautious as Tustarī was to point to Jacob's shortcomings, and they went so far as to blame Jacob's loss of sight on his grief for one other than God.[108]

Ṭabāṭabā'ī explains that when Jacob lost his sight because of his sadness for Joseph, he did not take his anger out on his sons or anyone else; rather, he kept his anger to himself. He states that the word used for anger is *asaf*, which means a mix of sadness and anger, described as 'the gushing of blood from the heart and an extreme wish for revenge'. Therefore, if this had happened to anyone with weaker belief it would have indicated anger, but for Jacob *asaf* resulted in melancholy and sadness. Ṭabāṭabā'ī interprets the word *kaẓm* as the 'coming out of ego' (*nafs*), therefore supressing his *kaẓm* meant that Jacob kept silent and did not allow his ego *(nafs)* to manifest.[109] As regards the word *bathth*,[110] he states that it connotes a kind of sadness that cannot be denied or hidden and is thus diffused, and 'what is diffused is *bathth*'.

He also adds that Jacob knew that complaining to anyone except God would be pointless, since ultimately it was only God who would not tire of his pleas and fail to address his grief (*ḥuzn*).[111]

Verses 28:8; 28:10 and 28:13, quoted below, are about the discovery of Moses in the river by Pharaoh's wife and also her wish to adopt him; the intensity of the stress experienced by Moses's mother on account of her separation from him; and their eventual reunion.

> *And the family of Pharaoh picked him up [out of the river] so that he would become to them an enemy and a [cause of] grief. Indeed, Pharaoh and Haman and their soldiers were deliberate sinners.*[112]

> *But there came to be a void in the heart of the mother of Moses: She was going almost to disclose his (case), had We not strengthened her heart (with faith), so that she might remain a (firm) believer.*[113]

> *So We restored him to his mother that she might be content and not grieve and that she would know that the promise of Allah is true. But most of the people do not know.*[114]

Ibn Kathīr gives a mainly literal explanation for verse 28:8 and adds that while Pharaoh himself had no wish to keep baby Moses, his wife managed to convince him by saying that the infant would be 'a comfort for the eye for me and for you…'. However, Ibn Kathīr explains that Moses turned out to be a comfort and a source of guidance for Pharaoh's wife, and not for Pharaoh himself, as he turned his back on Moses – a rejection which led to his ultimate destruction.

Ibn Kathīr's explanation for 28:10 is that when Moses's mother cast her child into the river, her heart became empty, meaning that she could not focus on anything except the loss of Moses. And had it not been for God, who filled the void in her heart with strength and patience, she would have disclosed her secret to others, which would have endangered her son's life.

Eventually, as stated in 28:13, Moses was restored to his mother so that she might be reassured that God always keeps His promise. His promise was that Moses would one day be returned to her and that he would be a Messenger of God. Ibn Kathīr explains the phrase 'but most of them know not' as lack of trust in God's wisdom. For on the surface, as the story of Moses demonstrates, things that happen may not appear to be good or of benefit, but ultimately, if decreed by God, then they are for the best.[115]

Tustarī opines that although Moses was adopted and raised to bring joy and happiness to the Pharaoh's household, little did they know that in fact, as decreed by God, he would actually become an enemy and a source of grief for Pharaoh and his followers. He adds that God filled the void in Moses' mother's heart in order to strengthen her belief and trust in God that her son would be returned to her.[116]

Mawdūdī concurs with Tustarī and explains that the mother of Moses was inspired by God to save her child and it was because of her total trust in, and submission to, God's promise that her child would be safe that she cast him into the river. And eventually, although nurtured in Pharoah's household, Moses became the very means for his destruction.[117]

Ṭabāṭabā'ī explains that Moses's mother kept her pregnancy and the birth of her baby a secret. She was inspired by God to continue to feed her baby until she sensed danger, at which point she was to put her baby in a basket and cast it into the river Nile. She was told that she should not fear that he would be killed, or be saddened on account of her separation from him, for God had promised that Moses would be returned to her one day and that he would have the status of prophet. He also points to the irony of Moses's becoming the enemy and the means of sadness for the very people who found him in the water and nurtured him in their household.

With regard to the emptiness in the heart of Moses's mother (28:10), Ṭabāṭabā'ī explains that this void was due to her fear and sadness on separating from him – feelings so overwhelming that she was on the verge of sharing her anxiety with others, which would have put Moses's life in danger. Thus the void in her heart was filled by the promise of God, through inspiration, that her son would be safe and would one day be returned to her. And so her heart was strengthened in order that she would be among those who have trust in God.[118]

Ṭabāṭabā'ī explains that the word *know* in 28:13 means that when Moses's mother sees her son with her own eyes, she will be reassured that God's promise is true. And the phrase '*most people do not know/understand*', he explains, means that most people tend to doubt God's promise because they are not totally convinced of it with their hearts. In the case of the mother of Moses, when she saw the baby with her own eyes, alive and healthy, she became convinced of God's unconditional promise.[119]

Comforting, consoling and reassuring the prophets and the faithful in times of ḥuzn

> *So let not their speech grieve you. Indeed, We know what they conceal and what they declare.*[120]

Ibn Kathīr expands on 36:76, quoted above, stating that God is commanding the Prophet not to be grieved by those who refuse to believe in Him and his Prophet. The Prophet is consoled too by God's affirmation that He is well aware of what they conceal, and by His reassurance that they will be punished for their false claims.[121]

Ṭabāṭabā'ī interprets this verse as God's commanding the Prophet not to be sad because of the idolatry surrounding him, as God is well aware of what they do and in no way will they be able to escape His punishment.[122]

Mawdūdī explains that this verse pertains to a deliberate plot by the unbelievers to create suspicion against the Prophet by branding him as a madman, a poet, magician or a sorcerer, in order to frustrate his mission. Therefore, Muhammad is being told by God not to be saddened by their plot as ultimately He is aware of what they are planning and will ensure that they fail in this world and receive punishment for their evil deeds in the hereafter.[123]

> Let not their speech grieve thee: for all power and honour belong to Allah: It is He Who heareth and knoweth (all things).

Verse 10:65, quoted above, is very similar to 36:76. Again, Ibn Kathīr gives a very literal interpretation of this verse, stating that Muhammad is being asked not to grieve on account of the remarks of the idolaters, but rather to trust in God, since ultimately all power and honour belong to Him.[124]

Ṭabāṭabā'ī explains that 10:65 is an example of God's sympathetic chastisement of Muhammad for allowing himself to be affected by the cursing and mocking of his religion by the polytheists. He is at the same time being consoled by being reminded that their ugly words do not affect God in any way, and he is urged not to take any notice of their false pride. There is no reason, God is saying, that he should be sad since God is aware of all their actions and will punish them if He so wishes.[125]

> *"O Messenger, let them not grieve you who hasten into disbelief of those who say, "We believe" with their mouths, but their hearts believe not...."*[126]

Ibn Kathīr interprets 5:41, above, as Muhammad's once again being commanded not to grieve on account of either those who rush into unbelief or hypocrites who express their belief verbally but not with their hearts.[127]

Ṭabāṭabā'ī states that this verse was sent to the Prophet in the form of consolation because of what he had to endure on account of the hypocrites who pretended to believe in God when in fact they strived in unbelief. He is being reminded not to grieve over these people as they are not true believers.[128]

Mawdūdī also affirms that the above verse was revealed in order to console the Prophet and to urge him not to grieve over those who scheme against him in order to defeat his mission. Muhammad is thus being reminded not to be disheartened and to continue patiently with his task.[129]

We know indeed the grief which their words cause you (O Muhammad SAW): it is not you that they deny, but it is the Verses (the Quran) of Allah that the zalimun ('polytheists and wrongdoers') deny.[130]

Ibn Kathīr states that 6:33, above, clarifies that it is not Muhammad whom people accuse of being a liar, but rather that it is the verses of God that they deny because they do not want to accept the truth. In 6.34, the Quran goes on to remind Muhammad that Prophets before him were also denied, but they bore it with patience until help came to them.[131]

Ṭabāṭabā'ī states that the above verse points to the fact that God does not force people to believe, as belief and unbelief constitute a matter of individual choice. He explains that Muhammad is being told not to be upset because in fact people are not denying him, as he is only a Prophet and a Messenger and not the message. Therefore, he is only a means of God's guidance. Consequently, their denial is targeted not at him but at God's signs. And because their denial stems from their oppression and not their ignorance, they will soon be answerable to their Lord.[132]

Mawdūdī explains that before Muhammad had begun to recite the revelation of God to the people, he was well respected as a truthful and honest person. And even after he began to deliver the message of God, he was such a righteous person that no-one, including even his bitterest enemies, was able to accuse him of lying with regard to the concerns of the world. Their rejection was thus levelled at the notion of his prophethood and not at him as a person. Mawdūdī states that in the above verse, God is comforting and reminding Muhammad that it is not he who is being rejected by people, and that what is actually being denied is God's message.[133]

But (a voice) cried to her from beneath the (palm-tree): "Grieve not! for thy Lord hath provided a rivulet beneath thee.[134]

Ibn Kathīr explains that in 19:24, quoted above, there is a difference of opinion between exegetes as to who '*cried to*' Mary. Some exegetes state that it was the baby Jesus himself, while others say that it was the Angel Gabriel, since Jesus did not speak until she brought him to show her people. Ibn Kathīr also points to the difference of opinion with regard to the Arabic word *sarīyyan* (stream), with some stating that it means river and others venturing that the word refers to Jesus. According to Ibn Kathīr, the first view is the most likely as in the next verse,[135] Mary is asked to shake the palm tree for dates, whereupon God provides her with both food and drink.[136]

Ṭabāṭabā'ī points to the verb *nāda* in the above verse, stating that it refers to Jesus and not Gabriel. Consequently it was Jesus who said to his mother '*grieve not*'. He adds that '*grieve not*' was God's way, through Jesus, of consoling and comforting Mary during the time that she was experiencing extreme sadness. He explains that Mary was a chaste and pure woman from an honourable family and the thought of dishonouring her family grieved her. And it was Jesus himself who instructed his mother not to speak, as he himself spoke for her in her defence.[137]

Ṭabarī's comments, quoted below, are in agreement with Ṭabāṭabā'ī that it was Jesus who comforted Mary by saying '*don't be sad*' and also that it was he who spoke out in her defence:

> When Mary became pregnant and in pain with contractions, she did not know what to do, so she decided to leave the city and sat under a dry palm tree – the pain was so much that she cried out loud wishing she was dead. It was then that Jesus became separated from her and said to her: don't be sad, God has provided a stream beneath you, shake the tree to obtain dates. And when she shook the tree it turned green and dates dropped from it so that Mary would eat from it and gain strength. Mary said: O lord, I am the Mary whom you provided summer fruit for in winter. People blamed Zakaria for Mary's condition. Zakaria stated that no man has touched Mary. They said, well where is this child from? Zakaria stated that you should ask her. Therefore, all the tribe went to Mary and asked: Where did you get this child from? But Mary did not respond as she had promised God not to speak to anyone. She pointed to baby Jesus who said that he was a servant of God chosen as a Prophet. On hearing Jesus, the people around him split into three groups: one group believing that Jesus was the son of God, one group saying that Jesus was God and the other group saying that this was witchcraft carried out by Mary.[138]

Mawdūdī does not discuss the source of the voice but focuses on the painful situation in which Mary found herself. He states that if she had given birth as a married woman, there would have been no need for her to observe the common Jewish custom of carrying out 'a fast of silence'. Therefore, she was comforted by being told that she would not have the responsibility to give any explanation, since God would take care of it.[139]

> *If ye help not (your leader), (it is no matter): for Allah did indeed help him, when the Unbelievers drove him out: he had no more than one companion; they two were in the cave, and he said to his companion, "Have no fear, for Allah is with us": then Allah sent down His peace upon him, and strengthened him with forces which ye saw not, and humbled to the depths the word of the Unbelievers. But the word of Allah is exalted to the heights: for Allah is Exalted in might, Wise.*[140]

In 9:40, quoted above, it is Muhammad himself who is reassuring his companion not to have fear. Ibn Kathīr sets the historical context as the year of migration from

Mecca to Medina. He states that during this time, the idolaters saw Muhammad as their enemy and were pursuing him in order to kill him. Having become aware of this, Muhammad, together with his companion, Abū Bakr, escaped and hid in the cave of Thaur. They stayed in the cave for three days in the hope that the Meccan polytheists would give up searching for them and return home. While in the cave, Abū Bakr feared that that they would soon be caught, especially as the enemy were lingering just outside the cave entrance. It was at this time that the Prophet reassured his companion by telling him not to be sad, as they have God on their side. In Ibn Kathīr's interpretation, God then comforted them by sending them aid from the unseen realm: the forces that were not visible to all were angels sent by God to come to the Prophet's and his companion's assistance. Ibn Kathīr also points to the contrast between the word of the unbelievers being the lowermost and linked with polytheism, and the word of God as the exalted or highest, linked to Divine oneness.[141]

Ṭabarī does not make any comment on the actual verse, stating only that Tabuk was a place near Medina where many people were killed, which is why it was referred to as the 'place of death' (*mutah*).[142] This possibly adds to the reason why the Prophet's companion was sad and fearful.

Ṭabāṭabā'ī explains the word *ḥuzn* in the above verse as stemming from fear. He states that Muhammad reassured his companion and told him not to be sad; Abū Bakr clearly feared their being alone and helpless, and was abundantly aware of the huge army of the enemy which had followed them and were lurking near the cave. Muhammad's assurance comes in the form of his emphasis on the importance of believing that God, who is *subḥān* (exalted), was on their side. He adds that it was because God sent *sakīna* (peace and tranquillity) to him that he was able to be protected from the enemy.[143]

Mawdūdī also explains the context of the verse. He states that this was at time when the unbelievers had decided to kill Muhammad; on hearing about this, Muhammad and his companion Abū Bakr left Mecca for Medina, to where most of the Muslims had already migrated. But noticing that the enemy were in pursuit, they decided to go southwards in order to hide in a cave known as *Thawr* for a few days. The enemies searched everywhere for them and eventually reached the entrance of the cave where they were hiding. Mawdūdī explains that it was at this point that Abū Bakr, sensing the huge army so close to their hideout, felt alarmed that they might enter the cave; consequently, Muhammad reassured his companion not to be sad as the important thing was that they had God on their side.[144]

Conclusion

This chapter began with a brief historical background on Quranic exegesis and information on the selected exegetes. This was followed by the various interpretations of verses from the Quran which are connected to the notion of the obviation of *ḥuzn*, together with interpretations of verses grouped together thematically. The chapter concludes by identifying and discussing the points of convergence and divergence in the various exegetes' understanding of *ḥuzn* in the context of the verses under discussion.

The opinions of the exegetes covered here are very similar with regard to the meaning of the words sadness (*ḥuzn*) and fear (*khawf*). They all concur that the concept of fear generally relates to the future, and in particular to the hereafter. There is also conformity of opinion with regard to sadness, which is interpreted in terms of loss of possessions, including the loss of loved ones in this earthly realm. Where they do differ in opinion, however, is in the way they emphasise particular components in these verses.

Ibn Kathīr approaches the issue of the obviation of fear and sadness by following guidance through the means of the prophets, the messengers and the 'clear discourse',[145] and thus interprets 'those who follow God's guidance' as those who follow what is contained in revelations which have been sent by all the Messengers.

Ṭabarī adds that the expulsion of Adam from heaven also applies to all human beings, in the sense that because Adam repented he was given the opportunity to receive guidance. And therefore, human beings also have the potential to receive guidance if there is sincere repentance on their part, and if they accept the 'clear exposition' as conveyed by His messenger, Muhammad.

Ṭabāṭabā'ī gives a more comprehensive analysis of 2:38 and identifies the breaking of the covenant made by Adam as the cause of his fall from heaven. However, all was not lost, for guidance now depended on repentance. He opines that just like Adam, all human beings also have the potential to be guided and hence saved. He stresses that the key to this guidance is humankind's acceptance of God's Mastership and humankind's own servitude. This acceptance means not only understanding, but also submitting to, the fact that God owns and controls everything in creation. Therefore, the pious believers who have submitted to God's commands will have no cause to fear about the future, and nor will they be sad about their losses in this world, for they will have realised that they did not own the things they 'lost' in the first place. Ṭabāṭabā'ī explains that in contrast, the unbelievers' assertion that they were their own masters places them in a position whereby they are in constant fear of what may happen in the future, and in which they are always saddened by loss of possessions, loved ones and opportunities.

The next criterion for the obviation of sadness and fear mentioned in verses 2:62, 5:69 and 6:48 consists of belief in God and in the Last Day, and the performance of acts of righteousness. These verses were addressed to everyone, including the Christians, the Jews and the Sabians. However, Ibn Kathīr interprets these verses differently to the other exegetes by adding that God does not accept deeds from just anyone, even if they are done with complete sincerity, unless those deeds conform with the law of Muhammad. Consequently, he explains that these verses are applicable only to the Jews, Christians and Sabians who existed before the time of Muhammad. Mawdūdī, Ṭabarī and Ṭabāṭabā'ī do not make this differentiation and stress that the emphasis in these verses is on sincere belief in God, resurrection and the carrying out of righteous deeds, rather than on connections to a particular group.[146]

The next criterion for the obviation of sadness or fear relates to submitting one's 'face' and being a 'doer of good' and remaining on the straight path.[147] Ibn Kathīr, Mawdūdī, Tustarī and Ṭabāṭabā'ī all opine that this means the performance of deeds with total sincerity, that is, purely for the sake of God and in accordance with the doctrine of *tawḥīd* and the laws of jurisprudence.

Another condition for the obviation of *ḥuzn* is to spend one's wealth 'in the way of Allah'.[148] Ibn Kathīr and Ṭabāṭabā'ī's interpretation of this verse is that charity must be given with sincerity, meaning without any expectations of return of favour. Ṭabāṭabā'ī elaborates that total sincerity is when there is a disconnection of the causal relationship – in other words, without any expectation of worldly benefit and purely for the sake of God. Consequently, this will not only result in spiritual harmony for the one who gives but will also contribute to a more equal and civilized society as a whole.

Ibn Kathīr links obeying and submitting to God's commands to being thankful and appreciative. He also says that it is this state of obedience which will result in the obviation of fear with regard to punishment on the Day of Resurrection. Ṭabāṭabā'ī's emphasis is on the evils of usury, which stands in opposition to belief, equality and justice. Therefore, he adds, those who believe and submit to God, and who give alms, while refraining from taking interest when trading, are behaving in a just way and will therefore have no cause for fear or sadness, since they are not responsible for upsetting the equilibrium in creation.

Ṭabāṭabā'ī explains that fear is the outcome of believing that the bounties enjoyed will eventually come to an end, while sorrow is experienced when misfortune has already occurred. However, in the case of those 'killed in the cause of Allah', who are enjoying everlasting happiness,[149] the bounties given to them by God will never diminish, and so there is no cause for them to have either fear or sadness.[150] Mawdūdī's interpretation of the martyrs' wish to be sent back to this world to enjoy the pleasures they missed goes against Ṭabāṭabā'ī's explanation of everlasting happiness.[151] It also gives the impression that the transient pleasures of this world are considered by the martyrs to be somehow superior to the everlasting happiness that they are experiencing.[152]

For Ibn Kathīr, the 'friends of God' are on par with those who fear God, namely those who have *taqwā*.[153] For these pious and God-fearing people there will be no cause to fear punishment in the hereafter; nor will they be saddened by what they have left behind in this world.[154]

Tustarī also links the word *taqwā* with 'the friends of God', explaining that these are people who constantly strive in the cause of God.[155]

Ṭabāṭabā'ī elaborates on Tustarī's understanding of *taqwā* as 'striving purely for the sake of God' by reiterating that 'the friends of God' are those who do not attribute anything to secondary causes and who see everything emanating directly from God. Thus, when there are no causes to blame and no concept of ownership to fall back on, the 'friends of God' will have no cause to fear anything or be saddened by any loss.[156] Ṭabāṭabā'ī states that this station of belief – the state of total submission (*taqwā*) – can indeed be reached in this world. He also adds that some exegetes opine that the state of fear and sadness is a normal condition, but that this is not the case for the 'friends of God', since they have reached such a high station of submission.[157]

It is not clear whether Ṭabāṭabā'ī interprets this state of belief as an ideal position liable to fluctuation or whether it is a permanent position for 'the friends of God'. The latter position would appear to contradict the verses discussed in this chapter in which even Prophets were advised not to be sad. This does not mean that sadness has to be seen in a negative light; rather, it also has the positive aspects of consolation, reminder and guidance.

Ibn Kathīr links the verse which says that God's devotees will not experience fear or sadness[158] to the day of resurrection, when everyone will be filled with terror apart from those who have believed in God's 'signs' and had submitted fully to God (*muslim*). Tustarī identifies God's devotees as 'the friends of God' and gives a similar explanation, stating that the 'devotees' are those who fully understand God's Oneness and who submit to Him in accordance with their belief.

Ṭabāṭabā'ī, however, states that the phrase 'those who believe in Our signs' differentiates God's devotees from others; these, he explains, are believers who have sincerely submitted to God, his Prophets and their miracles. It appears that Ṭabāṭabā'ī may not see the 'devotees of God' as being on par with 'God's friends', as he does not mention that the position of 'God's devotees' is also immune from fear or sadness.[159]

The exegetes' interpretation of the rest of verses on the concept of *ḥuzn* were categorized in accordance with the same themes of test, loss and separation, as well as God's giving of consolation and reassurance to the Prophets and the faithful.

Mawdūdī, Ṭabāṭabā'ī and Ibn Kathīr all agree that the grief given by God serves as a test, a punishment or a means guidance. Therefore for those who fled from the Battle of Uhud, for example, the loss of the battle can be seen as an opportunity to learn from mistakes.[160] In fact Ṭabāṭabā'ī interprets the 'grief after grief' (3:153) in a positive light, expressing how the second sorrow served to lighten the first one.[161] Another example of the kind of Divine trial or tribulation which can also be seen as a form of guidance is the verse about those who volunteered to fight alongside

Muhammad but were turned away as there were not enough mounts to go round (9:92). All the exegetes who commented on this verse agree that it is one's sincere intention that is important. Consequently, those who were unable to join the battle physically would still be rewarded for their good intention.[162]

As for the three categories of belief,[163] Mawdūdī, Ibn Kathīr, Ṭabāṭabā'ī and Tustarī concur that they cover all believers in the Book (Quran), but that the categories are differentiated in accordance with their different degrees of understanding and submission. However, Ṭabāṭabā'ī adds that the removal of sorrow applies only to the first two categories of believers, namely 'those who wrong themselves' and 'those who follow a middle course', because the third category – 'those foremost in good deeds' – did not have any sins in their book of deeds to be anxious about.[164]

The question which arises here is whether in this world, which is full of trials and tribulations, it is possible, even for those who have reached the highest level of belief, not to experience any sadness? As was discussed previously,[165] the Quran points to the fact that even prophets experienced sadness at certain times in their lives, and even those who fall into the third category of belief are still tested. However, this test is a source of hope, comfort and guidance from God. One must therefore question why Ṭabāṭabā'ī is inclined not to include the third category of believers with the first two categories, who will be relieved of their duties and difficulties once they depart from this world.

With regard to sadness on account of loss and separation, Ṭabarī only elaborates on the Quranic verses (12:84-86) and does not really explain why Jacob was so saddened by the loss of Joseph.[166] Ibn Kathīr also fails to explain why a prophet should be so saddened by the loss of his son. He does however state that Jacob's loss of sight was due to his suppression of his sadness and his refusal to share this sadness with anyone except God. Ibn Kathīr adds that when Jacob informed his sons that he had knowledge from God that 'they do not possess',[167] he was implying that he had received inspiration from God that Joseph was alive and that he would achieve his mission as a Prophet.[168] But if this is the case, one may ask why his sadness did not cease; in fact it actually reached such an extent that his sons were worried that he would die of grief.[169]

Tustarī does give a reason why Jacob was so sad with regard to his separation from Joseph.[170] His explanation is that firstly it was not Joseph himself that Jacob missed but, rather, the attributes of God which were manifested in him. Secondly, Jacob's great distress and anxiety were not on account of the loss of Joseph himself, but rather on account of his fear that Joseph might lose his faith.[171] This explanation does not really address the fact that Jacob knew that ultimately it was God's Divine Decree that this separation should take place and that this is why he admitted that he only complained to God and no one else, as he believed that ultimately God created these series of events. Therefore, since he knew for certain that it was God who ultimately caused this separation – which is why he attributed everything to Him, including his own sadness, in the first place –, it is highly unlikely that he would fail to attribute the protection of Joseph's faith to God.

Ṭabāṭabaī also stresses the non-attribution of effects to secondary causes by Jacob.[172] He explains that Jacob did not allow his anger and sadness to spill out, but kept it to himself, thus not allowing his ego to manifest. Although Ṭabaṭabāī does not give any further explanation, he does imply here that Jacob was aware of his own weakness, but kept it to himself, as he knew that ultimately this loss was a test of patience for him from God and that it would therefore be pointless for him to complain to anyone else except his Lord.[173]

With regard to verses 28:8, 28:10 and 28:13, all the exegetes above concur that the consequence of the separation of Moses from his mother was ultimately a good one, and a lesson that there are many wisdoms behind God's Decrees.[174] Therefore what appears to be unfavourable is in fact good. In this case the good outcome was evident: Moses was prevented from being killed and went on to achieve his mission as Prophet, standing up against Pharaoh's oppression. Another important point that Ṭabāṭabā'ī alludes to in his explanation is that the source of belief and guidance is God. This becomes clear through the example of Moses's mother, whose heart felt empty because of her separation from her son. She was on the verge of disclosing her sadness when God filled her heart with the promise that Moses would be safe. This implies that at that point she still had doubts, and that it was not until she actually saw her son alive and healthy that she reached the level of complete trust in God. This implies that the separation of Moses from his mother also had a good outcome for her, for it provided the opportunity for her heart to be strengthened.[175]

All the above exegetes concur that in verses 36:76, 5:41 and 10:65, God is commanding Muhammad not to be sad. They also agree that His order is also there to console Muhammad, and to remind and reassure him that God is aware of the actions of the unbelievers and that they will have to account for their deeds.[176] The exegetes also agree that in 6:33 God is again consoling Muhammad and reminding him that it is not he whom the deniers are denying, as he is only the Messenger. Rather, what these people refuse to believe– because it does not serve their immediate worldly interests – is the actual message or the signs of God.[177] Ṭabāṭabā'ī classifies their denial as a form of oppression, implying that unbelief itself is inherently oppressive.[178]

While there is agreement by all the exegetes that the call to Mary to '*grieve not*' (verse 19:24) is a source of comfort, consolation and reassurance for her, not all exegetes agree on the source of the call. Ṭabarī and Ṭabāṭabā'ī contend that the source of the cry was Jesus himself, comforting his mother, since he also later asks her to observe a vow of silence, telling her that he would take the responsibility from her by being answerable to the people and vouching for her purity.[179]

In 9:40 it is Muhammad who is comforting and reassuring his companion not to be sad. Ṭabāṭabā'ī links the word *ḥuzn* to fear – in this case, Abū Bakr's fear of being caught by the enemy. He concurs with Ibn Kathīr and Mawdūdī that the emphasis here is that they have God on their side; it is God's war, Ibn Kathīr states, that is the highest, in contrast to that of the unbelievers, which is the lowest. Although they are not explicit, the exegetes, and in particular Ibn Kathīr and Ṭabāṭabā'ī, imply that what Muhammad is actually saying is that the huge numbers of the enemy will not be a threat if God does not wish it to be. And since God is on their side, by having total trust in Him there will be no cause for them to be sad.[180]

With regard to the interpretation of the word *ḥuzn*, Ṭabāṭabā'ī, as discussed previously, has explained that sorrow is experienced when misfortune has already occurred.[181] In 9:40 the misfortune was the difficult situation in which Muhammad and his companion found themselves. However, that which Abu Bakr dreaded – namely, the fear of being caught and killed – had not yet occurred. Bearing in mind Ṭabāṭabā'ī's understanding of the concept of *ḥuzn*, when Muhammad told his companion 'not to grieve' since they had God on their side, this reassurance may also imply that Muhammad was reminding his companion about the pointlessness of being sad about a dreaded event which had not yet occurred.[182]

In short, the exegetes concur that the concept of *ḥuzn* is related to loss of possessions, including loss of loved ones, and that the *khawf* which occurs frequently with *ḥuzn* generally relates to the future, in particular to the hereafter.[183]

All the exegetes also concur that *ḥuzn* can be avoided only through the seeking of guidance, and that everyone has the potential to receive guidance if they are sincere in their belief. Ṭabāṭabā'ī explains this state of sincerity in terms of acceptance both of God's Mastership and of one's own servitude. The exegetes also concur that sadness given by God can ultimately be a positive experience if one has patience and trust, as in the case of the separation of Moses from his mother.[184]

However, none of the exegetes appears to give a clear explanation why most of the Prophets in general, and Jacob in particular, were so severely affected by their loss;[185] in the case of Jacob, for example, he was affected by Joseph's separation to such an extent that he lost his sight and his children were greatly concerned about his general physical health.[186]

The next chapter analyses work by Muslim thinkers who have written specifically on the topic of *ḥuzn*.

4

Ḥuzn in the Muslim Scholarly Tradition (Muslim Thinkers)

Introduction

In the previous chapter the points of convergence and divergence in a key selection of exegetical readings of the term *ḥuzn* were discussed. In this chapter, the works of Muslim thinkers who have written specifically about *ḥuzn* are explored. The aim is to compare the approach to the issue of *ḥuzn* by Muslim thinkers from both classical and contemporary periods with the approach to *ḥuzn* evident in the Quran in order to obtain a broader understanding of the concept. What emerges will later be compared with the interpretation of *ḥuzn* given by Said Nursi, which will be discussed in the final chapter.

As al-Kindī is considered to be the first Muslim philosopher, and given that he has written the longest and more detailed treatise on *ḥuzn*, his work will be discussed first. But before discussing al-Kindī's epistle on *ḥuzn*, major Islamic, Greek and Stoic influences on his work will be investigated in order to enable us to discuss his work in a broader context. However, it should be noted from the outset that he sought to follow only those Greek and Stoic ideas which were in conformity with the Quran. Also, because of his leanings towards the Mu'tazīlītes, this school of thought will also be discussed briefly below.

Early Muslim scholars and the notion of human psychology

Early Muslim scholars made exceptional contributions in their writings to the development of certain concepts that we would recognise today as psychological. Although psychology *per se* did not exist at that time, concepts such as the nature of the 'self' or 'soul' (*nafs*), similar to the Greco-Roman concept of the *psyche*, were discussed under the general rubric of philosophy, mainly within the sub-disciplines of metaphysics and ethics.[1] Metaphysics is a necessary framework for the subject of ethics. The concepts of being and existence are thus extremely important since they serve as a foundation in our understanding of the nature of the universe, the position of human beings in it, and consequently how ethical problems should be addressed.[2]

Although foreign or Hellenistic philosophy was frowned upon initially, mainly by the conservative Muslim theologians of the day, there was less hostility towards new ideas in the eighth century. The opening of gateway to 'free thinking' can be attributed in part to the Abbassid caliph al-Ma'mūn (813-933), who, on account of his interest in Greek philosophy, established 'a philosophical academy' (*bayt al-ḥikma*) to nurture interest in philosophical discourse and the translation of Greek philosophical works among Muslim scholars. It was at this time that scholastic theology, or (*kalām*), had begun to flourish, with two main schools of thought – the Mu'tazilites and the Ash'arites – paving the way. Ma'mūn himself was a staunch supporter of the Mu'tazilite school, whose main ideas will be discussed in brief below.[3]

The Mu'tazīlites

The Mu'tazīlites were followers of a school of theology which originated in the eighth century. The adherents of this school emphasized the legitimate role of reason in the pursuit of truth. The faculty of reason was given priority as it was considered to be the main tool for knowing God. However, they did emphasise that although intellect can lead to certain awareness, for example that there must be a God who is outside the realm of creation, revelation is needed to confirm such reasoning, as well as to inform about other aspects of belief such as the laws which God has imposed on human beings.[4]

The Sunni theologians were in general agreement with the Mu'tazīlites that belief in the existence of God has to be established rationally. There was, however, a difference of opinion among some Sunni theologians with regard to the whole discourse of rationalism itself. This difference was to be found mainly in the sphere of ethics. The Mu'tazīlites believed that generally, individuals can distinguish by reason alone what is morally good or evil. However, they did recognise the importance of revelation as a confirmation of this reasoning, and that there are some limitations to the scope and abilities of the faculty of reason. They recognised the fact that reason alone cannot distinguish all evil acts, for example, the things which have been made obligatory and which can be understood only through the Quran.[5]

The Ash'arites, on the other hand, rejected the idea that reason can recognise acts of justice or injustice by itself, stating that revelation is the sole foundation for discerning what is good or evil and that, owing to limitations in the human faculty of reasoning, it must fall in line with the Quran.[6]

The Mu'tazilites also defended the concept of free will, asserting that although in the Quran it is stated that 'God guides and leads astray those whom He wills,'[7] this does not mean that human acts are predestined by Him. They added that God gives man the ability to carry out an act in this world, but that the individual himself or herself has the choice whether to act on it or not. On the point of free will, they stood in complete opposition to the group known as the Jabriyya.[8]

The Jabrīyya

The Jabriyya school of theology was first introduced by Ja'd ibn Dirham (d. 736) and Jahm ibn Ṣafwān (d. 745). Contrary to Mu'tazīlite rationalism, Jabrism was founded on the belief that individuals are completely predestined, and hence powerless and unaccountable, since their actions are controlled totally by God. In order to defend their argument for predestination (*qadar*), they drew on specific verses in the Quran and on *ḥadīth* to demonstrate the fatalistic nature of human life.[9] Extreme Jabrism therefore suggested that everything is predetermined, hence absolving individuals of any responsibility.[10]

Greek ethics

Before discussing al-Kīndī's contribution to Muslim ethics, the Greek background and the Stoic tradition will be discussed in brief. Al-Kindī's epistle on sadness is influenced heavily by both of those traditions. Like Epictetus, for example, he stresses the importance of practical philosophy, and how physics and epistemology are intertwined inevitably with the subject of ethics.[11]

For Aristotle, ethics concerned the human good and how to attain happiness. It was therefore seen as a practical science of how to become virtuous rather than merely how one should understand the concept of virtue.[12] The emphasis of both Aristotle and Plato on the practical science of ethics was largely a result of their study of the Socratic notion of the human virtues.[13]

According to Socrates, humans may inflict harm on others physically, but they cannot impact upon the virtuous state of the soul. Humans therefore cannot be forced to be or do evil. Socrates stated that happiness can be obtained by cultivating four virtues in one's life, namely, wisdom, courage, justice and self-control; wisdom is the central component, for in order to be happy one must be virtuous, and it is not possible to be virtuous if one is not wise.[14]

The Stoics

Stoicism, founded by Zeno of Citium (332–262), was one of the new philosophical movements of the Hellenistic period. Despite the popularity of Stoicism in this period, very little information is available on the early Stoics. The history of Stoicism is generally divided into three phases: the 'Early Stoa', from Zeno to Antipater; the 'Middle Stoa', which includes Panaetius and Posidonius; and the 'Late Stoa', which includes figures such as Seneca and Epictetus.[15]

Zeno's beliefs were materialistic and deterministic rather than metaphysical, as he believed that nature was determined by cyclical natural laws. Zeno's God was the soul of the natural world, and individuals could be happy only if they were in harmony with it; the key, according to Zeno, for being in harmony with nature was to remain virtuous. He therefore believed that possessions, health and wealth were of no account, as these could easily perish; what really mattered was virtue, from which no one could be dispossessed.

For the Stoics, reason is considered to be the foundation for an ethical life, which means that through logic and self-discipline, one is able to free oneself of anguish and unnecessary suffering. Living according to reason (*logos*) is equated with living in accordance with the natural order of the universe.[16] Cosmopolitanism is also a distinctive feature of Stoicism, with all individuals considered to be a manifestation of the universal spirit; as such, they should therefore live harmoniously together and in accordance with their natural disposition. According to Epictetus:

> Each human being is primarily a citizen of his own commonwealth; but he is also a member of the great city of gods and men, whereof the city political is only a copy.[17]

Epictetus

Epictetus (55-135 AD) was a Greek philosopher and an exponent of Stoic ethics. Born a slave at the court of Nero, following the banishment in 93 AD or thereabouts of all philosophers by the Emperor Domitian, Epictetus fled to Greece and continued his studies there. It was there, in Nicopolis, that he established his own school and taught until his death 135 AD.[18] Epictetus's main work, *The Discourses*, was transcribed and compiled by his student, Arrian of Nicomedia. Arrian also compiled an abridged version of the *Discourses* entitled *The Enchiridion* ('Handbook'), to which he added quotations by other ancient authors.[19]

According to Epictetus, it is only through reason that one can avoid evil and become a truly rational human being and at one with the rest of nature. This gift of rationalization enables one to exercise one's power of choice, which, according to Epictetus, is a gift from the benevolent deity, Zeus.[20] Although Epictetus makes reference to various gods, Zeus is the one whom he considers to be the creator, administrator and designer of the whole universe. Zeus is considered to be immanent rather than transcendent, and so his inhering within nature enables him to be within the reach of all beings.[21] This is significant because the Quranic emphasis on transcendence contrasts with the Stoic emphasis on immanence. The main emphasis in the Quran is on God's oneness and absoluteness, in the sense that nothing resembles Him or has any share in His creative acts. God therefore does not have a corporeal entity, and because He is immutable and atemporal, His essence cannot be known. However, God is also immanent, in the sense that although at the level of His essence He cannot be known, at the level of His Divinity He can be fathomed through His attributes in creation.[22]

Epictetus's *Enchiridion*, begins with a discussion of the distinction between the powers human beings can and cannot exercise. Although individuals have no power over externals such as relationships, possessions and so on, that which places them above animals is their capacity to choose (*prohairesis*) without being impeded externally. Moreover, God's essence is considered to be pure goodness, and thus if humans wish to live a life without restraint, then they should, according to Epictetus, wish only what God wills. It follows that if one seeks happiness within oneself rather than externally, through material objects, then one will not suffer any anxiety, fear or grief.[23]

However, according to Epictetus, the cultivation of this mode of thinking, that is, to love without attachment and to comprehend and accept fully that all externals are transient, mortal and given to us only on loan, is not easy and requires training. Although this training or self-development can be made easier with the help of an expert, it is also possible to train oneself, since all individuals possess the faculty of reasoning and are therefore able to change their way of thinking and engage in self-teaching. The obviation of impulsive behaviour and bad practices can thus obtain only through change of habit and repeated practice.[24]

Although the moral aphorisms ascribed to Socrates and Aristotle were among the earliest texts translated into Arabic, there is less evidence of Stoic works being translated. However, there are indications that Epictetus's *Handbook* was translated into Arabic. One such indication is the belief that although al-Kindī (800-870) was not familiar with Greek, his epistle *On the Art of Dispelling Sorrows* contains quotes from Epictetus's *Handbook* and shares many of his ideas on how sadness can be obviated – something possible only, it is conjectured, if an Arabic translation of the work was in existence.[25] Al-Kindī is considered to be the first Muslim philosopher, and it was because of his admiration for the Greek philosophers that he played a key role in encouraging the translation movement. For al-Kindī, what was important was the truth itself, regardless of its source, and so he felt compelled to open the doors of

Greek philosophy to Muslim scholars. Before discussing his epistle on the subject of sadness (*ḥuzn*) at some depth, a brief biography of the author will be given.

Al-Kindī's life and work (800-870)

Al-Kindī (Latin 'Alkindus'), whose lineage can be traced back to the respected Arab tribe of Kinda, was born in Basra at the beginning of the ninth century AD.[26] He later moved to Baghdad and served as a scholar for the caliph, al-Ma'mūn (813-833). His philosophical career continued to gain momentum during the reign of al-Mu'taṣim (833-846), who admired al-Kindī's work greatly and promoted him to the position of a court astronomer.[27]

Al-Kindī gained the honorary title of 'the philosopher of the Arabs' in the ninth and tenth century on account of his contribution to scientific, philosophic and literary knowledge. With his extensive understanding and appreciation of the Greek scientific tradition, he contributed considerably to the translation movement, begun before his birth, by overseeing the rendering of many Greek scientific and philosophical texts into Arabic.[28]

A list of al-Kindī's work compiled by Ibn al-Nadīm (d. 995) a century later shows that he wrote 239 treatises on subjects as diverse as metaphysics, ethics, the study of the soul, mathematics and astronomy, as well as treatises on a range of miscellaneous subjects such as swords and perfumes.[29]

Despite the great number of al-Kindī's treatises, most are lost, with extant works having been collated into one manuscript. The paucity of al-Kindī's works is attributed to the political and cultural vagaries of the time, such as the destruction of intellectual creativity by reactionary movements; the political weakness of the Abbasid caliphs; and later the general decline in scholarly productivity in the Arab world. In 1932, however, a number of his epistles in the original Arabic were discovered by Helmut Ritter in Istanbul's Hagia Sophia library, including his epistle on sorrow (*ḥuzn*).[30]

Al-Kindī on metaphysics

Although al-Kindī makes extensive use of ideas from Neoplatonic philosophy in general and from Aristotle in particular, it is clear from his own admission that his aim was to demonstrate the fit between some of the ideas of Greek philosophy and the Divine truths of the Quran. His various treatises on monotheism and God's omnipotence were, for him, a proof that religion and philosophy can be reconciled.

> 'We ought not to be ashamed to applaud and accept the truth,' [he Affirmed], 'from whatever source, even if it comes from far-off places or foreign nations

> who have different cultures from ours. For nothing is more important to the seeker of the truth than truth itself.'[31]

Al-Kindī proposed the teleological argument for the proof of God's oneness and His administration of the universe, and believed in the creation of the universe out of nothing (*creatio ex nihilo*). Although he was in agreement with Aristotle on many issues, such as the attribution of effects to proximate efficient causes, namely, the heavenly bodies, where he diverged from Aristotle most conspicuously was on the question of the eternity of the universe. Al-Kindī likened the creation of the universe to motion, which, he stated cannot be eternal. He believed that just as everything in existence is finite, with the obvious exception of God who is outside the realm of creation, time and space must also be finite.[32]

On the subject of the soul and its nature, al-Kindī diverged from the ideas of the Epicureans and the Stoics, who believed that all substances, including the soul, are essentially material in nature. Al-Kindī believed that the essence of the soul is derived from the essence of God, and although separate from the body it acts with the body by striving to decouple it from material attachments. Through the process of detachment, a purified soul has the potentiality to reflect God's attributes at the highest level.

> When the soul attains the utmost degree of purity, it beholds in dreams a world of marvels, and it will be able to converse with those souls that have already separated from their bodies. It gains God's light and mercy, and it will partake of an eternal bliss superior to all other kinds of pleasures derived from food, drink, cohabitation, hearing, sight, smell and touch. These are sensual and defiled pleasures that end in pain, but its pleasures are divine, spiritual and heavenly that leads to the utmost nobility.[33]

Al-Kindī did not believe in eternal hell, opining that all souls, and not just the souls of Muslims, will eventually be purified.[34]

Al-Kindī on ethics

Al-Kindī emphasized that the human rational faculty alone is not sufficient for a complete understanding of the reasons behind one's existence, and that therefore revelation is also needed. Furthermore, he believed firmly in the compatibility of reason and revelation. It is on account of his emphasis on the importance of human reasoning that he was considered to have Mu'tazilite leanings.[35]

Contrary to the Stoics, al-Kindī did not identify God in nature; rather, he emphasised divine oneness and rejected the notion that He could have partners in

His Divinity. At the same time, however, he held that God's actions (*af'āl)* should be 'imitated'.[36] This indicates that al-Kindī followed the Islamic principle that God can be seen both as transcendent, insofar as He resembles nothing in creation; and as immanent, insofar as His Names and attributes are discernible in creation and may thus be manifested consciously by those who worship Him.

Al-Kindī defines philosophy in his treatise, *On First Philosophy*, as follows:

> The sublimest and noblest of human arts is the art of philosophy, which is defined as the knowledge of things in their realities to the limit of human power. The Purpose of the philosopher in his knowledge is to arrive at the truth and in his action to act in accordance with the truth.[37]

Al-Kindī's writings on ethics can be said to be influenced largely by Hellenistic thought, with the usual stress on the importance of action, but adding to this the importance of making small but key changes in order to ensure the conformity of ethics with Islamic principles. For example, with regard to the elements of virtue, he followed Plato, stating that these comprise wisdom, courage, continence and justice. However, where this differed was in his use of key Quranic terms such 'balance' or 'equilibrium' (*i'tidāl*), derived from the Quranic word for 'justice' (*'adl*), meaning neither excess nor deficiency, and connoting the idea of remaining in a moderate or middle-way position within one's true disposition.[38]

Al-Kindī's epistle *On the Device for Dispelling Sorrows* is particularly influenced by the Stoic ideal, especially as found in Epictetus, who also emphasized the importance of combining knowledge with action.[39] However, Al-Kindī stresses that these ideals should be carried out in accordance with Islamic principles, emphasising as he did his belief that religion and philosophy share the same aim.[40] One can conclude, then, that al-Kindī's emphasis on the importance of following knowledge with action was not an idea that he took from the Stoics alone; following only those philosophical principles which concurred with revelation, in the Quranic principle that belief should be followed by submission, he found a parallel, and thus acceptable, scriptural precept.

Real happiness, therefore, according to al-Kindī, can be obtained only through knowledge, which enables one to discriminate between good and evil and to live a virtuous life, thus preserving the purity of the soul. He also believed that human beings have a natural propensity to do good, stating that:

> What is just is appropriate to his nature, what is evil is only an accident.[41]

The Epistle of Ya'qūb ibn Isḥāq al-Kindī on the Device for Dispelling Sorrows (Rīsāla Ya'qūb b. Īsḥāq al-Kindī fī al-ḥīla lī-daf' al-aḥzān)

This epistle is the only complete treatise on ethics written by al-Kindī still in existence. It is written in the form of a letter in response to a friend's request on how to dispel sorrow. It deals with the concept, nature and causes of sorrow, and how it may be obviated. The epistle is arguably a very early contribution to the development of psychotherapy, since its focus is on understanding the nature of sadness (*ḥuzn*) and learning how to deal with it through self-training and behaviour changing.

In order to facilitate discussion and analysis, I will divide the epistle into four sections/parts.[42] The introductory section begins with a statement to the effect that in order to find the remedy for any kind of pain, one needs to know its causes. This is followed by a definition of *ḥuzn*, which includes the reasons for its occurrence. In the second section, al-Kindī discusses important rules and principles considered essential for the avoidance of sorrow. He also states that there are two kinds of sadness which must be distinguished from each other, since they require different remedies. This first kind of sadness is the sadness that is linked to the individual's own actions; the second kind is the sadness which is experienced as a result of the actions of others. The third section is an exposition of ten 'devices' for the dispelling of sorrow, and this is followed by the fourth section, which is his conclusion.[43]

Part One (Introduction to the Epistle)

The Izutsian analysis of *ḥuzn* in Chapter Two and the thematic analyses in Chapter Three revealed that *ḥuzn* is an outcome of loss pertaining to material goods as well as loved ones. It was also deduced from the analyses of the verses that *ḥuzn* can be positive insofar as it can be a means of guidance that leads to belief and submission. Ignored, however, *ḥuzn* can also be a precursor of despair.[44]

The chapter on the exegetical analyses of the concept of *ḥuzn* also showed that all of the exegetes in question concur generally that the concept is related to loss of worldly possessions and loved ones, and that sadness can be obviated only through belief and submission.[45]

Al-Kindī's definition of *ḥuzn* is also very similar. He defines it as:

> A psychological pain [*alam nafsānī*, lit. 'sickness of the soul'] occurring due to the loss of an object of love or the missing of things desired.[46]

However, al-Kindī provides no evidence for this definition. Given his knowledge of the Quran, one wonders whether his failure to refer directly to the position of revelation on the subject was deliberate or not. And if the failure was deliberate, a second question is raised as to whether this omission was an expression of his desire to demonstrate in true Mu'tazilite, rationalist fashion the fact that individuals are able to distinguish by reason alone that which is morally praiseworthy and blameworthy.

In his response to a friend's request for advice on how to dispel sorrow, al-Kindī relates *ḥuzn* to 'vice', 'pain' and 'tyranny' – all components of a state in which a noble friend such as his should not find himself. From this exchange it appears that sorrow is seen in a totally negative light as something which has to be obliterated.

The identification of the causes of sorrow sets the scene for an investigation into how it can be dispelled. Before discussing the 'devices' for dispelling sorrow, al-Kindī discusses a number of important principles that need first to be taken into account.

Part Two: Important principles for dispelling sorrow

After defining 'sadness', al-Kindī recommends that the causes of sadness be investigated in accordance with certain important rules and principles. The first principle concerns the fundamental distinction in al-Kindī's ethics between 'sensible' and 'intelligible' objects. He then points to the inevitability of experiencing the loss of loved ones on account of the ephemerality of this world. For him, then, intellectual reasoning indicates clearly that individuals should derive what they love from the 'world of the intellect' [*al-'ālam al-'aqlī*], which is permanent and not affected by death:

> Because constancy and permanence are non-existent in the world of generation and corruption in which we live; rather constancy and permanence exist by necessity only in the world of the intellect, the perception of which is possible for us.[47]

He then explains that unlike intellectual objects, which do belong to us, 'sensory possessions' are shared objects within the common domain and therefore do not necessarily belong to one individual. Seen in this light, it would be illogical to expect to obtain something from objects which do not possess what is demanded of them. In short, it makes no sense to expect or demand permanency from 'sensory possessions', which are by nature subject to change and decay. In other words, the important rule here for avoiding sorrow is not to expect things to be how we want them to be, but to see things for what they really are in order not to be disappointed:

> Then we are seeking from nature what is not in nature. And he who seeks what is not in nature seeks what is not existent. And whoever seeks what is not existent will be denied his quest, and whoever is denied his quest will be unhappy (*shaqī*). Thus who desires transitory things and that his acquisitions and loved objects be of them will be unhappy (*shaqī*).[48]

Al-Kindī advises that in order not to be unhappy (*shaqī*) we should live in the present, which means not having regrets over what has been lost in the past and seeking only those things which are accessible to us. By doing this, he advises, one would reach the station of 'noble kings' (*mulūk*) instead of the 'the low populace' (*ṣīghār 'ām*) who are characterised by 'meanness of spirit' (*īstīghnā*):

> We must neither long for them prior to our touching and observing them, nor, after their departure from us, burden ourselves with regret or preoccupation of mind. For such [is the disposition that] belongs to the morals of noble kings. They do not [longingly] anticipate an arrival nor [regretfully] bid farewell to whatever departs; rather, they enjoy everything that is a [present object] of observation to them with the firmest action, and with the clearest [indication] of not needing it. The opposite of this are the manners of the low populace and those of mean spirit and stinginess.[49] They would receive [with anticipation] every coming and bid farewell [with sorrow] to every departing.

We should not choose the permanence of sorrow [*ḥuzn*] rather than the permanence of happiness [*sūrūr*].[50]

Al-Kindī states that because of the transitory nature of this world, sadness (*ḥuzn*) over loss would be an on-going process, and thus there would be virtually no end to it. He also points out that two diametrically opposed feelings such as *ḥuzn* and *surūr* (happiness) cannot exist in the soul (*nafs*) at the same time. Consequently, he advises his readers not to be sad on account of any kind of loss, and to try to train themselves, through the use of 'beautiful habits' (*'ādatūn jamīla*), to be happy about, and accepting of, situations and circumstances that we have no power to change.[51]

The training of the soul

Al-Kindī explains that it is not the loss of objects and people that cause sadness, but rather that it is our attitude towards those objects which needs to be changed. For this, training of the soul (*nafs*) is required. He explains this point by giving examples of people who, drowned in their immoral habits to the extent that they do not question their attachments, value only their own perspective. The examples include: the effeminate or cross dresser, whom most people find distasteful, but who in his own mind imagines that others are missing out on such life adventures; the hedonist, who is attached to sensory pleasures and considers their absence to be a disaster; and the gambler, who despite the waste of so much of his time and money, imagines that any obstacle preventing him from continuing this habit would be a terrible situation to have to endure. Even brigands and outlaws (*shāṭīr*),[52] he argues, who visit monstrous brutalities on their captives, and who regard their own actions to be 'glorious and honourable', assume that not being able to continue their brutal ways would be a sorry state of affairs. Al-Kindī concludes that habits such as these are not inherent in human nature, but are acquired through habitual use.[53] It appears that al-Kindī is suggesting that in order to avoid sadness, people's thought perception needs to be changed, and that this requires the soul (*nafs*) to be cleansed of old habits.

Charles Butterworth's[54] recent criticism of al-Kindī is that he is too radical in his approach and that he does not actually discuss the nature of the habits of those 'noble kings' who, he advises, should be emulated; al-Kindī's arguments are, he concludes, more theoretical than practical.[55] However, there appears to be a contradiction in Butterworth's statement, for while he criticises al-Kindī's 'radical' expectation that people change completely their thought patterns and behaviours, on the other hand he states that he has not provided anyone with practical advice on how to do so. It should also be noted that al-Kindī does offer a way of escaping sadness, namely through the ten 'devices' which will be discussed shortly.

It may be, of course, that Butterworth expects al-Kindī to offer a new physical regimen for obviating sadness. As stated previously, however, al-Kindī's argument indicates that sorrow is caused not by the objects of attachment themselves, but by mankind's attitude towards them.[56] It is not about getting rid of old habits in order to acquire a ready-made set of new ones; the aim, rather, is to eliminate old, destructive habits in order to, through changes in attitude and reasoning, enable the soul to revert to its original, pristine state. As Groff explains, al-Kindī's use of the term 'rectifying one's character' alludes to the 'cleansing' the mirror of one's character in such a way that God's Divine attributes can be reflected therein.[57] Also, as discussed previously, the verb *aṣlaḥa* in verse 6:48 means 'to reform' or 'to correct one-self', [58] thus implying, as al-Kindī himself explains, that wrong habits should be changed or corrected through seeing the transient world for what it is and seeking permanence instead, which is the only way to obviate sadness.[59] Moreover, the word al-Kindī uses for 'training the self' – *tarbiyya* – is the key to the training of the soul. The verbal noun *tarbiyya* is an important Quranic term. It is derived from the verbal root *rabba*, which conveys the idea of 'fostering', 'bringing up', 'nourishing', 'regulating', 'cherishing', 'sustaining' and 'developing and bringing into maturity from the earliest state to that of the highest perfection'.[60]

According to al-Kindī, therefore, the training or regulation of the soul should be given a much higher priority than the training of the physical body. He opines that the soul is far superior to the body, since the body has a temporal existence while the soul is eternal. And yet there is a tendency for people to pamper their bodies and endure much physical pain to insure against illnesses. It appears hear that, by focusing more on perfecting the soul than on perfecting the physical body, al-Kindī is pointing to the importance of moving beyond the corporeal world and looking to the higher realms of existence.

Therefore straightening and healing the soul of its illnesses is much more required from us than remedying our bodies, since we are what we are through our souls, not through our bodies. The physical is common to everybody, but the animality of every living creature is in its soul. Our souls are personal to us and the interests of our personality are more important for us than the interests of the things strange to us. Our bodies are tools through which the deeds of our souls are made manifest. Thus remedying our souls is much more essential than remedying our tools.[61]

Al-Kindī adds that healing the soul is in fact much easier than healing the body, for rather than having to pamper oneself and engage in physical efforts round the clock, all that is required is 'steadfastness' (*al-'azm*), which obtains only as a result of firm determination.[62]

Butterworth also criticizes al-Kindī's idea that sorrow should be avoided, asserting that sadness is part and parcel of the natural human experience.[63] However, al-Kindī's argument revolves around the idea that sadness is innate to human nature, and that it is caused by attachment to transient things while seeking permanence from them. This becomes clear from al-Kindī's use of terms which have Quranic significance – terms such as the aforementioned *tarbiyya* and *takhalluq al-khulq*.[64] The term *takhalluq al-khulq* denotes the gradual rectification of one's character so that it reflects or embodies the 'character traits' of God. In other words, it means to relinquish one's imaginary ownership of the Divine attributes so that soul is able – *in potentia* – to reflect His names as a mirror reflects objects placed within view.[65]

The classification of sorrow

Al-Kindī maintains that sadness arises from either or both of two sources: our own actions and/or the actions of others. He rationalises in true Stoic fashion, asserting that if sadness occurs on account of our own actions, then we ought to do something about it, because continuing to act in a fashion that makes us sad runs counter to our inner desire not to be sad. However, if our *ḥuzn* is precipitated by the actions of others, al-Kindī says, then we should put an end to those actions if it is at all possible for us to do so. But in cases where sorrow is caused by actions of others which we cannot change, he prescribes a simple but extremely important strategy. Firstly, he says, we should not be sad before the event has actually occurred, secondly, if sorrow occurs during the actual causal event itself, then rather than be saddened, we should make every effort to try to dispel it. Thirdly, if sadness is absolutely unavoidable, we should employ any strategy that we can in order to cut short the sadness. It thus appears that al-Kindī sees sadness in totally negative terms, viewing it as an extremely painful and unnatural feeling which should be avoided at all cost:

> The most miserable of all the miserable is he who is unable to push distress away from himself in whatever way he can. And we should not accept being miserable when we are able to be happy.[66]

There is no discussion by al-Kindī on the source of sadness: he concentrates on his portrayal of the feeling as a wholly negative one, and as something which must at all costs be eliminated. If we compare al-Kindī's interpretation with the Quranic exegetical analyses carried out in Chapter Two, a clear and ineluctable difference in approach can be discerned. Although sadness is also portrayed in the Quran in negative terms, it is God who is identified as being the ultimate source of grief and sorrow.[67] Al-Kindī, however, appears to only locate the source of sadness in the ego (*al-nafs al-ammāra*) or in the misperceptions and incorrect thought patterns of individuals; whether sadness is given by God and whether, as a result, it may have positive aspects pertaining to guidance, are questions which he fails to address.

Al-Kindī then starts to offer ways in which sorrow can be dispelled.

SECTION THREE

Devices to dispel sorrow

Having located the source of sadness, al-Kindī proceeds to a discussion of ways in which the feeling may be dispelled. One 'subtle device' (*wa mīn laṭīf al-ḥīlah)* that al-Kindī prescribes is the use of memory to recall the things endured by us and by others in the past, in order to come to the realisation that just as those previous sorrows abated eventually, so too will the grief we are suffering at this moment in time. Al-Kindī is therefore offering consolation by pointing to the fact that while grief is a universal human condition, it can be overcome. He illustrates this point by relating the story of Alexander the Great, who, in order to console his mother as he lay dying, wrote a letter to her on his deathbed in which he is asking her not to grieve over his death, but to build a new city instead and invite everyone who had never experienced misfortune in their lives to commemorate his memory with joy. Disappointed when the day came and no one attended the memorial, she asked someone to explain to her what had happened. As soon as she was reminded that only those were invited who had never experienced sorrow, she understood that her son had been trying to console her by showing her that she was not alone in experiencing grief, since grief is something universal and unavoidable.[68]

Al-Kindī's second 'device' is to ponder or meditate on the principle that 'sorrow is by convention, not by nature',[69] meaning that *ḥuzn* is self-inflicted. He gives the example of people who are sorrowful on account of deprivation or loss of possessions such as money and family, juxtaposing them against those who have never had any money or family, and who are thus not sorrowful. He concludes that sorrow is created by the first kind of people themselves. He adds that since sorrow is bad, it would be madness for a rational human being to allow himself to be engulfed by such a state:

> He who creates for himself something bad is devoid of mind, and we should not be devoid of our minds because this would be the ultimate lowliness. Because there is no difference between him who has lost his mind and the irrational animals.[70]

Al-Kindī does not refer to the Quran directly, and so it is difficult to square his idea that sadness is linked to those 'devoid of mind' and those in 'ultimate lowliness' with the fact that the Quran is full of examples of the suffering of the Prophets and the faithful.[71]

There is also no mention that loss can be viewed as a test, a trial and possibly a means of guidance, or that the feeling of sadness may offer the opportunity to understand that it is the attachment to worldly possessions that is both the cause of pain and the means to understand the necessity of training the soul to detach itself from the toxins of worldly life.[72]

Furthermore, as discussed in Chapter Three, all of the exegetes apart from Ṭabāṭabā'ī are in agreement that sadness is a universal condition that is given for the purpose of educating (*tarbiyya*) the soul, thus implying that ultimately its existence is necessary. Ṭabāṭabā'ī's disagreement focusses on the distinction he makes between 'ordinary people' and the *walī* (lit. friend of God), a term used to describe one who has reached an elevated spiritual station. According to him, because the *walī* attributes all causes to God, he or she will be immune to sadness.[73] But, as has been discussed, even prophets, whose station is superior to that of the *walī*, experienced sadness at some time in their lives, hence showing that the reality of sadness may have a positive role to play.[74] Although al-Kindī admits that it is a universal condition,[75] his presentation of *ḥuzn* as totally negative is difficult to reconcile with the findings of the analysis of the Quranic understanding of the term, which indicate that *ḥuzn* may indeed have a positive role to play by serving as a form of guidance for believers.[76]

Al-Kindī's third device comprises the argument that one should accept that the transient nature of this world, which is a place of 'generation and corruption', necessitates disasters, and that in fact without 'decay', beings could not exist. Consequently, wishing for something which is impossible to obtain is akin to wishing for something which is 'non-existent'. He concludes as follows:

> Thus if we desire what is not in nature, then we desire what is non-existent; and he who desires what is non-existent will be deprived of his desire, and he who is deprived of his desire will be miserable (*shaqī*).[77]

The fourth device focuses on changing our thought perceptions with regard to the concept of ownership. Al-Kindī states that we are not necessarily entitled to possess the things around us, since possessions are common property and therefore we do not have a natural right to them. The only thing that is not shared by anyone else is our soul, and if there is a loss that we should grieve, that is the only one. To feel sad because other people have the possessions we want is to be envious, which is 'the worst of evils'.[78]

The fifth device is to focus on the concept of ownership and to internalise the fact that all possessions belong in reality to God alone; what we have is merely ours on loan, to take care of in the best possible way. If we accept this fact then it will be much easier to submit to the will of God, who is the Lender of all possessions, rather than complaining when He chooses to take back the things He has loaned to us. To be sorrowful if the Lender takes back what He has asked us to look after is to be unjust and ungrateful:

> He who has been lent something may think it is his own, but this does not show gratitude; the least that [one] must do in gratitude for what he was lent is to return the borrowed thing [if the lender wishes to reclaim it] with a generous spirit and delight and [to respond quickly] to the desire of the lender in reclaiming it. Thus he who feels sorrowful in returning what he was lent is ungrateful. Accordingly we should be ashamed of ourselves for this attitude which departs from justice.[79]

It is unclear whether al-Kindī has borrowed this understanding of possessions as a 'loan' solely from Epictetus.[80] He admits freely to following much of Greek thought, as he believed that it did not matter where truth was obtained so long as it did not clash with the precepts of the Quran. And even if al-Kindī has borrowed this concept from Epictetus, he has made it more 'Quranic' than 'Stoic', possibly by reflecting on those Quranic verses which also see possessions as things which are 'on loan' from the Creator.[81]

Butterworth criticises al-Kindī for what he calls the latter's 'passive attitude', by which he means not only his unquestioning acceptance of whatever happens to us as we go through life, but also his insistence on the importance of being grateful when experiencing loss and considering it to be a manifestation of justice. Al-Kindī's statement below is also problematic for Butterworth:

> It is also possible to think of the things common to all people as temporary possessions lent to us by the Creator, loans He can call back when He wishes. From this perspective, it can be argued that we need feel no shame when the Creator recalls a loan at His prerogative, not even if the Creator's collection agent happens to be our arch-enemy.[82]

Butterworth states that there are risks associated with this kind of stance, since there is no certainty that the so-called lender whom al-Kindī refers to is 'a bona fide agent'.[83] However, al-Kindī has pointed out that only when one is unable to change one's circumstances should one submit to God's will. He reiterates that when one is powerless to reclaim what has been taken, then it is pointless to allow one-self to fall into a state of grief and sorrow.[84] Al-Kindī's covert dependence for corroboration on the Quranic revelation becomes evident with his use of the words 'ungrateful' and 'justice', both of which allude to the importance of accepting God's Divine Decree and Determining. Therefore, all causes or 'agents' are in fact under God's command, and so the one who has been saddened because the Lender[85] has taken back that which was loaned has shown ungratefulness, and by wanting something which does not belong to him is behaving in an unjust manner. This accords with the Izutsian analysis of the word 'thankfulness' (*shukr),* which registered prominently in the semantic field of *ḥuzn* and showed that according to the Quranic interpretation, thankfulness is a necessary corollary of belief, which in turn is needed for the obviation of *ḥuzn*.[86]

The sixth device is a reminder that although external possessions may be reclaimed by God, the most precious thing – namely one's soul – is not reclaimed. Al-Kindī then reiterates that, owing to the fact that God has allowed the most precious thing to remain in the possession of individuals, there should be no room for sorrow; in fact individuals ought to be delighted that God has allowed that which is important to be retained.[87] Al-Kindī's central argument is that although sadness is a universal trait, it is acquired through habit and is thus not part of the innate disposition of human beings. His focus therefore is to change thought processes and to de-normalise that to which individuals have become accustomed. Al-Kindī is therefore endeavouring to train the mind to focus on the positive, largely through the rational argument which has it that worldly possessions are far less valuable than the soul.

What al-Kindī fails to explain, however, is that human reasoning may not lead automatically to belief. The Quranic example of Iblīs shows that human reasoning is insufficient, as submission of the heart (*qalb*) is also required. Iblīs was a jinn of very high status who resided in heaven among the angels. He was a believing servant of God who fell from paradise and was cursed because he refused to bow down to Adam. He used his own reasoning to argue with God, claiming that his status was higher than that of man since he – Iblīs – had been made from 'smokeless fire', while man was made from clay.[88] It was this excessive reliance on his own judgment which led to his downfall.[89] Similarly, the story of Moses's mother, whose heart is strengthened by God so that she does not disclose her secret,[90] also demonstrates the fact that, just as happiness and sadness are given by God, belief, too, is given by God out of His Mercy and Wisdom, and is not an automatic corollary of human reasoning.[91]

Al-Kindī's seventh device pertains to the absurdly contradictory situation of wanting to avoid sadness on the one hand and, on the other hand, insisting on forming unhealthy attachments with the things of this world. He concludes that the only way to avoid the constant recurrence of sadness is to acknowledge that sadness is the ineluctable outcome of attachment to transient material possessions. Through a number of anecdotes involving Socrates, Nero and the famous sea-voyage of Epictetus, al-Kindī tries to show that we should aim to reduce the number of possessions to which we are unhealthily attached, for the fewer one's possessions, the less sorrow one has to contend with:[92]

> It is related about the Athenian Socrates that it was said to him: 'Why is it that you are not sorrowful? He responded: 'Because I do not possess anything for the loss of which I will be sorrowful.'[93]

Al-Kindī's story of Nero concerns a precious gift that had been given to the emperor and a philosopher's subsequent warning that to own such a valuable gift is actually to display one's poverty, for if the gift were to be damaged or go missing, his grief would be palpable. And in fact this is exactly what happened: Nero lost the gift during a boat trip, and died before anything even vaguely resembling the piece could be acquired as a replacement.[94]

Al-Kindī relates another story about Socrates:

> An artist was present [when Socrates] said among other things: 'We ought not to be sorrowful.' The artist then asked him what if the jar [he was sitting in] breaks? Socrates replied: 'if the jar breaks, the place will not.' What the philosopher said is true, because for everything lost there is a replacement.[95]

Al-Kindī then goes on to explain that everything that creatures need is provided for them perfectly and in the right proportion; it is man who, despite having been appointed sovereign over all other creatures, exceeds the limits set for him and seeks to possess things which are not really essential for his survival. The outcome of wishing to acquire transient possessions will, al-Kindī maintains, end inevitably in sorrow:

> For this reason we say: he who occupies himself in increasing [possessions] that are out of his hands, will not gain eternal life; his temporal life will be disturbed, his illnesses will increase, and his pains will not cease.[96]

He illustrates this point further by warning once again against being dazzled by ephemeral objects – this time by adapting the ship analogy borrowed from Epictetus.[97] Al-Kindī likens man's life journey on this ephemeral earth to a voyage across the ocean with one's homeland as the destination. He describes in great detail the difference in behaviours of the passengers on board the ship. During the journey, the ship's captain stops briefly at an island so that passengers are able to obtain necessary resources. How the brief stopover is approached by the passengers shows that there are five basic types of traveller on board. One group consists of those who disembark at the stopover island and give themselves just enough time on dry land to obtain their required needs, before returning straight to their seats and enjoying the rest of a comfortable and peaceful journey. Another group is made up of people who are attracted somewhat by the beauty of the island scenery, but who return to their seats and continue their journey in relative comfort. One group comprises individuals who, dazzled by the beauty of the island, begin to gather shells from the beach and flowers from the forest in order to take back to the boat, only to find that their new possessions take up too much space and soon become the cause of discomfort and eventually lose their novelty value. Another group consists of people who are so attracted by the beauty of the island that they forget about the boat and wander, entranced, deep into the island's forests, hoarding more and more precious things and facing innumerable setbacks and disasters as a result. Some of them do eventually return to the boat but only to find that all the comfortable seats have been taken, and the cramped conditions during the rest of the voyage lead to many of them succumbing to various deadly diseases. And then there is the final group of passengers who, totally bewitched by the beauty of the island, venture so far into the forests that they are oblivious to the ship's horn and are left behind as the ship sails away; cut off from all links to their homeland, they perish on the island under horrifying conditions.[98]

Of the five groups of passengers mentioned by al-Kindī, only the first two arrive home safely; the others perish, either en route to or on the island, on account of their unhealthy attachments to material pleasures, which lead to their spiritual and physical deaths via the toxic allure of worldly possessions. Al-Kindī then explains that the boat journey is analogous to the passage from this world to the 'world of truth'.[99] His division of the passengers into different groups suggests that those who seek happiness in and from this ephemeral world will be faced inevitably with sorrow, while those who are successful in detaching themselves from such possessions will lead a happier and more stable life.

Butterworth criticises al-Kindī, however, for not basing his arguments for Divine activity and a homeland beyond this earthly existence on divinely revealed texts.[100] Although al-Kindī does not refer to the Quran directly, his emphasis on detachment from material possessions and his stress on the search for what is 'permanent' rather than that which is transitory are redolent of the Quranic focus on belief in One God and the concomitant abjuration of associationism (*shirk*). As discussed in the typology, belief in Divine oneness is the first and most important criterion for the avoidance of sadness.[101] According to Turner, the Quran's emphasis is not on proving the Creator's existence; rather, it is on proving that the Creator who exists is One.[102] Similarly, this journey of disassociating partners with God is akin to the journey al-Kindī proposes, which is one of detachment, by seeing the transient nature of worldly possessions for what it is, and seeking the Permanent.

Butterworth's criticism of the boat analogy is centred on al-Kindī's failure to clarify precisely the ship's ultimate destination: where, exactly, is mankind's true home?[103] However, al-Kindī explains, the sea voyage is merely an analogical representation of mankind's journey from this life to the next, with terms used for the world to come such as the 'realm of truth' (*'ālam al-ḥaqq*) and the 'true abode' (*ma'āl al-ḥaqq*). It becomes evident therefore that the true homeland is not mentioned by name because it is an allegory for the homeland that is man's eternal abode, namely the hereafter.[104] It appears that the aim of the analogy is to show that we should see the allurements of this world for what they really are, and that sadness is justified only if we are threatened with being cut off not from our material possessions, but from our 'true homeland' itself:

> We [also have to] close our noses to their putrid smells, to lower our eyes so that we do not see them because of their repugnance, and to distance ourselves from them in aversion to their proximity and being repelled by their sight. These are the things that sadden us and which indwell with us in this place. Thus if we are sorrowful, we should be sorrowful [indeed] because of being cut off from our true abode [*mahall al-haq*] and being on the high seas from where our boat will not take us to our true homeland where there are no disasters, as there are no perishables, nor regrets, because there are no things missed, for there is nothing but the truth.[105]

Al-Kindī's eighth device is the realisation that even the greatest loss, namely death itself, should not be seen in negatively since it is inherent in the human condition. He argues that what is bad is not death but rather the fear of death, which is totally irrational: after all, the very definition of man is that "he is a living, rational, mortal being'.[106] With this realisation, man should be able to train his mind to hate what is bad – namely the fear of death – rather than hating something which is part and parcel of the human experience, namely death itself. In order to demonstrate that death is a continuation of life rather than an end to it, al-Kindī gives the example of the journey of a sperm from the testicles to the womb, where, following its natural course, it ends up in a far more spacious, and thus much better, place. This analogy is used to posit the idea of death not as an end to life but, rather, as the gateway to a different kind of life and a superior realm of existence:[107]

> Similarly, while in this place, which is this world, it would be immensely fearful about departing from it. If it were to arrive at the rational place, which annuls sensory pains and possessions, that are sequential of all sensory and

> psychological pains, [the rational place] wherein reside all the good things that cannot be touched by [other] hands or by defects, then whatever possesses [the rational place] will not lose anything at all of its possessions. If it were said to it that it might be returned to this world in which it had been, its worry would be many times greater than when it was said that it was going to be returned from this spacious, mundane [world] to the womb.[108]

Although al-Kindī does not refer explicitly to the hereafter (*ākhīra*), his allusions to it are evident. He makes a distinction between 'this world' (*dunyā*) and the next, which he calls 'the rational place' (*maḥal 'aqlī*), and he links this world with sensory possessions while opining that in the next world there will be no flaws or defects, as it is a place where nothing can be corrupted by anyone.

The ninth device is a reminder that when we are faced with disaster, we should focus not on what has been lost but on what remains.[109] Again, al-Kindī here is advising his readers to change their ways of thinking and to focus on positives rather than on negatives. It is true that he does not refer to the Quran directly, but what he does appear to do is allude to the importance of being in a constant state of 'gratitude' (*shukr*).[110] For just as human beings are advised in the Quran to be grateful for what they have,[111] al-Kindī also says that instead of mourning that which has been taken away, one should rejoice in that which is still in one's possession.

The tenth and final device is the axiom that the less we have, the less we have to lose and, concomitantly, the less we are likely to be saddened as a result.[112] It is difficult at first glance to discern whether al-Kindī regards possessions or the *attachment* to possessions to be the cause of sadness. His previous examples of Socrates in the jar and the ship analogy give the impression that he is following the Neoplatonic line, which has it that possessions *per se* are negative. In the Quran however, the emphasis is on the recognition that whatever individuals possess is given to them as a loan from God,[113] and therefore that it is not possessions as such, but rather one's attachment to, and ownership over, those possessions, that is likely to result in sadness. For example, as discussed previously, the story of Jacob[114] showed that his loss of vision was connected to his attachment to Joseph;[115] similarly, just as Abraham was allowed to keep Ishmael so long as he was willing to sacrifice him for the sake of God,[116] Moses was restored to his mother because she had total trust in God.[117] This shows that from the Quranic perspective, it is not possessions as such, but rather one's attachment to possessions which is the cause of sadness.

Furthermore, according to the exegetical analyses of the Quran, fear and sadness are the outcome of *shirk*. Ṭabāṭabā'ī expands on the notion of *shirk* to explain its strong conceptual connection with ownership and attachment, explaining that this is why God's devotees (*'ibād*), who are totally submitted to God, and the 'friends of God' (*walī*), who see everything emanating from God, have no cause to fear the future or to be sad about any kind of loss, including the passing of loved ones.[118]

Part Four: Al-Kindī's Conclusion

In his conclusion, al-Kindī summarizes two points. Firstly, he reiterates that man should avoid becoming attached to material objects, which are innately perishable; and secondly, he says that rather than focusing so much on pampering the body, one should pay attention to freeing the soul of negative qualities such as anger and desire.

Conclusion

To conclude the discussion on al-Kindī's *Epistle*, on closer scrutiny one can understand that al-Kindī also subscribes to the Quranic notion of ownership as being linked to the 'attachment' to worldly pleasures and sensory objects. As discussed previously, according to al-Kindī, possessions constitute 'sensory things' which are not 'inherent in human nature'; to become detached from these 'bad' habits, self-training (*tarbiyyya*) is a must. He makes this clear by adding in the concluding part of the epistle, 'He who does not own what is out of his hands controls the things that enslave kings'.[119] He adds that negative qualities such as anger (*ghaḍab*) and desire (*shahwa*) are illnesses of the soul (*nafs*) which need to be cured; otherwise, if they are left unchecked they will take control and what is not inherent in human nature will become normalised. This is why he reiterates in his conclusion that the illnesses of the soul are much more harmful than the illnesses of the body. It is here that, speaking about the need to obviate *ḥuzn*, al-Kindī alludes to the Quranic states of the soul, saying that the soul should be trained (*tarbiyya*) in such a way that it is able to become detached from the 'lowest level', i.e. desire (*shahwa*), to the highest level of total detachment from sensory possessions.[120]

Main thoughts of other Muslim scholars on the concept of *ḥuzn*

Abū Zayd al-Balkhī (850-934)

In this section, background information on Al-Balkhī's life and work will be given before focussing specifically on his work entitled *Methods of Dealing with Sadness (ḥuzn) and Depression (jazā).*

Al-Balkhī was born approximately half a century after al-Kindī in Shamisitiyan, a small village in the Persian province of Balkh, now part of present day Afghanistan.

He authored more than sixty works in a variety of disciplines such as medicine, politics, theology, geography, astronomy, philosophy, literature, astrology, mathematics and poetry. Although he was recognised as a great physician and scholar in all fields, his fame pertained mainly to his work in geography. Sadly, the majority of Balkhī's work cannot be traced.[121]

According to Badrī, Balkhī experienced a spiritual crisis in his youth, first following the path of the Shi'ite Imāmiyya or the Zaydiyya, before aligning himself with the Mu'tazilites and finally reverting back to the Sunni school.[122] Balkhī had no desire to reach a high position in officialdom and appeared to be totally without ambition, at one point turning down an invitation from the ruler of Khurasan, who wanted Balkhī to work for him. He similarly rejected a ministerial position offered to him by the ruler of Balkh, al-Marwazī, accepting instead the humble post of secretary (*kātib*), which allowed him the time to carry out research in his areas of study which interested him.[123]

The only religious work of Balkhī's still in existence is his manuscript *Maṣāliḥ al-abdān wa al-anfus* (Sustenance for Bodies and Souls), which is located in the Hagia Sophia library in Istanbul.[124] The first part of the work is devoted to the physical aspects of health pertaining to the sustenance of the body, while the second part deals with the sustenance of the soul. Balkhī himself points to the uniqueness of his work, claiming that it is the first to combine discourses on both the body and the soul in one text.[125]

It is the second part of the work that I will be discussing here, with particular focus on the seventh chapter, which is on *ḥuzn*.

The first chapter serves as an introduction to the whole of the second part and focuses on the importance of sustaining the health of the *nafs*.[126] Balkhī points to the general obsession of physicians with physical illness, highlighting their lack of regard for the psychological aspects of illness, which can have a great impact on physical health.[127] He uses the word *ishtibāk* (intertwining), to describe the psychosomatic approach[128] – a preventative methodology which aims to keep the body and mind in a balanced state. He states that while the ailments that afflict the body have physical symptoms such as headaches and fevers, psychological ailments manifest themselves more through sorrow, fear, anger, panic and the like. He stresses, however, that the intensity of these feelings depends on individual coping strategies, hence the wide range of differences in reaction to these symptoms by different people.[129]

The second chapter is called 'Sustenance of Psychological Health' and is concerned mainly with mental health. Balkhī states that in order to preserve the calmness of the soul one should ensure continuous harmony by trying to avoid any kind of disequilibrium. He writes that just as the health of the body can be preserved to an extent both internally and externally, the health of the soul can also be protected in a similar fashion. He advises that one way of protecting the soul externally would be to avoid harmful outside elements which could induce symptoms such as anger, panic, sadness and the like, while in order to protect the soul internally one should aim to control the influence of negative thought patterns.[130]

Like al-Kindī, who portrays this world as one of 'generation and corruption',[131] Balkhī says that when one is in a serene mood and thus more likely to think rationally, one should convince one's heart and mind that worries and anxieties are an inherent part of this life.[132] Next, he says, one should generally train oneself not to overreact to minor incidents. He explains that just as the body can be habituated to tolerate minute increases or decreases in temperature, the soul, in accordance with one's capacity for endurance, can also be trained to be more accepting of unexpected painful experiences.[133] He acknowledges, however, that people differ in their capacity to endure difficulties and therefore suggests that individuals should first become fully acquainted with their own capacities. Subsequently, those of a stronger disposition may wish to confront their problems, while those who are weaker may try to steer clear of the things they cannot endure, even it means depriving themselves of certain pleasures.[134]

The third chapter is entitled 'Ways of Regaining Psychological Health When One Has Lost It'. In this chapter, Balkhī says that no matter how much one attempts to keep one's body healthy, bodily afflictions and illnesses are ultimately unavoidable; this world is, after all, the abode of sadness, anxiety, worry and calamity, and it is impossible for the soul to be in perpetual tranquillity.[135] Here Balkhī is pointing to the nature of the soul, which is creationally prone to these symptoms; he is also referring perhaps to the inbuilt ability of the *nafs* to change, and to move from the lowest animal state up, through various degrees of spiritual elevation, to the highest level of certainty.[136] He suggests, therefore, that because of the volatile nature of the soul, one should protect it as much as much as one can from emotionally disturbing influences, both internal and external.[137] He states that one way of combatting these psychological symptoms internally would be to 'neutralize' and 'desensitize' the symptoms by changing one's thought processes, that is, by thinking exactly opposite to those thoughts. This technique, referred to as 'opposite therapy',[138] was later adopted by Ghazālī in the eleventh century.[139] Balkhī compares the storage of positive thoughts in the mind with a medicine cabinet, ready to be used when negative symptoms present themselves.[140] The external approach he offers consists in seeking therapy through listening to the advice of a counsellor.[141]

In his fourth chapter, Balkhī enumerates the main symptoms of psychological ailments and their distinguishing attributes, which he discusses in detail in the rest of the chapters.[142] Chapter five focuses on anger and how it should be dispelled.[143] Chapter six is about 'tranquilizing fear,' with Balkhī emphasising that the best way to repel fear is to habituate our senses to those things which frighten us.[144] Chapter seven, called 'Methods of Dealing with Sadness and Depression' (*Tadbīr daf' al-ḥuzn wa al-jazā'*), will be discussed below.[145] The final chapter goes by the title of 'Mental

Manoeuvers that Fend off the Recurring Whispers of the Heart and the Obsessive Inner Speech of the Soul'.[146]

Balkhī's methods of dealing with sadness and fear

Balkhī states that sadness is the opposite of happiness and is caused by the loss of something that one loves or to which one is attached. As far as fear is concerned, it is future-directed, while sadness is linked to the past; if both fear and sadness are experienced together, they can result in an extremely unhappy and miserable life. However, Balkhī states that if one is saved from sadness and fear, then it is possible for one to lead a happy life. He stresses, however, that the nature of this world is such that no one can totally rid themselves of experiences of fear and sadness, and, unlike al-Kindī, he cites the Quran directly and explains that total happiness will be experienced only in the hereafter and only by believers.[147]

Also, unlike al-Kindī, who describes *ḥuzn* as "a bad thing",[148] Balkhī's views on *ḥuzn* seem to be less negative. While he stresses that in this world it is quite natural to have feelings of sadness, he nevertheless asserts that such feelings ought to be dispelled. In Balkhī's opinion there are two types of *ḥuzn*: the first type has an identifiable cause, such as the loss of a loved one or of possessions; the second type, he avers, tends to happen suddenly and without any obvious cause. He relates the second type of *ḥuzn* to physical conditions of the body and recommends as a remedy both physical and psychological treatment.[149]

Balkhī devotes the rest of the chapter to the first type of *ḥuzn,* which, he says, occurs generally on account of a reaction to loss, such as the loss of a loved one or the inability to obtain something that one desires desperately to possess. He states that this can be helped with mind exercises and requires both an internal and external approach. He advises that for the external approach, a medical practitioner may be needed – a counsellor or a wise preacher, for example, to empower the patient and raise their morale. The internal strategies, however, require mental mechanisms devised to train oneself to think optimistically in order to overcome sorrowful feelings.[150] He then offers seven strategies for changing negative thought processes into positive ones.

The first thought mechanism Balkhī offers is logical thinking. One needs to become aware, he says, of the physical harm that sadness can do to the body. He explains that the reason a person feels sad is linked ultimately to the self:

> The fact that a person feels sad and depressed for presumed loss is actually because he loves his body and soul and wants to please himself with what he failed to obtain or to stop the loss from happening. Destroying his health in agony over what has been lost, would be akin to someone selling out his capital to gain some little profit.[151]

Balkhī's second thought mechanism, similar to one of al-Kīndī's devices, is his invitation to the reader to internalize the reality of the world, which is one of generation and corruption, stressing that ultimately everyone in this world will have suffered some kind of loss. By understanding and believing that this world is not "the abode of perpetual joy and happiness" Balkhī believes that the mind will be more accepting of occasional loss and consequently more appreciative of the pleasures of life.[152] Badri attributes Balkhī's approach to the Prophetic Tradition (*ḥadīth*), which stresses the importance of being in a state of gratefulness by looking at other people who are worse off in this world, and, with regard to the hereafter, by considering the worship offered by others to be superior to one's own, thus encouraging oneself to be more thankful for what one has and more conscientious about doing more to prepare for the next world.[153] Considering that al-Kindī was a close mentor and teacher of Balkhī,[154] it appears that the latter is echoing the former, particularly on the issue of the ephemerality of the world and the inevitability of loss.[155] However, it is also possible that the psycho-spiritual religious cognitive approach that both of them espouse is influenced by Islamic teachings.

Balkhī's third thought mechanism is to accept that showing weakness when confronted with misfortune is worse than the misfortune itself. The reason he gives for this is that life is full of calamities, and if one were to respond each time with the same show of impatience, one would make life much more miserable and wretched for oneself. He advises that one should therefore discipline oneself to accept these losses in order that they become normalised in one's mind.[156]

In explaining the fourth mechanism, Balkhī describes those who lose their patience as "spineless cowards", while those who bear misfortunes with patience and endurance he praises as courageous 'heroes'. His fourth mechanism, then, is a question that people should ask themselves when faced with sad situations, namely, do I want to behave like a hero or like a coward?[157]

Balkhī's fifth mechanism is the realisation that the soul is the most precious thing that one possesses, and that it should therefore be the centre of attention and preservation.[158] Again, this seems to be almost identical to al-Kindī's body/soul comparison:

> Our bodies are tools through which the deeds of our souls are made manifest. Thus remedying our souls is much more essential than remedying our tools.[159]

The sixth mechanism is also very similar to al-Kindī's ninth 'device' for obviating *ḥuzn*, where the reader is advised to concentrate on what remains rather than on what has been lost.[160] Similarly, Balkhī advises his readers that in order to reduce the effect of a calamity, one should ponder the fact that it might easily have been more grievous, and thus more unbearable, and so rather than being in a state of despair, one should be grateful to God in one's heart for having been saved from what might have turned out to be a much greater misfortune. He states that we should be especially grateful that the most precious thing, namely the soul, has been spared, thus providing the opportunity and potential to make up for one's loss.[161]

Balkhī's final mechanism aims to turn the attention of the reader to his or her own sorrows in the past, as well as to the grief of others, in order to facilitate observation of how that grief has diminished or been. He states that by contemplating this and by accepting that the pain of loss will be gradually reduced and eventually forgotten, one will be able to engender feelings of comfort and reassurance.[162] Al-Kindī says more or less the same thing, but with a much more detailed explanation. While Balkhī only points to the fact that the pain of loss will be reduced as time goes by, al-Kindī expands on the idea that "sorrow is by convention, and not by nature" by giving examples. One such example is the observation that those who do lack something – those without children, for example – are generally content with their lot, which allows him to argue that it is not the thing itself which one possesses that gives one happiness. Al-Kindī is making an important distinction here for it seems that he is cutting off any causal relationship between the feeling of happiness and the material object which appears at first glance to be engendering that feeling. He is thus indicating that the feeling of happiness is given directly by God, which leads him to the conclusion that sorrow is something which the individual creates for himself or herself "in place of what he has been deprived of or has missed."[163] He then stresses that since sorrow is "a bad thing" we should acknowledge this and avoid creating such bad things.[164] Thus while al-Kindī does not attribute the creation of happiness to created beings, it appears that he does attribute the creation of sorrow to them.

Conclusion

Balkhī claims that his *Sustenance for Bodies and Souls* is unique insofar as it combines remedies for both body and soul in a single treatise. He stresses that his approach, which acknowledges the interaction between the body and the mind, has been lacking among physicians. Like al-Kindī, Balkhī is considered to be an early contributor to the field of cognitive behaviour therapy. However, what distinguishes Balkhī from al-Kindī is that Balkhī – like the German psychiatrist Emit Kraepelin a millennium later – makes a clear distinction between reactive and endogenous depression, although he does not use those exact terms. The first kind is related to the external world and comes with a known reason, such as the loss of a loved one, for instance, and is referred to today as reactive depression; the other presents with bodily symptoms, has no apparent known reason, and is referred to today as endogenous depression.[165]

Although Balkhī stresses the importance of a striking a healthy balance between mind and body, he states that human beings experience psychological symptoms more than they do bodily symptoms, and that if such symptoms are not halted they may lead to bodily illnesses.[166] Balkhī states that in order to preserve the health of the soul, both internal and external approaches are needed: the internal approach means the avoidance of negative thinking, while the external approach means the avoidance of elements which may arouse one's emotions.

Balkhī offers seven thought mechanisms designed to facilitate the obviation of *ḥuzn*. His approach is based on changing negative thought patterns into positive ones through logical reasoning. Firstly he argues that the fact we are sad is to do with the love of the self, in which case it goes against logic to harm the self physically and emotionally by being depressed. Secondly, he says that one should contemplate and accept the fact that sorrow is innate to human life and the world in which we live. Thirdly, he says that just as medication is kept in jars ready to use as a response to physical ailment, positive thoughts should also be stored in the mind and retrieved in order to deal with emotional stress whenever it occurs. Fourthly, he advises his readers to ask themselves, when facing sadness, whether they want to behave like cowards or like heroes. Fifthly, he says that we should try to understand and accept that the soul is the most precious thing we possess, and that we should therefore try to preserve it, with any loss being incurred being secondary in our consideration. Sixthly, he says that we should always bear in mind that the loss experienced might have been much worse, thus helping our state of sadness be transformed into one of gratitude. And finally, he advises his readers to console themselves with the fact that, with the passing of time, all sorrows are destined ultimately to be forgotten.

Unlike al-Kindī, Balkhī makes direct references to the Quran to support some of his arguments,[167] stating also that on account of the transient nature of this world, perfect happiness is not possible, reserved as it is for the believers in the hereafter.[168] He also offers two definitions of *ḥuzn*: one with an apparent cause and another without, or, in today's terminology, one that is reactive and the other, endogenous. Although he applies the same cognitive behavioural approach as al-Kindī, stressing that emotional disorder is simply a 'learning habit' which has to be unlearnt, and although he appears for the most part to be duplicating his methods, he does, however, express these ideas in his own unique way. Balkhī does not place the same emphasis as al-Kindī does on the negative nature of sadness, although he agrees with him that it ought to be eliminated. Furthermore, Balkhī does not really discuss the concept of ownership in connection with sorrow, whereas al-Kindī focuses on possessions from two aspects: firstly he identifies attachment to worldly possessions as the reason for grief, and advises his readers to emulate Socrates by ridding the self of unnecessary attachments;[169] and secondly, although unlike Balkhī he does not discuss God or quote from the Quran directly, he does however point to the fact that if one does not own certain worldly goods such as children or wealth, sadness is not felt, and that it is only when one loses those possessions that one becomes sorrowful. Through this example it appears that he is alluding to the fact that since happiness cannot be found in ephemeral beings, one must seek the Real Source of happiness instead.

Avicenna

Ḥakīm Abū 'Alī al-Ḥusayn 'Abd Allāh Ibn Sīnā (980-1037), known in the West as Avicenna, wrote around 450 works on a variety of subjects; around half of these, mostly on philosophy or medicine, are extant. He is regarded as the father of modern medicine on account of his famous medical works, namely *The Book of Healing (Kītāb al-shifā')* where his theories on the natural sciences, psychology, astronomy, music, metaphysics and logic were developed; and *The Canon of Medicine* (*al-Qānūn fī al-ṭibb*), which "because of its clarity, concision and order, became the most widely used comprehensive work on medicine in the Middle Ages."[170] The writings of Avicenna are influenced heavily by the Stoics, as well as by Neoplatonic philosophers such as Aristotle.[171]

The main difference between Avicenna and al-Kindī lies in the former's metaphysics. Although he believes that God is omnipotent, unlike al-Kindī he does not subscribe to the doctrine of *creatio ex nihilo*. According to Avicenna, the existence of contingent beings necessitates the existence of a necessary being who is the First cause, with the Creator giving form to pre-existent matter through the agency of the active intellect.[172]

Avicenna's work in the field of psychology includes his treatise *Repelling the Fear of Death* (*Risāle fī daf'-i ghamm al-mawt)* in which he uses his theory of the soul in support of his argument that there is no reason to fear death. Also attributed to him is a short piece on the treatment of sadness (*ḥuzn*), which also comes under the title of *Repelling grief and anxiety (Daf al-ghamm wa al-hamm)*. This manuscript – a photocopy and translation of which appears in Appendix – appears to be very similar to al-Kindī's epistle on sadness, but much shorter in length.

Avicenna's definition of ḥuzn

Like al-Kindī, Avicenna also defines *ḥuzn* as a psychological (*nafsānī*) pain which occurs as a result of the loss of objects or loved ones, as a consequence of not being able to attain what one is seeking (*ṭalab*).[173]

Avicenna's description of the soul

Although Avicenna generally follows the Greek philosophical ideas on the soul, particularly with regard to the way it is sub-divided into the vegetative, the animal and the human souls, he defines the soul not as a physical entity tasked with the organisation of the body, but rather as an independent substance in its own right. This dualistic perspective is illustrated in the thought experiment he designed known as the 'flying man', where he attempts to show the non-sensory nature of human awareness:

> One of us must suppose that he was just created at a stroke, fully developed and perfectly formed but with his vision shrouded from perceiving all external objects – created floating in the air or in space, not buffeted by any perceptible current of the air that supports him, his limbs separated and kept out of contact with one another, so that they do not feel each other. Then let the subject consider whether he would affirm the existence of his self. There is no doubt that he would affirm his own existence, although not affirming the reality of any of his limbs or inner organs, his bowels, or heart or brain, or any external thing. Indeed he would affirm the existence of this self of his while not affirming that it had any length, breadth, or depth. And if it were possible for him in such a state to imagine a hand or any other organ, he would not imagine it to be a part of himself or a condition of his existence.[174]

The essence of his thesis is similar to that of Descartes' *Cogito ergo sum* as the central point of both arguments focuses on making a distinction between the sensory world and the self or soul. However, for Descartes, even although there may be doubt about everything else, there can be no doubt about the fact that he thinks.[175] For Avicenna the world does not exist in and of itself; rather, it has a wholly dependent existence and is subject to decay, unlike the soul (*nafs*), which is immortal, which is driving force behind the attainment of various levels of perfection.

Avicenna's dualistic explanation of the soul is remarkably similar to that of al-Kindī, who stresses that although the soul, which is non-material and derived from the essence of God, is separate from the body, it nonetheless works with the body in order to detach it from material attachments. Al-Kindī makes a distinction between 'sensible' objects, which are shared within the common domain, and 'intelligible' objects, which are not shared and which remain in the permanent possession of individuals. He stresses that 'sensible' objects are subject to decay; the soul, however, is one of the personal possessions of individuals and therefore remains with them.[176] Avicenna's focus here is on the uniqueness of souls on account of their potential to achieve different levels of perfection in this world, and which will remain with individuals in the next.[177]

Detachment from worldly possessions

Like al-Kindī, Avicenna appeals to the human faculty of reason to argue that everyone is affected by loss because of the ephemeral nature of this world and all that it contains. He states that if we were to understand properly that ephemerality is part and parcel of all material objects, then we would not expect permanence from things which are subject to dissipation and decay.[178] Al-Kindī's discussion on the ephemerality of objects, including the human body, is essentially the same, but with much greater detail and elaboration. He spells out clearly that to attempt to obtain something which is impossible to obtain is akin to wishing something for that which is non-existent; consequently, any sorrow that follows such an attempt is 'by convention and not by nature', and is therefore self-inflicted.[179] While Avicenna uses the same reasoning to demonstrate the pointlessness of attaching oneself to the ephemeral, al-Kindī goes further by holding individuals solely responsible for their sorrow.

Unlike al-Kindī, Avicenna does not go as far as to equate sadness with those 'devoid of mind', although he does point out the importance of behavioural change and de-normalisation.[180] To change one's behaviour and to de-normalise means to accept and become accustomed to a world which is subject to change and corruption in order to decrease the likelihood of despair (*ya's*) when one is unable to obtain what one desires, as well as decreasing the likelihood of grief over loss.

Al-Kindī points to death as possibly the greatest loss human beings can imagine, arguing that since it is inherent in human nature then it is totally irrational to perceive it in a negative light. He opines that in fact what is bad is not death *per se*, but rather the fear of death.[181]

Avicenna does not discuss death in his discourse on sadness; death is a subject that he deals with in a treatise entitled *On Repelling the Fear of Death (Rīsāle fī daf' ghamm al-mawt)*, where he attempts to demonstrate the irrationality of those who fear death and dying.[182] Avicenna stresses that fear of death is linked to having the wrong ideas about what death actually is, and so attributes the fear of death squarely to ignorance. He states that fear stems from not knowing the meaning of death; from being uncertain about what happens after death; and from supposing erroneously that both the body and soul will cease to exist. He explains that just because the soul becomes separated from the body, it does not mean that it ceases to exist; rather, it continues on its journey to the eternal realm.[183] This is similar to the differentiation that al-Kindī makes between corporeal entities, which are ephemeral, and the soul, which is permanent; the task of the individual is to train the soul in preparation for its true destination or homeland.[184]

Avicenna also mentions other factors which can contribute to the fear of death: the belief that death is painful; the belief that one will be penalised after death; and the perception that with death comes an end to life's pleasures and enjoyments. He explains that death cannot be painful since pain is palpable only when one is alive, as sensory perceptions such as pain or happiness are felt only when the body and soul are together. He states that death therefore is simply the separation of the soul from the body.[185] As for fear of death due to impending punishment, he explains that in this case the fear is not about death *per se* but about one's deeds in this life. He suggests that instead of being frightened of death, the solution would be to refrain from committing sin. With regard to loss of pleasure after death, he reminds his readers that unlike the soul, which is permanent, worldly pleasures ultimately do not give satisfaction because they are ephemeral. However, unlike al-Kindī, who considers worldly attachments to be the cause of sadness and Socrates as a prime example of someone to be emulated in this regard,[186] Avicenna counsels against blaming sadness directly on possessions and in fact encourages – to an extent – the enjoyment of the pleasures of this world as long as it is not excessive.[187] He considers both pleasure and pain to be relative concepts since they differ in accordance with individuals' perception of them. He grades pleasure into three types: the sensual; the inward; and the intellectual, which he considers to be the most elevated kind. Unlike al-Kindī, who equates happiness with the world of the intellect alone,[188] Avicenna believes that it is possible to experience happiness on all of these levels to some extent. However, he appears to agree with al-Kindī that attaining intellectual happiness, that is, total happiness, is possible in this world only if one is able to detach oneself totally from material objects.[189]

Avicenna's remedy for ḥuzn

Avicenna does not suggest devices or mechanisms to dispel sorrow in the same way as al-Kindī, but concludes that one should possess only what is necessary, and when experiencing loss, continue to occupy one's mind with other things in order to distract oneself, instead of going to extremes to repossess those attachments. Avicenna likens this attitude to the morals of the kings (*mulūk*), as they do not give importance to what they gain or what they lose, unlike the 'common people' ('*ām*), who become very happy when they are in possession of things and sad (*ḥuzn*) when they lose them. Avicenna uses the same comparison as al-Kindī, who prefers the attitude of the 'kings', who live for the present instead of being preoccupied with what will happen in the future and sad about what has departed, over the attitude of the 'low populace', who longingly await 'every coming and bid farewell [with sorrow] every departing'.[190] Therefore similar to al-Kindī, Avicenna advises that since it is impossible for transitory things to last, then in order to avoid grief (*ḥuzn*) one must be satisfied with one's situation. However, unlike al-Kindī, he does not elaborate on the fact that the responsibility falls on the individual to use his intellect and to choose between the permanence of sorrow and the permanence of happiness.[191]

While Avicenna appears to be promoting a passive attitude by counselling acceptance of one's situation in order to dispel sorrow, al-Kindī's stance is more nuanced. In his opinion, grief can be avoided by doing something about the situation; if nothing can be done, then grief is pointless and one should submit to the circumstances. Furthermore, while Avicenna does not appear to make any reference to the Quran, al-Kindī alludes to the idea of Divine Determining and Decree by use of Quranic concepts such as the 'world of truth' and 'justice'.[192]

Abū 'Alī Aḥmad ibn-Muḥammad ibn-Ya'qūb Miskawayh

Miskawayh was born around the year 320/932 in Rayy, close to modern Tehran, and he died in 1030. He was a renowned scholar in many fields, in particular in history and ethics. His most important work in the field of ethics is *Tahdhīb al-akhlāq* ('The Refinement of Character').[193] Similar to al-Kindī and Avicenna, he adapts both the Platonic notion of the dualistic nature of the soul as well as the cardinal virtues of wisdom, courage, temperance and justice in this work.[194] *The Refinement of Character* consists of six discourses on the following subjects: 'The Principles of Ethics'; 'Character and its Refinement'; 'The Good and its Divisions'; 'Justice'; 'Love and Friendship'; and lastly 'The Health of the Soul'. The last discourse ends with a brief discussion on the remedy for *ḥuzn*, based heavily on al-Kindī's epistle *On the Device for Dispelling Sorrows*.

Miskawayh's *Tahdhīb al-akhlāq* serves as a training or educational manual for the purification of the soul. He states that in order to ensure that one has a good character and manifests that character through good actions, it is important to understand the soul and its purpose for existence, what keeps it pure and what corrupts it. According to Miskawayh, true prosperity can come about only through efforts that ensure the least corruption of the soul. In the sixth discourse, he offers advice on how this can be achieved.[195]

The concept of happiness according to Miskawayh

Miskawayh details the differentiation that Aristotle makes between *the good* and *happiness*. The former, he says, is something which is common to all whereas the latter, described as *a* good, is relative and has no definite essence. For Aristotle, happiness consists of five parts and the degree of happiness depends on the proportions in which these five qualities are possessed. They are: the health of the body; possession of fortune; fame; success in affairs; and good judgement and some belief in religion.[196] However, the philosophers who preceded Aristotle, such as Pythagoras, Plato and Socrates, believed that happiness and all of the virtues pertained to the soul alone, asserting that the faculties of the soul – wisdom, courage, temperance and justice – are adequate for happiness, with no need for any other virtue.[197] The Stoics, on the other hand, did not consider the body as merely a tool; they believed that happiness required both bodily as well as spiritual satisfaction.[198]

The ancients therefore differed in their opinions as to whether happiness can be realised in this world. Those who believed that happiness pertained only to the soul did not believe that complete happiness could be achieved in this world because of its attachment to the body. Aristotle, however, believed that happiness was possible in this world as long as one strives for a virtuous life.[199]

Miskawayh holds a combination of the above views. Unlike al-Kindī, he does not deny totally the need to satisfy sensory needs but, similar to Avicenna, stresses that the ideal is to aim to move beyond these and seek spiritual contentment. He describes two ranks of people only who are able to achieve happiness, adding that whoever is not within these two ranks resides at the level of the animals and is not able to achieve happiness. The first rank comprises those who are merely at the level of the corporeal but who desire and attempt to reach the spiritual level. Although the people at this level are able to attain happiness to a degree, they will not be totally free from sorrow because they are not completely detached from the world. The second rank consists of those who have reached the spiritual and who observe and learn from the corporeal level and, on account of their detachment, are able to achieve complete happiness:

> He is the one who does not mind being separated from his beloved in this world, nor does he regret the enjoyments which he misses in it.[200]

> He is the one who does nothing but that which God wants him to do, who chooses only that which brings him near to Him, who does not disobey Him by following any of his whims or base desires, who is not deceived by the deceits of nature, who does not pay attention to anything that hinders him from his happiness, who is not grieved at the loss of a beloved, and who does not regret his failure to attain a desire.[201]

Unlike the Muslim thinkers studied earlier, with the exception of Balkhī, the Quranic analysis showed, through the examples of the prophets,[202] that although an imperfect kind of happiness is possible in this world, perfect happiness or *beatitudo* as expressed by Thomas Aquinas[203] is not possible; this is because of the nature of this world as a place of test and as a journey towards perfection.

Miskawayh's sixth discourse

Miskawayh's sixth discourse on the health of the soul (nafs), its preservation and restoration

In this discourse, Miskawayh discusses the causes of a diseased soul and its remedy. He claims that all illnesses such as grief, anger, fear and the like are diseases of the soul. He states that although the soul[204] is an incorporeal reality it is connected to our physical being, and so damage done to the soul will naturally affect the physical body. He adds that just as one should do one's best to preserve a healthy body and try to restore what is lost, the same approach should be applied for preservation of a healthy soul.[205]

The preservation of the health of the soul

Miskawayh advises that in order to preserve the soul from corruption, it should avoid 'the wicked'. This is especially important for the youth, who are particularly at risk since they tend to be attracted more to physical pleasures, which, he opines, are a natural goal of human beings on account of their imperfections:

> The course of all of this is inborn in man on account of his imperfections. We are inclined to them and we covet them by our primitive nature and our original disposition, and it is only by means of reason's restraint that we keep ourselves from them, stopping at the limits which reason prescribes to us and contenting ourselves with what is necessary.[206]

As with al-Kindī, the focus here is on the power of reason, which should be used to save the soul from excessive indulgence.[207] Miskawayh states that just as the body needs exercise, the soul needs knowledge; without it, one's character can become corrupted. Unlike al-Kindī, who focuses on looking after the soul rather than constantly pampering the body,[208] Miskawayh, like Balkhī, emphasises the interdependence of the body and the soul and how the illness of the soul affects the physical body.[209] However, he concurs with al-Kindī with regard to the importance of preserving the soul, stating that the soul is where 'the great treasures' can be found.[210] He points to the permanence of the soul and highlights the futility of attempting to satisfy one's endless desires by seeking and attaching oneself to external objects, which, on account of their ephemerality, will ultimately bring nothing but sorrow:

> And even if they attain one of their desires, this is inevitably lost quickly or is exposed to loss and holds no hope of endurance, since it is external. What is external to us cannot be secure against the innumerable accidents which affect

> it; and, at the same time, its owner is in a state of intense fear, constant anxiety, and weariness of body and of soul, trying to keep what can in no way be kept and to watch over something where watchfulness is of no avail.[211]

Miskawayh concludes that external pleasures are impossible to sustain since 'dissolution' and 'annihilation' are part of their nature; internal blessings, however, are completely different: they are a gift from God and thus not subject to decay, and should be employed in the correct manner in order to facilitate elevation to a higher station before the Creator.[212] Al-Kindī and Avicenna both cite the high station of noble kings as one that should be aimed for, since kings tend to live in the present, giving no importance to what they gain or lose. This, they say, is in contradistinction to the 'low populace', who tend to grieve over past losses while craving future gains.[213] Although the terms 'noble kings' and 'low populace' are used metaphorically by al-Kindī and Avicenna to represent incorporeal beings and sensory objects respectively, the same terms are used by Miskawayah in a literal sense, and in a highly derogatory manner. Quoting the first caliph, Abū Bakr, he describes kings as 'the most wretched people in both this world and the next', adding that they deserve mercy because of the position they are in:

> It may be that some of those who attain to [a position of] kingship or rule are happy for a very short time in the beginning, until they become established in [this position] and look [at it] with open eyes, but after this stage, all that they possess becomes as a matter of course to them and they are neither delighted in it nor mindful of it. They then look beyond to what they do not possess, and, even if they come to own the [whole] world with all that it includes, they still long for another world, or their aspiration rises towards gaining the eternal life and the true kinship, with the result that they become weary of all that they have achieved and have been able to attain. For [the king] to maintain the things of this world is extremely difficult on account of the [predisposition to] dissolution and annihilation in the nature of those things.[214]

Miskawayh also asserts that the rational faculties of thought and discernment which have been bestowed by God upon His servants should not be used to serve the concupiscent and irascible faculties since this would be going against God's guidance and design. Hence one should avoid seeking past pleasures lest they become an end in themselves, bringing with them the risk of being enslaved by them and thus resulting in injustice against God's plan as well as against oneself.[215] Here Miskawayh is pointing directly to Divine Determination and Decree, and suggesting that anything that does not accord with God's plan is ultimately unjust. While al-Kindī and Avicenna only allude or make reference to verses in the Quran indirectly, Miskawayh, like Balkhī, refers to verses from the Quran directly and points to Traditions reported from the Prophet to support his arguments.[216] Furthermore, Miskawayh advises that for the preservation of a healthy soul, minute attention should be paid to all of one's plans and actions. What he adds to the advice given by Balkhī, Avicenna and al-Kindī is that apart from using one's faculty of reason to deal with all situations, one should also reproach and penalise oneself for transgressing and going against one's own resolution.[217]

Al-Kindī, Balkhī and Avicenna's training of the soul focuses mostly on changing thought processes, whereas Miskawayh combines abstract thought with practical suggestions in an attempt to train the soul to resist temptation. He states that in order to preserve a healthy soul, which is key to the prevention of sadness, one should pay attention to all of one's actions instead of following routines simply as a matter of habit. He advises that if our actions go against our intended resolutions, such as succumbing to anger, laziness and so on, then one should penalise oneself in order to return once more to a state of harmony and balance. He gives non-adherence to a self-imposed diet as an example:

> Whoever finds himself in this position should fix for himself penalties to counteract such misdeeds. If [for instance] he suspects himself of seeking some kind of harmful food, or failing to adhere to a self-imposed diet, or eating unwholesome fruits or pastries, he should penalise himself by fasting and should only break his fast by taking the lightest and the smallest amount of food...[218]

Miskawayh gives similar examples when discussing how to train oneself against anger and laziness, stressing that whoever learns self-control from childhood will be in a better position to control his passions and will have the ability to deal with difficulties in life more easily.[219] He urges us as his readers to accustom our bodies and souls to be virtuous by constantly being on our guard and changing our behaviour when necessary. In order to be able to do this, he says, one needs certain qualities:

> This preparation consists of accustoming ourselves to being patient where patience is necessary, to forgiving those whom we should forgive, to abstaining from wicked desires, and to mastering these vices before they rage, for then the task would be very difficult if not utterly impossible.[220]

Miskawayh does not agree with Galen in *Man's Understanding of His Own Defects*[221] where the latter advises that in order to become aware of one's faults it is advisable to encourage a close friend to point out those faults. Miskawayh says that in such a situation, enemies may be more useful, for on their part there would be no reluctance to enumerate someone else's faults. Miskawayh recommends that in order to become aware of one's faults and also be reminded of good deeds, it is best to follow the advice of al-Kindī rather than that of his predecessors:

> The seeker of virtue should look at the images of all his acquaintances as if these images were to him mirrors in which he can see the image of each one of these acquaintances as each of them undergoes the pains which produce misdeeds. In this way, he will not fail to notice any of his own misdeeds, for he will be looking for the misdeeds of others. Whenever he sees a misdeed in some one, he will blame himself for it as if he had committed it and will reproach himself exceedingly on its account.[222]

We should not be content to become like notebooks and books, which convey to others the meanings of wisdom while remaining themselves devoid of such meanings, or like the whetstone which sharpens [other instruments] but does not itself cut. Rather let us be like the sun which benefits the moon. Whenever the sun shines on the moon, it causes it to shine out of the emanation of its light and exerts its effect on it exactly in that way which makes it resemble itself, though not so radiant. The same should be true of us if we transmit virtues to others.[223]

Discussion of the restoration of health to the soul when health is missing

On his discussion on the nature of virtue, Miskawayh combines Aristotelian and Platonic ideas with his own theory.[224] The moral development that he recommends is based on virtues of wisdom, courage and temperance, which, when employed in a balanced and proportionate manner, will result in justice.[225] He makes a distinction between Divine Justice, which is permanent, and human justice, which, on account of its contingency, takes a different form in the realm of multiplicity.[226] Although Miskawayh ranks spiritual happiness more highly than earthly happiness, he does nevertheless state that one can be assured of happiness in this world as well as the next so long as one uses one's reasoning in accordance with the precepts of one's nature.[227] But if human justice is contingent, and if its definition is subject to changes dictated by the norms of different societies, it remains questionable whether in an ephemeral world it could ever be possible to attain perfect happiness and true justice, however carefully one employs the virtues of wisdom, courage and temperance.

Miskawayhs' idea of the 'perfect man', endowed with the potential to reach the highest level of just behaviour, is comparable with the Quranic notion of the 'friends of God'. According to the interpretation of the exegetes, 'friends of God' have neither fear nor sorrow. Recognising their existential impotence, these individuals are at one with their innate dispositions and, through belief and submission, become mirrors which manifest God's Names and will eventually attain eternal bliss.[228] However, the journey to reach such a stage, be it for the 'friends of God' or for the 'perfect man' as described by Miskawayh, Avicenna and al-Kindī, is not an easy one, for as discussed in earlier chapters, even the Prophets were admonished at times and cautioned not to be sorrowful.[229]

Miskawayh discusses the main diseases affecting the soul and which are connected to the four virtues of wisdom, courage, temperance and justice. He points to recklessness and cowardice as being the two opposite extremes of courage; to profligacy and frigidity as the opposites of temperance; to ignorance and stupidity as the opposites of wisdom; and to tyranny and servility as the antitheses of justice.[230] He then discusses the causes and treatment of various diseases of the soul connected to the above virtues and their opposites, such as anger, fear, death anxiety and grief, some of which will be discussed below.

Fear: its causes and remedy

Miskawayh considers excessive and unjustified fear to be one of the diseases of the soul and related to the same faculty as anger. The Izutsian analysis in Chapter Two showed that Quranically, fear is related to anxiety about the future or the unknown.[231] The exegetical analysis in Chapter Three also showed that fear is linked to something which has not yet taken place, on account of "either the anticipation of an evil or the expectation/of a danger".[232] Miskawayh also links fear to events that may take place in the future, in which case they may be either necessary or contingent. He states that contingent events should not be feared as they have not yet taken place – and it is pointless to be fearful about an occurrence which may or may not ever happen.[233] This is similar to the point made by al-Kindī, who says that it is totally illogical to be anxious about an event which has not yet occurred.[234] With regard to fear of things which are bound to happen, such as old age, Miskawayh suggests that the remedy is to anticipate the inevitable and to view it in a positive way.[235]

Fear of death: its causes and remedy

Like al-Kindī and Avicenna, Miskawayh blames fear of death on ignorance, before going on to explain what death means. Death, he says, is not an evil; it is merely the detachment of the soul from the body, whereupon in leaving its corporeal shell the soul reaches completion and, once separated from the ephemeral world, becomes cleansed and experiences complete happiness.[236] Miskawayh also concurs with Avicenna that fear of death on account of the pain it will entail is baseless, for without the soul the body cannot experience any pain.[237]

On the issue of fear of death which stems from anticipation of impending punishment, Miskawahy agrees with Avicenna[238] and al-Kindī.[239] He explains that in this case it is not death but rather the punishment itself which is feared. He advises therefore that one should remind oneself that God is just and punishes individuals only on account of their bad deeds, in which case the remedy for such fear would be found in the avoidance of bad deeds.[240] He states that fear of leaving this world because of having to separate from one's loved ones and possessions stems from the inability to understand the difference between what is corruptible and what is permanent. His explanation of the inherent nature of man as 'a living, rational and mortal being' is exactly the same as that of al-Kindī.[241] He therefore arrives at the same conclusion as al-Kindī, namely that to cling on to what is ephemeral while expecting permanence from it is nothing more than self-delusion.[242]

As discussed in Chapter Three, all of the exegetes studied here associated the word fear (*khawf*) with the future, and in connection to the hereafter in particular. Ṭabāṭabā'ī explains clearly that when the Quran states that God has removed 'general fear' from a person or people, it means that He has favoured those who believe and who submit with His bounty of happiness, and that this bounty is everlasting and not subject to deterioration.[243] Al-Kindī also describes death as a journey to a place where there are no defects or corruption, and refers to the next world as the 'rational place' (*maḥal 'aqlī*) as opposed to the 'worldly life' (*dunyā*).[244] While Avicenna does not discuss the existence of a physical paradise, he does point to different levels of happiness in the next world and links the rational soul to the source of highest pleasure, since it is at this level that the soul has the potential to understand essences which are not polluted with matter. This seeking of pleasure is linked to all physical beings' innate yearning for perfection, which is oriented ultimately towards God, as only His essence is perfect and complete. According to Miskawayh, the worldly abode offers the opportunity for the soul to detach itself from material objects and prepare for the next stage of life. Seen in this light, death is not an end but a completion or perfection since it is a return journey to the Creator of the universe.[245]

What al-Kindī, Avicenna and Miskawayh have in common therefore is that through the use of human reasoning they all point to the ephemerality of this world as opposed to the permanence of the hereafter. In true Sufi fashion,[246] al-Kindī and Miskawayh in particular encourage the training of the body and the soul in order that the latter may detach itself from the world, and recognise that the innate need of human beings for permanence points to a permanent abode.

The remedy for grief (ḥuzn)

Mīskawayh's remedy for grief appears to be more a brief summary of al-Kindī's epistle on sorrow rather than an original contribution in its own right. In fact Leaman questions the originality of Miskawayh's work generally and accuses him of presenting "a mixture of ideas and theories which were not properly integrated, and which consisted of a ragbag rather than a synthesis".[247] But it is possible of course that he adopted the same approach as al-Kindī, that is, focussing on the truth itself rather than being concerned about the source. For as Waltzer opines:

> After all, he is not a Greek philosopher but a Muslim who uses the discoveries and the experiences of the Greeks for his own way of life and wants to naturalize the spiritual religion of the Greek philosophers within the world of Islam, as other Muslim Philosophers did in their own time and in their own way.[248]

In fact in the last section of the sixth discourse, Miskawayh quotes al-Kindī's remarks on grief directly and therefore only the first part, on the remedy for grief, will be discussed here.[249]

Miskawayh defines grief as "a suffering of the soul occasioned by the loss of a dear one or the failure to fulfil a desire."[250] Again this definition is in line with all previous definitions of *ḥuzn*. Miskawayh identifies its root cause as attachment to material objects and bodily desires, which bring about grief on account of man's deluded belief that these objects of attachment are permanent. The remedy for grief that he advocates is the realisation that all material objects are subject to decay and that stability can be attained only from those things which belong to the world of the intellect:

> He will direct his efforts to ends that are pure and limit his attention to the seeking of permanent goods only. He will discard all that is not by nature stable and enduring. When he obtains any of these goods, he will immediately put it in its proper place and take only as much of it as is necessary to remove the pains which we have enumerated, such as hunger, nakedness, and similar exigencies. He will not try to treasure up these things, or to seek to accumulate them or to show them off and boast of them. He will not entertain the hope of amassing them, nor will he long for them. If he loses them, he will not regret them, nor care about them. Whoever accepts this advice will feel confident rather than distressed, joyous rather than grieved, and happy rather than miserable.[251]

Miskawayh reiterates that the failure to accept the corruptibility of material objects will always end in "constant distress and unabating grief."[252] On the other hand, for those who are satisfied with what they have and are not affected by material loss, theirs will always be a joyful state. Without elaborating on them, Miskawayh uses the same examples as al-Kindī, namely the gambler, the swindler and the effeminate,[253] in order to demonstrate the delusionary state of people who imagine that they are happy, but who have in fact merely become accustomed to a particular routine and way of life. Miskawayh's remedy for grief is to stay on the path of virtue rather than clinging to earthly attachments and the world of the 'insane'.[254] Again, unlike al-Kindī and Avicenna, who only allude to Quranic verses, Miskawayh ends his work on the remedy for grief by quoting directly from the Quran: "Verily, God's friends – no fear shall be on them, nor shall they be put to grief."[255]

Miskawayh sees no contradiction between philosophy and Divine Law and even uses philosophical arguments to interpret the Quran. He refers to 10:62 to illustrate the point that 'God's friends' are those who follow the course of virtue, while God's enemies are those who stray in the 'darkness of their own ignorance'.[256] Thus unlike Ghazālī, who criticized philosophers for over-dependence on their own powers of reason,[257] Miskawayh believed that philosophy was an excellent tool to use in order to understand the truths of the Quran; had he been alive at that time, one supposes that he would have been an advocate of Averroes (1126-1198), who responded to Ghazālī's attack by supporting the argument for the compatibility of philosophy and revelation.[258]

Abū Bakr Muhammad ibn Zakarīyā al-Rāzī (Rhazes)

Abū Bakr Muḥammad ibn Zakarīyā al-Rāzī (864-925) was born in Rayy, near modern-day Tehran. He is seen mostly as a famous physician, although he defended his position as a philosopher and believed that to be a good physician, knowledge of both medicine and philosophy is needed. This is in line with the stance of other philosophers at that time, who believed that medicine comprised both bodily and spiritual aspects, in the same way that philosophy covers both practical and the moral.[259]

With the Arabic translations of Greek medical and philosophical texts at his disposal, al-Rāzī wrote over two hundred books on philosophy, medicine, logic, cosmology, theology, mathematics and alchemy, as well as penning a commentary on Plato's *Timaeus* and summaries of Aristotle's writings on logic, the *Aphorisms* of Hippocrates and the medical works of Galen and Plutarch.[260]

Among al-Rāzī's most famous books on medicine is his *Kitāb al-Manṣūrī*, which was also translated into Latin. All his work on medicine were valued greatly by medieval physicians and used as a popular source of reference. The reason why his philosophical work did not earn him the same respect is that some of his opinions were considered out of line with the teachings of the Quran and were subsequently condemned as heretical, in particular opinions expressed in his *On Prophecy*, which shocked both orthodox and heterodox Muslims of the time.[261] In this book, which for obvious reasons is no longer extant, he is said to have expressed the view that reason was superior to revelation, in contradistinction to the general Quranic understanding all human knowledge is inspired directly by God. He is also said to have rejected the idea of prophetic mission, prophetic miracles and the imitability of the Quran.[262] However, as Walker explains, some aspects of al-Rāzī's thought may have been misunderstood. He did not reject the sacred nature of the Quran, and believed that the Quran's incomparability is due to its uniqueness, and that it is for this reason that it cannot be compared to anything else. Consequently, he added, the demand that it be compared with other writing is absurd.[263]

Al-Rāzī demonstrates his passion for human reasoning over blind acceptance by pointing to the fact that all human beings, including prophets and religious figures, are by nature equal: no-one is superior to anyone else and it is only by the dint of the extent to which they apply their knowledge and investigative powers that differences between them appear. Al-Rāzī concludes that no one should follow religious figures blindly and uncritically.[264]

Because of the censure which met al-Rāzī's metaphysical doctrines, most of his scholarly output, and in particular his non-medical work, has not survived. Two treatises on ethics remain, namely *The Philosophical Life (al-Sīra al-falsafiyya)* and *The Spiritual Physic (al-Ṭibb al-rūḥānī)*. For al-Rāzī, ethics was akin to psychological medicine – the medication with the potential to restore and bring back balance to the individual. Balance for al-Rāzī was the key, for although he believed that one should lead a disciplined life, he was totally opposed to the idea of extreme self-abnegation. Consequently he did not oppose a pleasurable life as long as it was not taken to extremes. When he was accused of not following the ascetic model of Socrates, he responded by pointing out that Socrates did eventually return to public life, giving up the initial, extreme position which he had adopted.[265]

Al-Rāzī fashioned his metaphysical doctrine out of five 'eternal principles': God, the soul, space, matter and time. Contrary to al-Kindī he did not believe that God created the world from nothing (*ex nihilo*); rather, he held that the Creator utilised the principles already in existence in the universe. According to al-Rāzī, the soul is cast into the world, only to be saved by the gift of the intellect. Ironically, however, and contrary to other philosophers who followed the Neoplatonic and Aristotelian doctrines, al-Rāzī did not consider the intellect to be one of the eternal principles.[266]

Al-Rāzī's Spiritual Physick

Al-Rāzī's *Spiritual Physick* contains twenty chapters, beginning with 'The Superiority of Reason', which he believed to be the most important topic, since he held that reason is the only tool that can help man save himself from his own passions.[267] Other chapters include 'Of Conceit', 'Of Envy', 'Of Repelling Anger', 'Of the Fear of Death' and 'Of Repelling Grief'. Although focus here is on the chapter on 'Repelling Grief', references to other chapters will be made where necessary. It should be noted that before al-Rāzī, al-Kindī had written a book entitled *Spiritual Physick*, which is apparently lost.[268]

In his *Spiritual Physick*, al-Rāzī deals with what he classes as the evil qualities of the soul such as uncontrolled passion, which invites people to enjoy immediate pleasures without any thought for the consequences. He likens the animal passions to uncontrolled beasts which need to be trained and educated.[269] He defines pleasure as follows:

> Pleasure consists simply of the restoration of that condition which was expelled by the element of pain, while passing from one's actual state until one returns to the state formerly experienced.[270]

Al-Rāzī explains that pleasure cannot be perceived without prior pain. It is only when one departs 'from the state of nature' that one is able to appreciate a return to the former state. He concludes that the idea of endless pleasure is therefore a delusion, since it cannot exist without its opposite.[271]

He further adds that those who are engaged in a life of constant indulgence and gratification are never satisfied, and are always hungry for more. They become so habituated to this situation that leaving the circle of endless desires becomes almost impossible, and results in them being sorrowful rather than happy. He then asks, rhetorically, "So what difference is there between them and the man who deliberately sets out to destroy himself?"[272] Like al-Kīndī he advocates the use of reason rather than being a slave of animal appetites, saying that man should "utilize and improve the reason, and not be slave and lackey of the calls of nature."[273]

Al-Rāzī explains that listening to one's rational soul and labouring to wrestle with one's appetitive soul will prove to be worth-while eventually. For even if one were to own half the world, one would not be happy, for one would fear at all times the loss of what one has, while yearning constantly for more:

> If any man should possess half the world, his soul would still wrestle with him to acquire the remainder, and would be anxious and fearful of losing hold of as much as it has already gotten; and if he possessed the entire world, nevertheless he would yearn for perpetual well-being and immortality.[274]

Although al-Rāzī is intimating that the ephemerality of worldly possessions means that man's endless desires will never be satisfied, he makes no reference or allusion to divine revelation. Al-Kindī, however, follows the exegetes in stating clearly that all possessions in fact belong to God and are ours only on loan until the time that they are to be returned to their rightful Owner, and that bearing this in mind, we should not complain when He chooses to take them back; to complain would be to show ungratefulness and injustice on our part.[275] Also, unlike al-Kindī, who followed Socrates in the view that possessions are generally a hindrance and an obstacle to training the soul to detach itself from this worldly life,[276] al-Rāzī considers both excess and deficiency, even in practice of religion, to be harmful, and recommends moderation in all things. He defends the enjoyment of certain necessities in life by referring to Socrates, who in later life did enjoy certain possessions such as home and family life.[277]

Al-Rāzī's 'Of Repelling Grief'

Al-Rāzī does not give a definition of grief as such, although he does explain the cause:

> "When the passion through the reason pictures the loss of a beloved associate, grief thereby follows"[278]

Here, unlike al-Kīndī, Balkhī, Miskawayah and Avicenna, as well as the exegetes of the Quran, who connected grief to loss of possessions as well as loss of loved ones, al-Rāzī does not appear to include possessions at all, reiterating that "the substance out of which sorrows are generated is simply and solely the loss of loved ones".[279] However, he is in agreement with al-Kindī and the other early Muslim thinkers that grief clouds the thought and the powers of reason, and thus it is harmful to the soul as well as the body and should be reduced or preferably diminished. The strategies he offers for accomplishing this task are either to guard against it before it actually occurs, or, if it has already taken place, to try to repel it.[280]

Precautions against the occurrence of grief

Al-Rāzī explains that loss of loved ones brings about grief because they are not eternal but, rather, subject to 'generation and corruption'. And this is why the person affected most severely by grief will be the one who has the greatest number of loved ones and the deepest attachment to them. He states that a person thinking rationally would address the reason for his grief by cutting himself off from its source. He gives an example similar to one given by al-Kindī,[281] namely that "A man who has no children cannot be so grief-stricken as the man who loses his child."[282]

Al-Rāzī explains that while one's loved ones are in one's possession and one has become habituated to them, the pleasure that this affords is recognised only when one has lost those loved ones; it is only through the grief occasioned by loss that one becomes truly aware of the pleasure afforded by that particular attachment. He says that this is because "nature accounts and reckons all that long enjoyment as her due and right".[283] Although al-Rāzī is alluding here to the idea that one does not have a natural right to one's possessions, he makes no reference to revelation and does not rationalise as al-Kindī does that all possessions are merely on loan from God and must be returned eventually to their rightful Owner.[284] Instead, the remedy he suggests for the obliteration of grief is, quite simply, that one should forego such attachments:

> This being so – since the pleasure and enjoyment felt in having loved ones, while they are there, is something so poor, so obscure, so feeble and inconsiderable, whereas the grief, distress and anguish of losing them are so palpable, so huge, so painful and ruinous; what is one to do, but get rid of them altogether, or assert one's independence of them, in order that their evil consequences, their train of hurtful, wasting griefs, may be destroyed or at least diminished? This is the highest level that can be reached on this topic, and the most effective in amputating the very substance of grief.[285]

Al-Rāzī also offers an alternative for those who are weaker in resisting their passions: acquire more than one beloved, so that when one is lost there is another to take its place. In this way, he explains, "it is possible for his sorrow and grief not to be extreme over the loss of any of them."[286] However, he provides no logical reasoning for this argument. It is questionable whether, if one has many children for example, that the loss of even one of them would not cause extreme grief.

After suggesting these strategies for the avoidance of grief, al-Rāzī outlines a number of ways in which grief may be repelled or lessened once it has occurred.

The manner in which grief may be repelled or lessened

Al-Rāzī appeals to the use of reason to argue that when individuals understand and accept fully the fact that everything is subject to 'generation and corruption', it is easier to accept the loss of a loved one. Seen in this light, he opines, one will make most of their existence while they are still present, rather than take them for granted. He reiterates that it is the expectation of permanence from the ephemeral which causes grief.[287] He then argues that sorrow passes and life continues, and happiness does eventually return. He explains that just as we see people who have faced terrible calamities in life, but who have picked themselves up again, it is possible to leave sorrow behind and become accustomed to one's new circumstances.[288] Similar to al-Kindī and Balkhī, al-Rāzī is recommending here a conscious change to one's thought processes. Firstly, he says that there must be acceptance that in this world nothing lasts; secondly, he gives reassurance that loss can eventually be overcome. However, while al-Kindī alludes to revelation and the hope of an eternal abode where there is justice and everlasting happiness,[289] al-Rāzī does not use the same arguments as a consolation for loss. In fact in what remains of al-Rāzī's work there is scant reference to the concept of justice.

Although he acknowledges that human beings are created not merely to satisfy their physical needs but rather to acquire knowledge and practice justice, he does not specify a clear criterion for justice, apart from equating it with moderation:

> True virtue consists in taking of every need so much as is indispensable, or so much as will not involve pain exceeding the pleasure thereby procured.[290]

Al-Rāzī adds that one can reduce the impact of grief by reminding oneself that one is not the only person who grieves; grief, after all, is a state that is universal. Again, this is similar to the example given by al-Kindī of Alexander, son of Philip, the Macedonian King, who on his death bed tried to reduce his mother's grief by demonstrating that she was not alone in experiencing grief, which is a feeling experienced by all.[291]

Al-Rāzī then adds other ways in which grief can be lessened. Firstly, one should reflect on the ways in which others have coped with affliction and the various methods they have used to console themselves. Secondly, one should consider one's own situation and reflect on the coping mechanisms one has used when trying to console oneself for past afflictions. Thirdly, one should consider the fact that the loss of a loved one has the potential to make a person stronger and thus more able to cope with similar afflictions in the future. Finally, he gives the example of "the intelligent and perfect man" who "follows only the dictate of reason" rather than following his passions, which would lead him to the wrong direction. This status of the 'perfect man', whom he describes in his *Kītāb al-ṭibb al-rūḥānī* is attainable only by a 'supreme philosopher' who follows reason in denying his passion and who thus has complete control over his grief.[292] Similar to other early Muslim thinkers, al-Rāzī appears to be saying that grief is not God-given but, rather, is something totally negative and self-induced which must of necessity be repelled. But for al-Rāzī, only supreme philosophers, are able to reach the highest stage of total liberation from their passions, which he considers to be the sole source of grief.

Conclusion

In this chapter, al-Kindī's epistle *On the Device for Dispelling Sorrows* was chosen for analysis and was compared with the work of other Muslim thinkers who have written on the subject of *ḥuzn*. The epistle is in the form of a letter in response to a request from a friend on how to dispel sorrow, but it serves as a piece of general advice on spiritual medicine for anyone who may be suffering from the same affliction.

Although this epistle is based heavily on Stoic ideas and analogies, al-Kindī develops only those ideas which are compatible with revelation. His detractors consider this work simplistic,[293] while in fact his use of Quranic terms takes this work beyond the generic to another level entirely. His allusions to important concepts, some of which will be discussed below, are almost Sufi in tenor and require a deeper analysis than that offered by his critics.

Al-Kindī's definition of *ḥuzn* as "psychological pain occurring due to the loss of an object of love or the missing of things desired"[294] falls in line with the Quranic definition offered by the exegetes. Other Muslim thinkers are of the same mind, with the exception of al-Rāzī, who does not include possessions, defining sadness as being the result exclusively of the loss of loved ones.[295]

Before offering remedies for dispelling sorrow, al-Kindī clarifies an important point relating to the ontological understanding of existence, that is, the emphasis on the distinction between the 'sensible' and the 'intelligible' – a distinction that has to be understood and internalised completely if one is to dispel sorrow.[296] All of the exegetes and Muslim thinkers studied here agree with his argument that this world is one of 'generation and corruption',[297] and that this transience will always be conducive to disasters. Al-Kindī adds that the inclination towards permanence is a natural human disposition; permanence should therefore be sought in that which is permanent, namely the soul, which he conceives as immortal and separate from the body, rather than in material objects, which are transient and ephemeral. He then outlines ten 'remedies' for the 'tarnished' soul, designed to de-normalise one's immoral habits and refine one's character.

While al-Kindī's idea of 'self-training' (*tarbiyya*) is similar to the Stoic ideal of self-liberation and cultivation, his use of this term, with its connotations of 'guiding' and 'directing', together with his use of the term *takhalluq khulq* (rectifying one's character),[298] shows that his approach has more in common with the Sufi notion of the 'purification of the self', [299] in which one's soul, through total submission to the Divine, becomes a polished mirror for the manifestation of God's Names and Attributes. This entails moving beyond the realm of multiplicity and attributing everything to one God.

Whilst supporting the Stoic idea of unity with nature, al-Kindī sees beyond the limited boundaries of nature and in fact speaks of the world pejoratively, pointing to the hereafter as the place of permanence and mankind's true home.[300] He uses Platonic and Stoic analogies with great skill to demonstrate that earthly life, with all of its trials and tribulations, is merely a journey from the ephemeral world to the world of permanence.[301]

The ten coping mechanisms suggested by al-Kindī all concentrate on detachment from the worldly life. He calls attachment to ephemeral objects a kind of 'delusion' and 'madness', while sorrow is seen as an evil which must be obliterated.[302] While most of the Muslim thinkers under discussion in this chapter appear to see sorrow in a negative light, the Quranic analysis shows that both sorrow and happiness are directly from God. Moreover, sorrow can play a positive role, serving as a reminder and a means of direction and guidance.[303] In fact it may, if read in the correct way, serve as a guide rather than as a hindrance.

Yet there seems to be an apparent contradiction in al-Kindī's concept of sadness, for on the one hand he states that sadness is self-inflicted and thus not part of man's innate disposition; while on the other hand he opines that grief is a universal condition, and can be changed only through proper moral training.[304] Al-Kindī does not explain why the inclination to sorrow has been given to human beings in the first place. Furthermore, he states that sadness is a negative attribute that stems from man himself, thus implying that it is not God-given.[305] However, one should note that the Quranic analysis suggests that such inclinations are given by God [306] and can serve as a form of guidance and a sign that is to be read and acted upon in order to facilitate the purification of the soul.

Al-Rāzī opines that one becomes aware of pleasure only after it is lost; pain, thus, is an inevitable co-requisite of pleasure.[307] If this is the case, then logically it follows that in order to be able to experience pleasure, the existence of pain and sorrow is necessary. This means that spiritual pain and sorrow have positive roles to play. And yet both al-Rāzī and al-Kindī appear to depict sorrow as totally negative, adding that its cause – for al-Rāzī the attachment to loved ones and for al-Kindī the attachment to all possessions not necessary for human survival – should be removed.

While all the Muslim thinkers studied here, with the exception of al-Rāzī, who has a more liberal view, and possibly Balkhī, who does not pin the blame for grief on possessions directly, appear to promote the Socratic imperative of physical detachment from material objects and loved ones, the Quranic analysis suggests that it is not possessions *per se* that are the problem; rather, it is one's sense of ownership over these possessions that gives rise to sorrow. The Sufi saying attributed to the Prophet, 'Die before you die!', encapsulates the idea of self-annihilation[308] and detachment from the illusory life of this world, in such a way that the soul becomes a place for the unalloyed manifestation of God's Divine Names.

Although al-Kindī depicts sorrow in a totally negative way, his stance reflects the Quranic notion of the soul as a potential place of manifestation for the Divine attributes, albeit once the soul has been accorded priority over the body and has detached itself from sensory objects as a result of the training (*tarbiyya*) it has undergone in order to de-normalise acquired habits such as anger (*ghaḍab*) and desire (*shahwa*). This convergence of Greek and Islamic ideas in al-Kindī's discourse is not far removed from the Sufi idea of self-annihilation/self-mastery that is pursued in order to liberate oneself from worldly desires and, in so doing, to transform the soul into a perfect mirror in which God's attributes may be made manifest.[309] However, al-Kindī never mentions openly that there may be wisdom in having been given the inclination for desire (*shahwa*) itself, or the fact that if it were not given by God in the first place, how human beings would be able to train their soul to resist their animal appetites in order to reach the high level of total detachment. Although sorrow from the Quranic perspective is considered on the whole to be negative, the fact that Divine admonition in this respect comes in the form of guidance means that sorrow has a positive use.[310] Moreover, the usefulness of sorrow is indicated fact that it is given by God, who, the Quran asserts, brings about nothing in vain.

All of the Muslim thinkers discussed in this chapter agree that happiness is possible in this world; however, owing to the corruptibility of the world, total or perfect happiness is reserved for the hereafter alone. For al-Kindī, happiness relates to both dimensions of existence – both this world and the next. But the latter is considered by him to be the most important, and he advises his readers to use their powers of reason in order to decouple themselves from worldly attachments and prepare their souls for the true home that is the hereafter.[311]

Unlike al-Kindī, who equates perfect happiness with total detachment from worldly attachments, and Balkhī, who also asserts that total happiness can be experienced in the hereafter by believers only, Avicenna posits three kinds or levels of pleasure – the sensual, the inward and the intellectual – and states that it is possible to experience happiness at each or all of these levels.[312] Miskawayh states that only two kinds of people will be able to achieve happiness in this world: those who are at the level of the corporeal but who desire to reach the level of the spirit; and those who are at the level of the spirit. He states that while the former are able to attain a certain degree of happiness, only the latter will have the capacity to achieve complete happiness.[313]

For al-Rāzī, happiness is associated with 'people of knowledge' and not necessarily with prophets.[314] Although all of the Muslim thinkers and exegetes agree that true happiness can be found only in one's knowledge of God, and that the animal soul must be subjugated to the rational soul, the Quranic analysis has shown that just as happiness and sorrow are God-given, true knowledge and wisdom are also gifts from God; as such they are not acquired independently and without recourse to revelation.

The Quranic analysis shows that in this world, which is seen by the revelation as a training ground for the next world, perfect happiness is impossible. But while perfect happiness – or, in the words of Thomas Aquinas, *beatitudo* – cannot be had in this world, an imperfect kind of happiness (*felicitas*) is attainable.[315] The analysis of the Quran and the interpretations of all of the exegets apart from Ṭabāṭabā'ī,[316] show that even the prophets, although infallible in conveying the message, were not immune to human error.

To conclude, while the Muslim thinkers studied here understand sorrow for the most part as the Quran understands it, tensions between the approaches remain:

Although all of the Muslim thinkers agree with the exegetes that the only way *ḥuzn* can be obviated is through decreasing one's attachment to the body and focusing more on the training of the soul, most of these thinkers, when explaining their arguments, tend to appeal to the reader's power of reasoning rather than referring openly and directly to revelation.

The majority of the Muslim thinkers appear to portray *ḥuzn* in a negative light, with al-Kindī going as far as to associate the experience of *ḥuzn* with those 'devoid of mind',[317] regardless of the fact that, as the Quranic analysis shows, even prophets experienced it.

The Muslim thinkers generally appear to agree that *ḥuzn* is self-inflicted.[318] This concurs to an extent with the findings of the Quranic analysis. However, the thinkers do not discuss the possibility that ultimately, happiness and sorrow may have an important role to play.

Said Nursi has written extensively on the issues of trials and tribulation, his 'Message for the Sick'[319] being a salient example. However, since *ḥuzn* is the main subject of enquiry here, it is Nursi's conceptualisation of that concept, and not his wider discourse on illness as tribulation, that will be discussed in Chapter Six, with the aim being to resolve some of the tensions mentioned above.

5

Said Nursi's Life and Works

Introduction

Before we turn to the resolution of the tensions summarized in the previous chapter,[1] it is important that we familiarise ourselves with the life and times of our final interlocutor, Said Nursi. This chapter will thus serve as a contextual backdrop against which Nursi's teachings are to be understood; it will also serve as a background for Chapter Six, which focuses specifically on the term *ḥuzn* as conceptualised by Nursi in his scholarly output.

Nursi's *magnum opus*, the *Risale-i Nur* or 'Treatises of Light' is not only an extended commentary on the Quran; it is also in a sense a reflection of his own life experiences. Nursi claims to have been inspired by his own life story and in his work he involves the reader in the narrative provided by his life journey and the lessons he has learnt. As we shall see in Chapter Six, in providing a window on his personal life, Nursi teaches the reader to not to look superficially at events but rather to go beyond the external and the apparent and to treat everything that comes into existence as a message and source of guidance from God.

The account of his life story will show that it is impossible to pin Nursi down as a follower of a particular group or ideological movement. As we shall see, Nursi stressed the importance of rational thought yet realised its limitations; he had a Sufi-inspired upbringing both at home and at school, yet never felt compelled to self-identify as a Sufi. And while he disagreed with the assumptions and conclusions of secular science, he believed that they should be taught alongside the so-called Islamic sciences.

Throughout his whole life it seems that Nursi neither identified with, nor could be linked to, any particular group, his only source of inspiration being the Quran. It is possible therefore that Nursi's withdrawal from the 'worldly' life in which he found himself actually provided the impetus needed to write the *Risale*.

This chapter will examine Nursi's transition from the 'Old Said' to the 'New Said', following the demise of the Ottoman Empire. It was this second stage of his life, described by Nursi himself as a period of spiritual rebirth in which he turned his back on the world, which facilitated the writing and appearance of the *Risale-i Nur*. Towards the end of his life came the period of the 'Third Said', in which Nursi was to emerge from relative isolation and engage once more – albeit in a limited capacity – with social issues and political life. It is these transitions that led Nursi to take the Quran as his sole guide and to focus directly on the question of belief. It is important, therefore, to examine some of Nursi's key works in the context of his life and worldview.

Historical context

It will help us gain a better insight into Nursi's mindset if we consider the historical backdrop to his life and look very briefly at some of the events in his story in order to understand whether – and, if so, how – the difficulties he encountered during his life journey shaped his perception of the world in any way, and whether his personal suffering served as a form of inspiration for his teachings and writings.

Though not a classically trained scholar as such, Nursi nevertheless earned the title of *Bediüzzaman* or 'nonpareil of the age',[2] since he was considered to be a reviver (*mujaddid*) of Islam at a time when secular materialism was at its peak and when science and philosophy were being used to draw the young people away from religion. It was the secularising currents of the newly founded Turkish republic that were partly responsible for driving Nursi to write the *Risale*.

Nursi's life spans significant historical periods, including two world wars, the birth of the Turkish Republic, and the secularising reforms of Kemal Ataturk. Ataturk's endeavour would lead to the collapse of the Ottoman Empire and the birth of the Turkish Republic. Nursi's *Risale-i Nur*, a commentary on the Quran, was written over a period of six decades and reflects the gradual transformation of the Ottoman Empire, which successfully retained a multi-ethnic and multi-religious demographic, into a westernised, secular republic. The aim of the *Risale* was to concentrate on the truths of belief and, contrary to the secular sciences, to empower people to read the 'book of the universe' by focusing on the Divine names and attributes in order to move beyond the apparent with the aim of understanding the meaning and purpose of creation.

Nursi was born in 1877 in the predominantly Kurdish area of Eastern Anatolia. Ottoman rule was by this time almost six centuries old and covered three continents – from Asia Minor to the Middle East, into south-eastern Europe and across North Africa. Its greatest years were the fifteenth to the seventeenth centuries when, with Islam as its *raison d'etre*, the arts and sciences were able to flourish. Indeed, it was believed that what gave strength to the empire was Muslim unity, which enabled it to bring together all the different tribal factions and ethnic minority groups.[3]

By the end of the nineteenth century, however, Europe had gained dominance over much of the Muslim world; by the end of the First World War, the Ottoman Empire was crumbling. There had been a sense of decline since the opening decades of the nineteenth century, when the autocratic Sultan Abdulhamid[4] tried to rescue the ailing Empire with a series of reforms known as the *Tanzimat* or 'Restructuring' (1839-1876), covering the military, the state bureaucracy and the educational system. These reforms were the result of pressure exerted by Europeans and European-educated elites to modernise the Empire and to adopt European values, in an attempt to save the Empire from its perceived 'backwardness' and decline.[5] Although the reformist groups had conflicting ideas and objectives, they were united in their opposition to Abdulhamid's despotic reign and their insistence on constitutional rule.[6]

The announcement of the Constitution, which came into effect in 1908, was greeted with jubilation, but the period of freedom it engendered was not to last long. In fact, the rule of the CUP [7] lasted only nine months, whereupon discontent began to brew, leading to the notorious uprising known as the 'Thirty-First of March Incident'. According to one explanation, it was the liberals (*aḥrār*) backed by the British who were behind the revolt.[8] Another explanation, propounded by Said Nursi, was that the revolt was engineered by those factions that favoured a speedy secularization and westernization programme, with fingers of blame pointed at members of the CUP whose attitude towards religion had now become extremely lax.[9]

With the Second Constitutional Era (1909-1922) came the period in which the 'Turks', under Western influence, found their national identity as a single people, in contrast to Ottoman rule, which had united the different ethnic groups under the banner of Islam. After World War I, Mustafa Kemal, a nationalist and a staunch proponent of Western philosophical materialism, headed the new secular republic. This new political entity was given the name *Tűrkiye* ('the land of the Turks'), which suggested tacit disregard for the ethno-cultural diversity of the new republic.[10]

Family context

Bediuzzaman Said Nursi, the fourth of seven children, was born in 1877 in the village of Nurs, a small hamlet in the province of Bitlis, one of the six eastern provinces of the Ottoman Empire. He grew up on a smallholding worked by his father, a Kurdish mullah named Mirza, and his mother, Nuriye. Nuriye, who came originally from a small village called Bilkan, three hours away from Nurs, died during the First World War. All of his brothers and sisters, save for the youngest, Abdulmecid, predeceased him. Both his parents were devout Muslims. Mirza was addressed as 'Sufi Mirza' on account of his affiliation to the Khālidiyya branch of the Naqshbandi Sufi order;[11] he died in the 1920s and was buried alongside his wife in the cemetery at Nurs.[12]

Nursi's educational background

Nursi spent his early years with his family in Nurs, but unlike the rest of the family, who followed the Naqshbandi order, he was never affiliated to a Sufi brotherhood, and would later describe Sufism as being inappropriate for the needs of the modern age. Nevertheless, he was influenced considerably by the teachings of the renowned mystic Abd al-Qādir al-Jīlānī (d. 561/1165-6). He was also influenced and inspired by the spiritual changes he had witnessed in his elder brother, Abdullah, and was eager to emulate him. And so, at the age of nine, under Abdullah's supervision, he began to study the Quran, before moving on to works on Arabic grammar and syntax. Initially, the young Said attended the religious school (*madrasa*) in the nearby village of Tag, near Isparit, before going on to attend many similar schools in eastern Anatolia. The rate at which he changed schools reflects his general dissatisfaction with the education he was receiving, most of which was provided by members of the Khālidī brotherhood. He also got into frequent quarrels, not only with other students but sometimes with the teachers themselves, to whose teachings, standards and expectations he refused to conform.[13]

The young Said's rebelliousness notwithstanding, his early studies gave him a good grounding in the religious sciences, upon which he was able to build the foundations of his later work. Eventually he was able to complete his studies and obtain his diploma, earning himself the title 'Molla Said'.[14] Impressed by Nursi's intelligence and his ability to memorize voluminous religious texts, another teacher, Molla Fethullah of Siirt, conferred upon him the title 'Bediüzzaman' or 'The Wonder of the Age'. However, unlike most of the other school teachers in the *madrasa* system at this time, Nursi was not afraid to push boundaries and cross lines. During his time at the Beyazıt *madrasa*, for example, he spent day and night not only studying philosophy and religion but also teaching himself the new secular sciences.[15] In order to learn self-discipline, he also tried for a short time to follow the extreme asceticism of the Illuminationist (*Ishrāqiyyūn*) philosophers.[16] [17]

Nursi gradually became very popular. Unafraid to voice his opinions so long as they were grounded firmly in belief, he began to draw large crowds whenever he gave sermons in mosques. But his increasing fame aroused the jealousy of established local scholars; subsequently, unhappy with Nursi's activities, the governor of Mardin expelled the sixteen year-old and sent him under armed guard to Bitlis.

At the invitation of Tahir Pasha, who was both governor of Bitlis and a respected official of Sultan Abdulhamid II, Nursi made his way to Van, where he was to remain for fifteen years. In Van, while Nursi spent most of his time teaching, the reputation for fearlessness and fair-mindedness that he was making for himself among government officials and intellectuals meant that before long he was being called upon to act as arbitrator in tribal disputes. It was also at this time that he taught himself the modern sciences. And, not content with being competent in three languages Kurdish, Arabic and Persian – he began to learn Turkish.[18]

The atmosphere created by endeavours such as the Tanzimat, occasioned by European pressure on the Ottoman Sultans to emulate the secularising programmes of the West by driving a wedge between state and religion, was such that Nursi's eyes were soon opened to the importance of incorporating the new sciences into the Islamic curriculum. The call for reform and the trend towards secularization that ensued was beginning to impact negatively on the mind-set of the educated, Western-oriented Ottoman elites, and particularly on their views with regard to religion. It was inevitable that comparisons would be drawn between Europe and the Muslim world, and Islam had already come under fire as a probable factor in the Ottoman Empire's perceived backwardness. Without the sciences as a key component of public education, Nursi reckoned, it would be extremely difficult to deflect criticisms levelled at Islam.[19] But these were not the only considerations which influenced Nursi in his choice of direction, as we shall see.

Intellectual and spiritual influences

As we have seen, Nursi received his early education at various *madrasas* in eastern Anatolia, tutored mainly by shaykhs from the Naqshbandi/Khālidī orders. Despite the fact that most of his relatives and teachers were followers of that order, Nursi neither submitted to a shaykh nor identified himself as a member of a brotherhood; rather he took 'Abd al Qādir al-Jīlānī (d. 561/1165-6) and Shaykh Aḥmad Sirhindī (d. 1034/1624), whom he called 'the highest saints', as his spiritual guides.[20] Although not opposed to Sufism *per se*, Nursi believed that it was inappropriate for the modern age.[21] The reason for this is that he believed that it was time for a new method – one which blended science with the truths of religion. His dissatisfaction with the curricula of the Khalīdī *madrasas* gave him the determination to reform *madrasa* education by updating the religious sciences and introducing modern science alongside them.[22]

During his visit to Mardin in 1892, Nursi encountered two dervishes: one was a follower of Jamāl al-Dīn al-Afghānī (1839-97), who had been brought to Istanbul at that time by Sultan Abdulhamid to help further the latter's pan-Islamic policies; the other was an adherent of the Sanusiyya order. Although the sources are unclear on the identity of these dervishes, it is evident that their emphasis on the importance of Islamic unity and education had a tremendous impact on Nursi. Inspired by them, he was determined to unite Muslims and revitalise Muslim civilization, but through constitutionalism and educational reform.[23]

Nursi's attempts at educational reform

External influences, especially during the period of the Second Constitution (1908-1918), also influenced Nursi's thinking. These influences included the liberal ideas being adopted at this time by the majority of Ottoman intellectuals together with the spread, particularly among some of the elite, of positivism and materialism – trends originating in the West which were already finding their way into the curricula of the new secular schools. For Nursi, the only way to halt the expansion of these materialistic ideologies was through educational reform in general, and through the endeavour to combine modern sciences with religious sciences in particular, for he believed firmly that science did not contradict religion; rather, he claimed, it supported the truths of belief. Nursi hoped that his idea of educational reform would come to fruition by uniting three educational traditions with a view to establishing a university, which he named Medresetüz-Zehra. Educational reform was to be effected by combining the education provided by the *madrasas* with that provided by the *maktabs* (new secular schools), and the *tekkes* (Sufi gathering places), so that each would be able to complement and also "complete the deficiencies of the other."[24] Nursi said that the teachings at the new university and the new *madrasas* should be tri-lingual, stressing that Arabic language should be "compulsory", Kurdish "permissible" and Turkish "necessary", in order make it as accessible as possible and thus preserve unity.[25] He felt that combining the religious and the modern sciences was particularly important at this time, as many of the clerical class (*'ulamā*) believed that modern science was at odds with certain precepts of Islam, hence the inclination to keep the two separate. However, Nursi saw no contradiction between the findings of science and the teachings of religion, believing that the only way the truth could become manifest would be by combining the two. Nursi tried to lift the veil of prejudice against science and to challenge the dualism of those clerics who talked about a world that was divided between 'the religious' and 'the irreligious' – a binary similar to that of the sacred and the profane – by reassuring his audience that Islam and science are not irrevocably opposed to one another; on the contrary, for Nursi, science and religion were mutually sympathetic, with Islam able to comprehend science completely:

> This is strange, to say the least, for how can something be in conflict with the very phenomenon that has given rise to it? For it is Islam which has shepherded the sciences, and even given birth to many of them. Yet the fallacy of conflict between Islam and science continues to prey on our minds, driving many to

> hopelessness and serving to close the doors of knowledge and civilization to many of the Muslim people.[26]

The benefits of this educational reform, namely the preservation of unity, were what preoccupied Nursi more than anything else. The '*ulamā* would still be involved in the education in the Eastern provinces, while the introduction of the new, 'natural' sciences would help to uproot superstitions and false assumptions made about modern science in general, thus dispelling the erroneous belief that they contradicted elements of Islamic teachings. Furthermore, this educational strategy would help to facilitate the spread what Nursi believed were some of the more useful aspects of constitutionalism. One such aspect was possibility of creating a consultative council, which would run under the guidance and mutual consultation of the three divisions of Islamic education, namely the *madrasas*, the *maktabs* and the *tekkes*, with the Medresetüz-Zehra University representing this ideal. Nursi believed that this multifaceted form of education would encourage debate and reduce the likelihood of "scholastic despotism."[27] Right up to the outbreak of the First World War it was these educational issues with which Nursi was mostly preoccupied, his aim being the eventual publication of his ideas on educational reform.

It was around June 1908 that Nursi presented his ideas on educational reform to the palace; by November 1908 the text was printed in *The East and Kurdistan Gazette*. In the article he stated that the policy of the new secular government schools to teach only in Turkish would alienate young people: Kurdish children had not learnt the language yet and feelings of separation would lead to disorder and uncivilized behaviour. He suggested that as a starting point, three educational establishments should be set up in different areas of Kurdistan for different tribes where both religious and modern sciences were to be taught side by side. In this way the basis of education would be established and the Kurds' needs would not be ignored.[28] However, not only were Nursi's attempts at unity and inclusiveness rejected, they were seen as impertinent meddling with His Imperial Majesty's educational policies, and led to his arrest. Subsequently he was examined by state affiliated doctors and sent to *Toptasi* mental asylum. But after a short period, and discussions with the hospital doctor, Nursi was released, as the doctor who examined him found no deficiencies in his mental health.[29]

The confirmation by the hospital doctor that Nursi was not insane did not please the palace, and the decision was made to send him back to prison. However, with the help of the Young Turks, somehow he managed to escape. Safely out of prison, Nursi stayed as a guest of some of the CUP's leading figures.[30]

Discontent with Abdulhamid's despotic regime meant that there were many uprisings in the Balkan provinces and so finally the Sultan had to give in and reinstate the Constitution, which he did on 23rd July, 1908. Thus, the Young Turk Revolution had achieved its objective. People from all different minority groups came together and celebrated the victory of constitutionalism in the streets. However, although during the first days of the Constitutional Revolution Nursi worked closely with the CUP – mainly because he had the same aims of educational reform – this was not to last, and it was not long before he began to be disenchanted with them.[31]

Furthermore, Nursi's solution to the main enemy of ignorance – the building of the *Medresetu'z-Zehrā* – did not come to fruition. Funding had been approved and the foundations laid at a site near Lake Van but unfortunately on account of the breakout of the First World War, the project came to a halt and never resumed. Nursi fought in the war as commander of a militia force on the Caucasian Front; his military endeavours were later to earn him a medal. The inspiration for his work *Signs of Miraculousness* came during this war and while in active combat.[32]

The 'Old Said': Nursi's involvement in politics

Three days after the military coup against Abdulhamid, Said Nursi, with the support of the CUP, delivered a speech in Salonica and also Istanbul. Entitled 'Address to Freedom', Nursi's speech stressed the importance of constitutionalism, but in a form that would be consonant with the precepts of the *sharī'a*. He believed that absolutist government and despotism were among the major causes of internal and external conflict and disunity, and that the only way freedom and progress could be achieved would be to ensure that the *sharī'a* was its foundation, since Islam itself, he claimed, contained the necessary requisites for progress and civilization.[33]

Nursi had first become politically aware in the early 1890s during his stay in Mardin, but it was only now that he was becoming fully engaged. Inspired by Namik Kemal, who had guided him and showed him what he called the 'middle way' (*muktasid mesleğī*) in politics[34], Nursi strove to fight against what he believed were two extremist reactions: many people, it seemed, either recognised the freedom of the 1876 Constitution or they went to the other extreme by expressing the opinion that Islamic principles should be abandoned altogether and European civilization as a whole taken as a model for emulation. Nursi was thus at pains to point out that the liberal principles of constitutionalism were in fact in conformity with Islamic principles and thus wholeheartedly supported the constitutional cause.[35]

The short period of freedom brought about polarity of ideas and much discontent. Said Nursi believed that constitutionalism could still be achieved if unity could be preserved and public order maintained. He did not take part in the 'Thirty-First of March Incident'; indeed, he tried to use his influence to persuade others not to join. Nevertheless, he was arrested, only to be acquitted once it was proven that he had no part in it.[36]

In November 1922, Mustafa Kemal, President of the Grand National Assembly, invited Nursi to Ankara to congratulate him for the role he had played in the victorious War of Independence. Mustafa Kemal was also keen to offer him a governmental position, but Nursi refused as he was extremely dismayed by the situation in Ankara. The government was mired in secular politics, while religious obligations were being abandoned and replaced by atheistic ideas of philosophical materialism. Aggrieved by events in Ankara, Nursi returned to Van, where he spent the summer in contemplative isolation and the winter preaching in the Nursin Mosque, where he attracted large groups of both religious scholars and students to his speeches and sermons. At this time his talks were less about politics and more about the fundamentals of belief.[37]

In February 1925, Nursi was approached by the Naqshbandi leader, Shaykh Said of Palu, to join him in a revolt against the government. Despite his concerns over the direction in which the country was being driven politically, Nursi refused the request, stating that he was opposed to internal disunity; it was simply wrong, he said, and at odds with the spirit of the *sharīʿa* for 'brother to fight against brother'.[38] Nursi believed that the only hope for salvation was to use the truths of the Quran and belief as guidance, and that focus should be placed on the extirpation of ignorance, which had always been the greatest enemy. Despite the fact that a large group of people in the Van area heeded Nursi's warnings, the Shaykh and his followers went ahead with the revolt, which resulted in imprisonment, exile or execution for all those involved.[39]

Although Nursi took no part in the insurrection, he was nevertheless accused of having links with the rebels, and along with hundreds of other people was exiled to south-western Anatolia. This marked the beginning of a period of twenty-five years of imprisonment, exile, house arrests and unlawful harassment for Nursi, all engineered by the state. While in Burdur, Nursi continued to attract the attention of local people by giving sermons in the mosque. These sermons were later collated into a book called *Nur'un Ilk Kapisi* ('The First Door of the *Risale-i Nur*'), which, according to Vahide, would be the seed of the *Risale-i Nur* collection.[40] Worried by Nursi's growing popularity in south-western Anatolia, the authorities exiled Nursi for eight and a half years to Barla, a small village in the mountains near Isparta. These years marked the transformation of the 'Old Said' to the 'New Said' and heralded the emergence of the *Risale-i Nur*.

Before exploring further the emergence of the 'New Said', some of the works written by him prior to this transformation will be examined briefly.

The works of the 'Old Said'

Before 1921, Nursi published twelve pieces of work, mainly in the form of pamphlets; any works published after this date, including the *Risale* itself, he attributed to the 'New Said'.[41]

It was between 1908 and 1910 that Nursi was able to take advantage of a short period of press freedom, engaging with the public and making speeches without let or hindrance. At this time he was fully active in political life and spent much time and energy advocating constitutionalism, inviting questions from the public and offering answers in order to erase any doubts that constitutionalism might not be consonant with Islamic principles. These debates were collated into two volumes: *Muhakemat (The Reasonings)* published in 1911; and *Munazarat (The Debates)*, published in 1913.[42]

Nursi's political involvement also included efforts to preserve unity, both internally and externally, under the banner of the *sharīʿa*. It was with this in mind that, early in 1911, he travelled to Damascus, where he gave his famous sermon on what he described as 'six dire sicknesses in the social and political life and their cure'.[43] These sicknesses, he said, are despair and hopelessness; the death of truthfulness; the love of enmity; the lack of Islamic unity; despotism; and egocentricity. To cure these diseases, Nursi said, it was imperative that the people should not abandon hope; rather, they must try to ensure that values such as truthfulness, trust, mutual love, mutual consultation, solidarity and freedom prevail in the global Muslim community. For these values to become widespread, Muslims must follow Islamic principles; after all, he asserted, it is only in Islam that true civilization can be found.[44]

It was during World War I that Nursi began to write his partial commentary on the Quran, *Isharat al-I'jaz* (*Signs of Miraculousness*). Other works published during this time include *Sunuhat* (*Inspirations*) (1920); *Hakīkat Cekīrdekleri* (*Seeds of Truth*) (1920); *Nokta* (*Points*) (1921); *Işarat* (*Indications*) (1920-21); and *Lemeat* (*Gleams*) (1921). All of these focused on the causes of decline of the Muslim world in general and the Ottoman Empire in particular. *Sunuhat*, for example, was written as an attempt to awaken the Muslim world to the importance of belief. Nursi begins by stating that although the 'externals' of religion are clearly important, they have served to act as a veil over crucial issues linked to the fundamentals of belief, which form ninety per cent of the religion's teachings, with the 'externals' accounting for only ten per cent.[45] Nursi goes on to blame the indifference of many believers to the Quran on their inability to understand that it is more than a sacred book – it is the speech of God and it addresses them directly.

> If the Quran had been shown directly in the fundamentals of religion, the mind would have naturally perceived its sacredness, which urges conformity (to the precepts of religion), is the rouser of the conscience, and is [the Quran's] inherent property. In this way the heart would have become sensitive toward it, and would not have remained deaf to the admonitions of belief.[46]

Nursi also had to address the approach of those who judged Islam through superficial understanding. Saddened by the obsession of many of the elite and the 'educated' with secularization and westernization, in *Lemeat*, a collection of writings on a range of subjects, Nursi makes a comparison between European literature and the Quran, attributing the destruction of Western civilization to its separation from true Christianity – a tragedy which, he says, has led to inequality, dissipation and immorality, and, as a consequence, the distress and corruption of individuals and society.[47] Nursi connects this corruption of society to modern man's tendency to see the world as the work of 'nature' rather than as a work of divine art, as it is depicted in the Quran. Nursi's ideas on 'true civilization' will be discussed in greater detail in Chapter Six.

The 'New Said' (1926-1948)

Nursi's inner struggles and spiritual rebirth

Nursi's mental and spiritual transformation began at some point during the second half of 1920 and was more or less complete by the end of the following year.

It was after his escape to Istanbul from the Russian prison camp that Nursi underwent a radical spiritual change. He had suffered greatly, both physically and mentally, on account of the harsh conditions of war and captivity, the loss of many of his students and also the events that had followed, such as the defeat of the Ottoman Empire and the subsequent growth of secularism and materialism. This, together with his growing awareness of death, separation and the transitory nature of the world, prompted Nursi to seek solitude and search for direction.[48]

Nursi was middle-aged when this profound existential crisis and his eventual 'spiritual awakening' occurred. Towards the end of his life he described the experience to one of his students, Mustafa Sungur:

> Sixty years ago, I was searching for a way to reach reality that was appropriate for the present age. That is, I was searching for a short way to obtain firm faith and a complete understanding of Islam that would not be shaken by the attacks of the numerous currents. First I had recourse to the way of the philosophers; I wanted to reach the truth with just the reason. But I reached it twice with extreme difficulty. Then I looked and saw that even the greatest geniuses of mankind had gone only half the way, and that only one or two had been able to reach the truth by means of the reason alone. So I told myself that a way that even they had been unable to take could not be made general, and I gave it up, then I had recourse to the way of Sufism and studied it. I saw that it was truly luminous and effulgent, but that it needed the greatest caution. Only the highest of the elite could take that way. So, saying that this cannot be the way for everyone at this time, either, I sought help from the Quran. And thanks be to

> God, the Rīsale-ī Nur was bestowed on me, which is a safe, short way inspired by the Quran for the believers of the present time."[49]

Nursi identifies two 'spiritual guides' – 'Abd al-Qādir al-Jīlānī and Shaykh Aḥmad Sirhindī – as bearing some of the responsibility for his transformation to the New Said. Firstly, he said that reading Jīlānī's *Futūḥ al-Ghayb* effected a kind of 'drastic surgery' on his soul, thereby 'smashing his pride'.[50] Secondly, Sirhindī's *Maktubat* (Letters) made him feel, he claimed, as though it was addressing him directly, especially when he read "Take only one *qibla!*" ; this he interpreted as a call for him to take only one master, for only one master is necessary and there is no need to follow anyone else.[51]

Nursi's transformation happened in three stages. First came the realisation that he had put too much importance on "human philosophy". This was followed by a period of intense self-examination, in which he questioned his own intentions and mistakes. And finally, there was his Sirhindian epiphany, showing him that the only guidance he needed was from the Quran itself. Nursi came to believe that it was only through the guidance of the Quran and the engagement of both heart and mind that his spirit could be healed, allowing him to banish doubts and reach the truth. And so, by his mid-forties, Nursi's spiritual crisis was over and he believed that he had found what he was looking for.[52]

The New Said's Life and Works

Nursi had by this time turned his back on politics. The difference in the sermons he gave now was that as the New Said, he had stopped trying to integrate politics into Islamic principles and was now focusing more directly, and with much greater intent, on shoring up the foundations of belief.[53] It is not totally clear whether Nursi came to believe that religion and politics were incompatible *per se*, or whether he felt that in the modern secular era a new way had to be found to spread the message of the Quran. What is certain, however, is that Nursi began to realise that religion played no part in the ideologies prevalent in modern Western civilisation; as Abu-Rabi points out, despite the mainstream understanding which takes a positive view of 'modernism', the minority Third World discourse points to the destructive origins of modernity,[54] which Nursi described as having "drawn far from the religion of Jesus"[55] and being based on "waste and destructive competitiveness." [56] It was partly this realisation, together with his awareness of the need for the Quran to speak for itself rather than have its truths grafted on to some foreign system, that occasioned the transformation from the 'Old Said' to the 'New Said', and the change in his approach.

Although Nursi endeavoured to eschew both political and social life as much as possible, he nevertheless experienced very harsh conditions, as we shall now see.

Conditions during Mustafa Kemal's rule

Mustafa Kemal's positivist ideology led him to believe that the key to progress was 'science'; in his view, religion was a serious obstacle and thus Islam had to be eliminated or at least rendered ineffectual. With all opposition now silenced, Mustafa Kemal was eventually able to gain absolute control over the state. In 1924 he officially abrogated Article Two of the Constitution, which recognised Islam as the state religion. He then abolished the Sultanate, dismantled the Caliphate and continued apace with his radical, Westernizing reform programmes. His aim was to eliminate Islamic rituals, culture and traditions altogether and replace them with Western secular ideas under the banner of nationalism. The disestablishment of Islam meant radical structural changes which began with the state's ideological appropriation of the education system, replacing Islamic institutions, religious schools and Sufi gathering places with a wholly secular secondary school and higher education system.[57]

The primary goal of the new Turkish education system was to sever all connections with the 'backward' Islamic past. This was accomplished very astutely by changing the concept of time and space itself. In 1926 the twenty-four-hour clock was adopted in place of the *hijrī* system and the traditional calendars were changed to the Western Gregorian system. In 1935, Sunday replaced Friday as the weekly holiday. But the changes did not stop there. Young people had to be cut off from the past completely, and so by 1928 the Latin alphabet had replaced the Arabic alphabet and attempts were being made to 'purify' Turkish by taking all foreign words – Arabic and Persian in particular – out of the language. But the change that caused the greatest resentment was the change of the call to prayer – the *adhān* – from the original Arabic to Turkish.[58]

While Mustafa Kemal was successful in changing many of the outward expressions of Islam, it was generally perceived that the one thing that he was unable to eradicate was belief itself. Although the 'New Said' was no longer actively involved in politics, he was nevertheless engaged in what he termed the 'greater jihad', that is, the 'war of the pen'. Through the teachings of the *Risale-i Nur* he tried to show the destructive nature of materialist philosophy, pointing out that the only way to progress, felicity and salvation was to follow the criteria of the Quran.[59] As Al-Attas argues:

> Western civilization is constantly changing and 'becoming' without ever achieving 'being'. Its values pertain to the secular, material and physical realities of existence.[60]

When Nursi talks about the 'literature of civilization' it is the above aspect of Europe that he is criticizing.[61] Reviving belief in God was always Nursi's mission, but the important change that occurred in Nursi was the realisation that the Quran was all that was needed. The rest of Nursi's life was devoted to promoting this cause.

Persecution of the 'New Said'

Nursi was at this time busying himself with an exposition of the principles of belief and although he neither took part in any revolt against the state nor encouraged others, his students in particular, to do so, he was still seen as a threat to the new government on account of his fame and influence. It was thus important for the authorities that he be kept out of sight and under tight control. Although he was exonerated from all claims of involvement with the Shaikh Said Revolt of February 1925, he was nevertheless ostracised from society and exiled under the most oppressive conditions.[62]

Nursi's first place of exile was Burdur, a small town in south-western Anatolia. Unhappy with his activities and popularity, the authorities moved Nursi again. In 1926 he was sent to a small city called Isparta, to the east of Burdur. But since Nursi continued to attract the attention of local people, he was exiled again, this time to a remote village called Barla, which nestles on a hillside on the north-west shore of Lake Eğirdir.[63]

Barla was not a village that could easily be reached; access by car was impossible and people could get there only after a long trek on foot or horseback. In 1928, the government granted an amnesty for all those who had been exiled for actively opposing the government; Nursi, however, was not included, and repressive measures to isolate him continued. He remained in Barla for another eight years and was allowed no books apart from the Quran. He was also permitted to receive the occasional visitor. But Nursi looked at this situation as a mercy from God for it was here that he was able to write most of the *Risale-i Nur*:[64]

> In addition, although 'the worldly' left all the influential and powerful leaders and shaykhs who could interfere in their world in the towns and cities and permitted them to meet with their relatives and everyone, they wrongfully isolated me and sent me to a village. With one or two exceptions they gave permission to none of my relatives and fellow-countrymen to visit me. My All-Compassionate Creator transformed that isolation into a vast mercy for me. It left my mind clear and was the means of my receiving the effulgence of the All-Wise Qur'an as it is, free of all malice and ill-will.
>
> Also, 'the worldly' considered the two commonplace letters I wrote in two years at the beginning of my exile to be excessive. And now even, they do not

> look favourably on one or two visitors coming to me purely for the sake of the hereafter once every ten or twenty days or once a month; and they have harassed me because of this. My All-Compassionate Sustainer and All-Wise Creator transformed that tyranny into mercy, for He transformed it into a desirable solitude and acceptable retreat for me during these three months, which will gain a spiritual life of ninety years. All thanks be to God for all conditions, my condition....[65]

In April 1935, Nursi and a number of his students from all over Turkey were taken to Eskişehir prison, accused of organizing a political movement and undermining and challenging the regime of the day. Nursi was imprisoned for eleven months; fifteen of his students were sentenced to six months and the rest were acquitted. The conditions in the prison were very harsh, particularly for Nursi, who was placed in solitary confinement. Nevertheless, in emulation of the prophet Joseph, who had managed to reform prison life during his own confinement, Nursi saw his own incarceration as the means whereby his own situation and the situation of his cellmates might be transformed into something positive. Eventually, his prison stay was referred to as the 'school of Joseph' (*medrese-ye Yusufiye*), and it was here that he was able to complete The Flashes and write another five treatises that formed part of the fourth part of the *Risale*, known as *Şualar* (The Rays).[66] In 1936, Nursi was released from prison as there was no evidence of his having been politically involved in the state's affairs. He was nevertheless seen as a threat on account of his continuing popularity and at the age of fifty-nine he was exiled to Kastamonu in central-northern Anatolia. He was to spend the next seven years there, during which time he completed *Şualar* and wrote a new treatise called *Âyet'ŭl Kŭbra* (The Supreme Sign).[67]

Nursi claims that he wrote *Âyet'ŭl Kŭbra* for himself.[68] In it he describes himself as a traveller observing the universe in order to become acquainted with its Owner and to emulate the saints by moving gradually from the stage of 'imitative belief' (*taqlīdī īmān*) to the stage of *'ayn al-yaqīn* (vision of certainty) or even *haqq al-yaqīn* or 'absolute certainty'.[69] In effect this means moving away from a materialistic vision of the world to one in which everything is connected to the Wise and All Knowing Creator. Here again Nursi strives to prove that belief in the Creator is the only cure for the illnesses of individuals and society at large.[70] Some of these writings are discussed in greater detail in Chapter Six.

In 1943 Nursi was arrested again, charged this time with creating a new Sufi order. This accusation was linked to a section in *Şualar* about Prophetic Traditions which discuss the signs of the end of time.[71] Once again Nursi transformed prison life into a 'school of Joseph' and, with great difficulty since there was no paper available, wrote the last main section of the *Rīsale* on the *Fruits of Belief*.[72] With Nursi having once again made prison life bearable for both the inmates and, consequently, for the prison guards and officials, the guards turned a blind eye to the transcription and distribution of the writings in the prison:

> My friends who are studying together with me in this School of Joseph! Since the reality is this and the Rīsale-ī Nur proves it so clearly and decisively, like sunlight, that for twenty years it has broken the obstinacy of the obdurate and brought them to believe; we should therefore follow the way of belief and right conduct, which is easy and safe and beneficial for both our own worlds, and our futures, and our lives in the hereafter, and our country and nation; and spend our free time reciting the suras of the Qur'an that we know instead of indulging in distressing fancies, and learn the meaning from friends who teach them; and make up for the prayers we have failed to perform in the past, when we should have done; and taking advantage of one another's good qualities, transform this prison into a blessed garden raising the seedlings of good character. With good deeds like these, we should do our best to make the prison governor and those concerned not torturers like the Angels of Hell standing over criminals and murderers, but righteous masters and kindly guards charged with the duties of raising people for Paradise in the School of Joseph and supervising their training and education.[73]

Once again Nursi and his students were acquitted by the court as he was able to show clearly that his writings were religious in nature and not political at all. Nevertheless, he continued to be seen as a threat by the authorities and was harassed constantly, spending much of the rest of his life under surveillance or house arrest.

In 1944, Nursi was exiled to Emirdağ, where he continued to write. It was here that the *Risale-i Nur* came under close scrutiny by the authorities. Unable to fathom exactly what Nursi was trying to say in his work, the Committee from the First Ankara Criminal Court claimed that he was suffering from hallucinations.[74] This was not the first time Nursi had been accused of mental illness: the Old Said had once had to prove his sanity to a hospital doctor.[75] But unfortunately for Nursi and fifty-four of his students, the court in Afyon did not agree with the Denizli court's decision regarding their release, and in 1948, Nursi and his students were once again imprisoned, this time under much harsher conditions, with Nursi again kept in solitary confinement. Nursi was now over seventy years of age and in addition to the harsh conditions he had to endure for nearly a year while in custody, he also had to put up with several attempts on his life. During his periods of exile and imprisonment, Nursi was allegedly poisoned seventeen times.[76] However, although Nursi grieved initially over the terrible conditions he experienced, and while events such as the death of his nephew and the destruction of his home town added to that grief,[77] he states that through the guidance of the Quran he was able to attribute his sorrow to his own heedlessness and see beyond the apparent:

> The heedlessness arising from my intense grief showed me the world to be terrifying, empty, desolate, and about to collapse over my head. My spirit sought a point of support in the face of innumerable hostile calamities. Its endless desires which stretch to eternity were seeking out something to satisfy them. While awaiting consolation in the face of the sorrow and grief arising from those endless separations and deaths, that endless devastation, suddenly the reality was manifested of the All-Wise Qur'an's verses:
>
> *Whatever is in the heavens and on earth - let it declare the praises and glory of God; for He is Exalted in Might, the Wise. To Him belongs the dominion of the heavens and the earth: it is He Who gives life and death; and He has power over all things.*

It saved me from that pitiful, terrible, sad, separation-stained imagining, and opened my eyes. I saw that the fruits at the tops of the fruit-trees were looking at me as though smiling. "Note us as well," they were saying. "Do not only look at the ruins." The verses' reality brought the following thought to mind:

> Why does an artificial letter written in the form of a town by the hand of man, who is a guest on the page of Van's plain, being wiped out by a calamitous torrent called the Russian invasion sadden you to this extent? Consider the Pre-Eternal Inscriber, everything's True Owner and Sustainer, for His missives on this page of Van continue to be written in glittering fashion, in the way you used to see. Your weeping over those desolate ruins arises from the error of forgetting their True Owner, not thinking that men are guests, and imagining them to be owner.
>
> A door to reality opened up from that error, from that searing sight, and my soul was prepared to accept the reality completely. Like iron is plunged in the fire so that it softens and may be profited from, that grievous sight and terrible state were fire which softened my soul. Through the reality of the above verses, the Qur'an of Miraculous Exposition showed it the effulgence of the truths of belief, causing it to accept it.[78]

Throughout his life, Nursi was either imprisoned under very harsh conditions or exiled to small and scarcely accessible villages. Initially, Nursi suffered greatly from the harsh conditions that he experienced. He admits to five kinds of exile which impacted on him most tellingly: the realisation that he was ageing; the sense of loneliness he felt on account of attachment to the things he loved; being alone on the mountains at night; the alternation of the seasons, which always reminded him of separation from his homeland and his family; and, of course, his own spiritual exile.[79] Despite all of these trials – or what he refers to as 'heedlessness' on his part[80] – Nursi began to see that, ultimately, his situation was decreed by God and that it was only through his own experiences and the attempt to understand them through the guidance of the Quran that he was inspired to write the *Risale-i Nur*.

As Abu-Rabi opines:

> Nursi reached the peak of his creativity in times of great sadness. This is why his most dynamic and moving writing seems to have been accomplished as he withstood great distress.[81]

The 'Third Said' and the last years of his life

It was during the 1950s, when the Democratic Party was in the ascendant, that Nursi underwent another transformation, moving from the second stage of his life when he was totally disengaged from politics to a stage that would be referred to later as the period of the 'Third Said'. During the last ten years of his life he saw fit to become more involved in the social and political life of Turkey. This change in approach came about because he considered the policies of the Democratic Party to be an improvement on those of the Republicans. The Democrats might have been secular in outlook, but they were opposed to communism and were more supportive of the freedom of religious activity. Nursi offered the government his services as a consultant on guidance religious matters as it was important, he believed, that politics should serve religion and not the other way round. He did not, however, engage actively in politics himself, and also cautioned his students against such involvement. Nursi's method of fighting unbelief remained the same, with emphasis on a spiritual struggle or 'jihad of the word', with the goal of safeguarding belief in accordance with the criteria of the Quran.[82]

Nursi was now eighty years old and wished to spend the last few years of his life in Urfa, in south-eastern Turkey. And so, in 1960 he asked a few of his closest students to take him there. People gathered in crowds to welcome him. Yet despite his age, Nursi was still considered to be a threat and the authorities, concerned by the attention he was receiving, issued orders that he be moved to Isparta. Too ill to be moved, in the early hours of Wednesday, 23rd March 1960, Nursi passed away in his sleep. Thousands of people came to Urfa for the funeral, but even in death Nursi was not left to rest. On 27th May 1960 a military coup took place and many Democratic Party officials were sent to prison. Subsequently the new government had Nursi's corpse disinterred and taken to an undisclosed location.[83]

It was always Nursi's wish that he should not become the focus of attention, and that his followers should use the *Risale-i Nur* and not him as a guide to Quran, in order to understand the meaning and purpose of their creation.[84] The fact that he is buried in an unknown place is an indication, perhaps, that his wish was granted.

Conclusion

In one sense it can be understand that Nursi's whole life was one of continuous exile and alienation from the world. Although he had much respect for his family, he did not follow the same Sufi order as they did, and although he owes much to his schools for his religious education, he was not totally content with their pedagogical approach. He felt that too much emphasis was put on the externals of religion and very little emphasis on the inner meanings of the Quran. He also disagreed with the dualistic approach towards science and religion.

Not only was Nursi dissatisfied with the religious schools that regarded the 'natural sciences' with suspicion, but also he felt alienated from many of the young intellectuals who either associated Islam purely with its 'externals' or attributed the decline of the Ottoman Empire and its failures – Abdul Hamid's despotic reign in particular – with the 'backwardness' of Islam. Nursi felt that ignorance and prejudice were the cause of these two extreme views, hence the need for educational reform.

The emphasis of the 'Old Said' on science and philosophy at this particular point in time – the beginning of the twentieth century – came in response to the onslaught of secular western ideas that were finding a foothold in Ottoman society and impacting on the minds of the elite and the young alike. For Nursi it was important to counter these new materialistic and secular ideologies that were emerging and which, with their supposedly definitive scientific proofs, were being used to deride the idea of belief in God. Nursi felt that at this time, the unfounded claims of science had to be answered, and refuted, with the language of science itself.

Nursi also found himself out of kilter with both the Ottoman Empire in general and the initiatives of the Young Turks in particular. His initial support for the Ottoman Empire was contingent upon its continued support for the *sharī'a* as well as western technology. Thus, while in essence he supported the Empire, he believed that reform was necessary. Being against the despotic regime of Abdulhamid, Nursi sided with the Young Turks, who favoured constitutionalism – something which he thought would be inclusive of all approaches, enabling a refreshing exchange of ideas. However, Nursi's involvement in the constitutional movement was brief. His engagement was due not to political aspiration or nationalist zeal but, rather, to his belief that a democratic system would engender more tolerance and understanding between different factions and, as a result, enable changes to be brought about in the school curricula, where all educational disciplines could be offered.

After the Turkish victory in the War of Independence, Nursi began to notice a distinct lack of enthusiasm for Islamic principles on the part of the leaders of the new regime. He believed that this lack of enthusiasm was in a way a silent display of consent to the arrival of Ataturk's secularization and westernization programmes. For a brief period, Nursi was in spiritual turmoil; then, he says, the Quran came to his rescue and facilitated the transformation of the 'Old Said' to the 'New Said', bringing with it the understanding that he should withdraw from political life. His new mission was to wage a 'jihad of the word' – an internal jihad by way of the exposition of Quranic truths rather than any kind of struggle with weapons.

However, despite the fact that Nursi was no longer involved in politics in any way, he was still seen as a threat throughout his life; his ideas concerning belief simply did not fit in with the new secular materialist current. He was therefore accused of suffering from mental illness on at least two occasions in an attempt, through hospitalization, to keep him out of the way and thus deprive him of an audience. When attempts to prove his insanity failed, other strategies were pursued in order to silence him.

Nursi believed that the *Risale* served as a means of guidance not only for him but also for his fellow prisoners; he believed that it was the perfect antidote for the sicknesses of today's 'civilized' societies, which imposed secularism within all their institutions.

Inspired by the Quran, Nursi was able to write his *magnum opus*, the *Risale-i Nur*, which he claimed would address the main ailment of modern times, namely the need for belief, and allow for spiritual development through the understanding of the 'self' vis-à-vis the creation. He believed that this was something which all individuals and all societies needed, even though they were not aware of this need. Despite the constant persecution that Nursi suffered at the hands of the authorities, he tried to avoid all disputes and confrontations that might cause disunity, and he continued to take a positive stance at all times in order to promote belief. Nursi promotes the *Risale-i Nur* as the safest and the most direct and accessible way to belief, enabling individuals at all levels, as it enabled him, to read 'the book of creation' in the correct way.

6

The Concept of Sadness (*ḥuzn*) in Nursi's Works

Introduction

From his brief biography in the previous chapter, we have seen that *ḥuzn* was something of which Said Nursi was experientially well aware, living as he did in what were often the most soul-destroying of personal circumstances. But how did Nursi approach *ḥuzn* conceptually, and in what sense, if any, is his approach unique? To what extent, if at all, does the Nursian take on *ḥuzn* contribute to a clearer understanding of the concept? It is to these questions that we now turn. To this end, Nursi's use of the term will be analysed in much the same way that the Quranic usage of the term was analysed earlier in the book. We will then be in a position to compare and contrast his understanding of the term with both the Quranic and Muslim philosophical understandings.

In his semantic analysis of certain Quranic terms, Izutsu has shown that all semantic fields in the Quran are connected directly to the concept of *Allah*.[1] The exegetes in this study also concur with Izutsu.[2] Therefore since ontologically *Allah* is the central focus of all the concepts in the Quran including *ḥuzn*, this chapter will also examine Nursi's understanding of Divine Unity. Alternative views of 'sadness' and 'happiness' such as those of certain Christian scholars and Sufi mystics will also be discussed briefly, in order to obtain a broader understanding of the concept. Furthermore, the subject of free-will will be discussed in relation to the issues of Divine determining (*qadar*) and evil (*sharr*) in order to understand how Nursi reconciles human sovereignty with the absolute sovereignty of the Divine.

Before turning to Nursi, however, it may help if we remind ourselves of our findings so far. The main conclusion of the typological analysis was that in order not to have *ḥuzn* in the negative sense there should be no deviation from belief in one God.[3] This belief in one God would as a corollary necessitate belief in resurrection and the hereafter; submission with total sincerity in carrying out righteous deeds; and regular prayers and giving charity. The terms 'God's devotees' and 'the friends of God' are used in the Quran to denote those who have reached a state of *taqwā* (trust and submission) by following the criterion that is the Quran rather than their *nafs* (ego). The thematic categorization of *ḥuzn* in the typology also showed the positive aspect of this concept as a means for the Divine test and a means of reassurance and guidance for believers, often through the experience of a calamity such as loss of goods or loved ones (*balā*). It also showed that *ḥuzn* has the potential to be a means of guidance or misguidance depending on whether one chooses to follow the path of the Quran or to remain heedless through the covering (*kufr*) of the truth.[4]

The Izutsian analysis served as an important tool for identifying other members of the semantic category of *ḥuzn*. According to the findings, *ḥuzn* had a strong semantic relation with the word 'belief' and its opposite, 'unbelief'. The semantic field of these two terms provided other useful categories related to *ḥuzn* such as the connection of belief to 'belief in one God', the 'hereafter', 'guidance', 'thankfulness', 'trust', 'submission' and 'happiness'; as opposed to 'unbelief', which was connected to the concepts of 'associationism' (*shirk*), 'denial of the hereafter', 'misguidance', 'ungratefulness' and 'misery'.[5]

Furthermore, the Izutsian analysis of *ḥuzn* revealed the fact that there are many words in the Quran with similar meanings to *ḥuzn*, but that when these concepts were examined in accordance with the Quranic *Weltanschauung*, the different nuances of these concepts became apparent. It became clear that *ḥuzn* has a strong connection with loss, such as the loss of belongings or loved ones. It also became clear that if the Quran is not used as the criterion (*furqān*) that one follows in life, then one will have sadness in the negative sense, as one's imbalance and alienation from the truth – and by extension the whole universe – will lead to corruption (*fisq*), oppression (*ẓulm*) and ungratefulness (*kufr*). The analysis also revealed the positive side of *ḥuzn* as a feeling given by God, without which there could be no concept of happiness, and showed also how belief in One God, i.e. submission to Divine decree and determining (*qadar*) and the non-attribution of effects to causes through having total trust in God (*taqwā*) can be a means of comfort, reassurance and guidance.[6]

Most of the exegetes studied in Chapter Three also interpret the concept of *ḥuzn* in terms of loss of possessions, including loved ones. They concur that *ḥuzn* can be obviated if one follows God's guidance through the criterion of revelation. According to the exegetes, the key to guidance is acceptance of God's Mastership (*rubūbiyya*) and one's own servitude – in other words, the giving up of all ownership and the concomitant attribution of all things to their rightful Owner. They agree that it is attachment that is the cause of sadness and that detachment from ephemeral things is the only way to obviate *ḥuzn*. They also conclude, as does the Izutsian analysis, that accepting God's Mastership comes through belief followed by submission, that is, performing prayers, carrying out righteous deeds and giving charity in total sincerity and trust (*taqwā*), with *taqwā* implying the performance of those acts purely for the sake of God and not for the sake of the self (*nafs*).[7]

All the Muslim thinkers studied in Chapter Four, with the exception of al-Rāzī, also define *ḥuzn* in a manner similar to al-Kindī as "psychological pain occurring due to the loss of an object of love or the missing of things desired".[8] Al-Rāzī does not appear to include possessions in the definition and says that sadness is caused solely by the loss of loved ones.[9]

The solution offered by all of the Muslim thinkers for the obviation of *ḥuzn* is the use of reason in order to save the soul from excessive indulgence. Consequently, most of them focus on the importance of changing thought processes in order to facilitate behaviour modification. Their reasoning begins with the understanding that all possessions – including loved ones – are given to us on loan to look after, and must be given back to their rightful Owner whenever He asks for them.[10]

All of the Muslim thinkers studied are of the opinion that *ḥuzn* occurs as a result of wrongly expecting permanence from transient things. Miskawayh states that 'dissolution' and 'annihilation' are part and parcel of the nature of transient beings; al-Kindī concurs, adding that 'sorrow is by convention and not by nature', and so to expect something to behave in a manner which is not in conformity with its nature is to adopt the attitude of those 'devoid of reason'. It appears that most of the Muslim thinkers are in agreement that grief is not God-given but is self-induced, and that it should be repelled through the use of reason.[11] As we shall now see, however, Nursi argues that there is a limitation to human reasoning, the point being that since the Quran is *the* criterion for truth, human reasoning has to be subservient to it.[12]

Nursi on the limitations of 'human reasoning'

Human beings are defined as rational animals who are able to use their powers of judgment, discrimination and clarification in order to understand universal truths.[13] In the chapter on the Izutsian analysis, we saw that words are symbols that are charged with meaning and which therefore cannot be understood in isolation; since they represent a whole 'world-view', it is important to go beyond the dictionary definition in order to understand what they signify.[14] And in the Quranic analysis it was shown that while God is deemed to be the source of knowledge and guidance, it is the soul which interprets that knowledge.[15] Therefore, as Al-Attas puts it, knowledge is merely "the arrival of meaning in the soul".[16] This is exemplified by the verse in the Quran in which God commands Muhammad, who is illiterate, to "Read!", whereupon he asks, "How should I read?" God then instructs him to "read, read in the name of your Lord..."[17] It is clear the reading referred to here is related not to the prophet's functional illiteracy but to the reality that anyone has the potential to read and understand the 'book of creation' if it is seen as a sign or symbol pointing to something other than itself. However, the doctrine of atheistic naturalism erected a barrier that prevented anyone from reading and interpreting the world transcendently. Nursi saw the encroachment of materialism as a huge threat, especially since it was hidden under the deceptive guise of 'advancement' and 'progress'. This was a time when the Ottoman Empire had come to an end and Ataturk's new Republican Turkey was encouraging its youth to leave the 'outdated' religion behind and emulate instead the 'civilised' countries of the West by following the 'modern' and 'scientific' doctrines of materialistic naturalism.[18] The secular scientific view regarded the universe in purely physical and materialistic terms, with all existent beings seen as referring only to themselves. Viewed in this light, devoid of real meaning and without any connection to a transcendent source, the manipulation of material beings for the sake of self-interest could be justified quite easily. Nursi used the term 'self-referential' (*ismī*) to describe the attitude which saw material beings as having meaning only in and of themselves, while the attitude which understood every created being as pointing to other than itself – with 'other' meaning God – he described as 'Other-indicative'. He objected to the fallacious claim that this atheistic stance followed 'scientific knowledge' when in fact its view of existence went only as far as the shell, missing out on the kernel or the true source of knowledge.[19]

Like the Quran[20] and the Muslim thinkers studied here,[21] Nursi asserts that one must investigate (*taḥqīq*) truth claims rationally rather than accept them blindly through imitation (*taqlīd*). Emulating the approach of the Quran, Nursi either poses rhetorical questions or appeals to his readers' ability to reason, urging them thereby to see beyond the apparent face of existence:

> Is it possible that another hand could share in this amazing order and all-comprehensive organisation based on an absolute measure and balance? Who other than the Unique One of Unity, the Absolutely All-Wise and All-Powerful One, could share in this art, this regulation and government, and this raising and sustaining?[22]

Although Nursi does not deny the possibility of reaching revealed knowledge through interaction with nature, it must be said that he agrees to an extent with Ghazālī in his critique of Muslim philosophers, concluding that too much importance is given to the faculty of human reason, and that in actual fact, human beings have freedom of choice and thus cannot be compelled by reason anyway.[23]

For Nursi, true happiness cannot be obtained if human reason is not subservient to Divine revelation, for in order to understand important concepts pertaining to the unseen (*malakūt*), such as angels and the hereafter, revelation is needed. However, he stresses that the corporeal or visible realm (*mulk*) is also necessary since it serves as a mirror or mirrors for God's manifestation; without it, the connection between the two would be impossible.[24]

Before discussing Divine Unity, which sits at the heart of all Quranic concepts, including *ḥuzn*, the Nursian definition of *ḥuzn* is examined.

The Nursian concept of sadness

The definition of *ḥuzn* according to Said Nursi

According to Nursi there are two kinds of *ḥuzn*. He describes the first kind in terms of total disconnection:

> [It is] a dark sorrow arising from the lack of friends, that is, having no friends or owner, which is the sorrow produced by the literature of civilization, which is stained by misguidance, enamoured of nature, tainted by heedlessness....

He describes the second kind of *ḥuzn* in more positive terms:

> This arises from the separation of friends, that is, the friends exist, but their absence causes a yearning sorrow. This is the guidance-giving, light-scattering sorrow which the Qur'an produces.[25]

Ḥuzn due to the 'literature of civilization'

Nursi's comparison of what he calls the 'literature of civilization' with the Quran throws further light on the differences between the two kinds of *ḥuzn*. In the 'literature of civilization', *ḥuzn*, he asserts, is characterised usually as "the dark grief and hopeless wailing of a motherless orphan and the low uproarious song of a drunkard", while the Quranic approach is one which sees *ḥuzn* as "the yearning, hopeful sorrow of an elevated lover, arising from a temporary separation and patriotic songs urging victory or war and high self-sacrifice." Nursi uses the term 'civilisation' pejoratively here, referring to moral decadence and the decline of religion, and not to scientific progress. In other words, Nursi stresses the fact that literature divorced from revelation is an art form that will ultimately lead to misguidance and grief. According to Nursi, therefore, the literature of Europe, despite its apparent glamour, if disconnected from revelation can lead only to the corruption of society. By contrast the literature of the Quran does not deceive but, rather, helps to unveil reality. The 'literature of civilization' looks at the universe through the prism of nature, while the Quran looks at creation from the point of view of 'Divine Art'.[26] Nursi then goes on to explain that both these paths produce sorrow, but the sorrow connected to the 'literature of Europe', that is, a world-view disconnected from belief, is a worldly sorrow, unlike the 'sorrow of love' produced by revelation:

> The literature born of Europe excites a pathetic sorrow [*bir ḥüznü*] arising from the lack of friends, from being ownerless; not an elevated sorrow [*ulvī ḥüzün*].
>
> For it is a woebegone sadness [*hüzn-ü gamdar*] inspired by deaf Nature and blind force. It shows the world as desolate, not in any other way.
>
> It depicts it in this way, holds the sorrowing [*maḥzūn*] man there, places him ownerless among strangers, leaving him without hope.
>
> Due to this feeling of consternation it has given him, he gradually sinks into misguidance; it opens up the way to atheism, from whence it is difficult to return. Perhaps he never will return.
>
> Qur'anic literature produces a sorrow [*bīr ḥüznü*], but it is the sorrow of love [*âşıkane ḥüzündür*], not of orphans. It arises from separation from friends, not from the lack of them. Its view of the universe, in place of blind Nature, is as conscious, merciful Divine art; it does not speak of Nature.
>
> Instead of blind force, it describes wise and purposeful Divine power. The universe, therefore, does not take on the form of a desolate wasteland.[27]

Nursi further asserts that the aspect of the 'Quranic *ḥuzn*' which he calls 'a yearning sorrow' (*ḥüzn-ū müştakane*) brings about feelings that are elevated in comparison to the kind of sorrow that engenders 'dejected mournfulness' (*gamlı bir ḥüznü*), and enables, through its connection to the Creator of the universe, a positive view of love rather than distress. Nursi adds that it is because of this that the melancholic (*maḥzün*) person feels once again connected to society.[28] As discussed above, Nursi contrasts this with the 'literature of Europe', which promotes 'worldly life' as glamorous and eternal, and he states that in fact this claim is a lie, a deception and a cause of sadness on account of the impermanence and transience which lie at its heart.[29]

> ...a mendacious tongue in mankind's mouth, attached a lustful eye to its face, dressed the world in a scarlet petticoat, and does not recognize sheer beauty.[30]

By way of comparison, Nursi states that the 'literature of the Quran' does not stir up desire but, rather:

> It imparts a sense of love of the truth, a passion for sheer loveliness, an appreciation and taste for beauty, a desire for reality. And it does not deceive. It does not look at the universe from the point of view of Nature; it speaks of it from the point of view of Divine art, with the colouring of the Most Merciful. It does not confuse the mind. It instils the light of knowledge of the Maker. It points out His signs in all things.[31]

An example of positive *ḥuzn* can be seen in Nursi's description of the Prophet Muhammad's prayer in the quote below. He explains that just as our acknowledgment of the need for food means that eating and drinking are never a chore, our acknowledgment of the need for prayer should have the same effect, for prayer is a means of sustenance for the heart, the spirit and the subtle faculties of the soul. Describing the prayer of the Prophet, he says:

> And he supplicates with such want, so sorrowfully [*ḥazinane*], in such a loving, yearning, and beseeching fashion that he brings the whole cosmos to tears, leading them to join in his prayer.[32]

Nursi also appears to be pointing to the positive understanding of *ḥuzn* when he describes the crying of the cats and the songs of the nightingales – all creatures, in fact – as they recite God's Names. Like the supplications of Muhammad, their mournful (*ḥazīn*, the adjective derived from *ḥuzn*) sounds are, he says, part of their inherent recognition of their Creator. He explains that their 'sorrowful song' is merely their way of giving thanks to God:

> However, the nightingale's small wage is the delight he experiences from gazing on the smiling, beautiful roses, and the pleasure he receives from conversing with them and pouring out his woes. That is to say, his sorrowful [*ḥazin*] song is not a complaint arising from animal grief, it is thanks [*shukr*] in return for the gifts of the Most Merciful. Compare the bee, the spider, the ant, creeping insects…[33]

According to Nursi, the obviation of *ḥuzn* is possible only by understanding the nature of created beings, which, by virtue of their impotence and dependence, point to the One who is neither impotent nor transient. Since it is Nursi's belief that the oneness of the One is the key to belief – and, by extension in this particular context, the key to resolving the issue of *ḥuzn*, it is to his understanding of Divine Unity (*tawḥīd*) that we now turn.

Nursi on Divine Unity (*tawḥīd*)

When the Quran talks about Divine Unity, it talks about a God Who is 'absolute' (*muṭlaq*), meaning that the Creator is self-subsistent, all-encompassing and neither divisible nor temporal. He is also transcendent and immanent, meaning that although God's essence can never be known, He can be understood to an extent through the manifestation of His Names in creation. Only human beings, by dint of their being created in *imago Dei*, have the potential to attain the most comprehensive knowledge of Him and thus manifest His Names at the very highest level, as vicegerents.[34]

Nursi's emphasis in the *Risale* is that spiritual progress is not about becoming 'more God-like'; rather, it is more about realising that all of the Names and Attributes reflected in creation belong not to themselves but to the Divine: they are signs pointing to Divine Unity, and therefore spiritual progress is more about stripping off or disowning these attributes, and 'returning' them to their rightful Owner, than it is about emulating or becoming more like Him.[35]

For Nursi the aim of writing the *Risale-i Nur* was that it should serve as mirror or a prism for the light of the Quran; this is why he refers frequently to the verses of the Quran for inspiration and explanation. Nursi considered the Quran itself as the most beneficial and much needed 'salve' for the darkness and wounds of the age.[36] Of particular concern to Nursi was not the kind of misguidance which came from a genuine lack of knowledge, but the kind of misguidance that was fomented and promoted by spiritual miscreants who used the tools of knowledge with the specific intention to spread mischief and misunderstanding:

> You know that if misguidance arises from ignorance, it is easy to dispel. Whereas if it proceeds from science and learning, it is difficult to eliminate. In former times, the latter were one in a thousand, and of these only one in a thousand could come to the way through guidance. For such people fancy themselves. And they do not know, but they suppose that they do know. I think that Almighty God has bestowed the Words at this time, which are flashes of the Qur'an's miraculousness, as an antidote to this atheistic misguidance.[37]

Although the *Risale-I Nur* is not a systematic exegesis of the Quran in the classical sense, it is nevertheless considered to be a commentary on the Quran that is accessible to today's audience, whatever their background and intellectual level. The *Risale* covers all the major themes in the Quran, focussing in particular on the concept of *tawḥīd*.

Mirroring the Quran, *tawḥīd* is the kernel of Nursi's arguments and reasoning. He indicates clearly that it is the key to happiness and the only means whereby 'negative' sadness may be obviated.[38] For Nursi, therefore the only way that human beings can attain the highest level of perfection as God's vicegerents on earth, and thus become the happiest and most valuable of all animate beings, is through the affirmation of *tawḥīd*. He stresses that it is only through this affirmation that existence becomes meaningful; without this connection the universe would resemble 'a house of sorrows', 'a ruin' and 'a place of utter confusion'.[39]

> Indeed, all man's perfections and his lofty aims are tied to the affirmation of Divine Unity and find existence through its meaning. For if there was no unity, man would be the most unhappy of creatures, the lowest of beings, the most wretched [*ḥüzünlüsü*] of the animals, the most suffering [*azāblisi*] and sorrowful [*gamlisi*] of intelligent beings.[40]

According to Nursi, therefore, true belief in one God means not only recognizing God's Unity, but also submitting through trusting in, and not ascribing 'partners' to, Him.

Belief and unbelief

As discussed previously, the 'line of philosophy' or so-called 'civilization', which sees everything as self-referential (*ma'nā-i ismī*), [41] obscures the connection to the transcendent, thus reducing the value of beings merely to the sum of their parts; creation seen as Other-indicative (*ma'nā-i ḥarfī*) on the other hand, that is, as signs pointing to God, or, as Nursi describes it, as "officials charged with duties and bearing meanings…" brings the whole cosmos to life, demonstrating a sense of purpose in existence.[42]

The Izutsian analysis and the works of exegesis analysed earlier have shown that belief comes down to having trust (*tawakkul*) in God, which is something that can come about only if the knowledge gained is actualised through submission.[43] Consequently, acknowledging the truth requires not only the faculty of reason but also the heart – the intuitive faculty that has to be open always to guidance. The Nursian schema also focuses on the interdependence of belief and submission, with the emphasis that belief should be through investigation (*taḥqīq*) and followed by submission. Nursi also stresses that belief is not static but subject to change; no-one can claim that he or she has reached belief and is no longer susceptible to wrong-doing.[44]

According to Nursi, then, the only way in which *ḥuzn* can be obviated is through belief. Nursi uses the Quranic concept pair of light and darkness in order to demonstrate the difference between belief and unbelief. Worldly enjoyment is very brief, he says, and is like "poisonous honey"; the only route to true, pain-free pleasure is through belief in God.[45] Moreover, because unbelief views the past and future as a dark void, it can bring no real pleasure; the light of belief, on the other hand, illuminates both the past and the future, resulting in everlasting contentment.

> As for life, if it is without belief, or because of rebelliousness belief is ineffective, it will produce pains, sorrows [*ḥüzünler*] and grief [*kederler*] far exceeding the superficial, fleeting enjoyment it brings. Because, since, contrary to the animals, man possesses a mind and he thinks, he is connected to both the present time, and to the past and the future. He can obtain both pain and pleasure from them. Whereas, since the animals do not think, the sorrows [*ḥüzünler*] arising from the past and the fears and anxieties arising from the future, do not spoil their pleasure of the present. Especially if the pleasure is illicit; then it is like an altogether poisonous honey. That is to say, from the point of view of the pleasure of life, man falls to a level a hundred times lower than the animals. In fact, life for the people of misguidance and heedlessness, and indeed their existence, rather their world, is the day in which they find themselves. From the point of view of their misguidance, all the time and universes of the past are non-existent, are dead. So, their intellects, which connect them to the past and the future, produce darkness, blackness for them. Due to their lack of belief, the future is also non-existent. Furthermore, because they think, the eternal separations resulting from this non-existence continuously produce darkness for their lives. Whereas, if belief gives life to life, then through the light of belief both the past and the future are illuminated and find existence. Like present time, it produces elevated, spiritual pleasures and lights of existence for the spirit and heart – in respect of belief.[46]

And so according to Nursi, lack of belief brings a sense of powerlessness since the desire for happiness can never be fulfilled completely in an ephemeral world, and it is this expectation of permanence in a world of transience that results in profound feelings of alienation. When the world is seen through the eye of belief, however, this 'orphan-like' state disappears and the universe becomes alive and meaningful:

> The view of unbelief sees human beings, powerless as they are to secure their desires, as ownerless and without protector; it imagines them to be grieving [*ḥüzün*] and sorrowful [*keder*] like weeping orphans on account of their impotence. The view of belief on the other hand, sees them as living creatures; not as orphans but officials charged with duties; as servants glorifying and extolling God.[47]

In the Izutsian analysis, in order to obtain a deeper understanding of the Quranic usage of the word *ḥuzn*, its opposite – 'happiness' – was also discussed. We shall now discuss Nursi's definition of happiness, looking in particular at the post-Enlightenment period, when the discourse on happiness, focused hitherto on the possibility of salvation in the next world was now trained more on the right to pursue happiness while still in this world.

Nursi's definition of happiness

Before the Enlightenment, the dominant Protestant view was that being in a hopeless state of sadness is a sin, while happiness was considered "a sign of God's grace" to be "pursued into every crevice of the self." Although religious sanction was given for the pursuit of happiness, the insistence that sadness was a sin inevitably made the task of becoming happy a burden. By the end of the seventeenth century, with the advent of the Enlightenment, a number of less religiously inclined scholars began to argue that happiness was also intended for this world.[48] The Enlightenment emphasis on human agency and the pursuit of happiness in this world, as an end in itself, brought about a change in individuals' expectations. As noted by Porter, the question "How can I be saved" was now less relevant than "How can I be happy".[49] The quest for this-worldly happiness thus became a 'right' – a natural human condition for which all human beings were entitled to aim. Jean-Jacques Rousseau followed the Jacobin constitution that the goal of society should be 'common happiness'.[50] He made a distinction between pleasure and happiness, stating that the sensations and sentiments used purely for the satisfaction of human needs are pleasure and do not result necessarily in human happiness, whereas happiness is linked more to a 'psychological state' of balance between one's needs and one's powers.[51] Nevertheless, Rousseau connected happiness not to the next world but only to the here and now, refusing to believe that happiness was in any way connected to an understanding of the ultimate cause of creation. Although he would later admit that total happiness is unattainable, he believed, nevertheless, that the aim of society should be to work towards it, even if it meant having to change the world and human nature in the process. Rousseau's *The Social Contract* outlined how society should be organised in order to give the maximum opportunity for happiness to all individuals.[52] When Nursi criticises Western civilization or the literature of Europe, it is clear that it is this 'misguided philosophy' of the Enlightenment, which limits knowledge to the sensible world alone, that he finds corrupting. Nursi stresses that the expectation that the ephemeral will be able to satiate mankind's desire for eternal happiness is an illusory one: beings which are transient can never be in a position to satisfy anyone or anything, and thus such expectations will always end in pain. "All worldly happiness," he says, "is but a fleeting flash of lightning in relation to an eternal sun."[53]

Nursi's explanation is similar to that of al-Rāzī, who says that the idea of endless pleasure is an illusion since pleasure cannot exist without pain, and, is perceptible only after it has departed.[54] Nursi adds that the desire for eternal happiness is part of mankind's natural disposition and therefore possible, but that the quest for this has to go beyond the gratification of instinctive desires. He therefore defines happiness as being of two kinds: one kind which stimulates the self/ego; and the other kind which silences it:

> Joy (*neş'e*), too, is of two sorts. One stimulates the desires of the soul. This is the mark of civilization's literature in the fields of theatre, cinema, and the novel. While the other joy silences the soul, and is subtle and mannerly, innocently urging the spirit, heart, mind, and subtle faculties to attain to sublime matters, to their original home and eternal abode, and their companions of the hereafter; it is the joy the Qur'an of Miraculous Exposition produces. It fills man with eagerness for Paradise and eternal happiness (*Neşe*) and the vision of God's beauty.[55]

As discussed previously, the key to happiness according to Nursi is to love what is reflected in the mirror of creation rather than to look for eternal happiness in the mirror itself, which is transient, or, as Nursi describes it, an empty 'shell' to be thrown away after the truth within it has been uncovered.[56] His description of worldly enjoyment in his passage on civilization's literature is similar to al-Kindī's boat analogy,[57] with both of them emphasizing that those who look for happiness in the ephemeral world will be faced with inevitable sorrow. While al-Kindī, however, does not refer directly to the Quran as the source of happiness, Nursi's arguments are based on verses from the Quran, which he describes as a salve for every kind of spiritual disease.[58]

While al-Kindī equates happiness only with the world of the intellect, recommending total detachment from worldly life,[59] Avicenna does not deny that some happiness is attainable by all, including those within the 'sensual rank'.[60] Miskawayh takes the middle position, stating that apart from those who have reached the spiritual rank, happiness in this world is achievable by those at the level of the corporeal, but only if they aspire sincerely to the spiritual ranks.[61] Nursi approaches the interpretation of happiness somewhat differently. While he does not deny that everyone experiences happiness in this world, his emphasis is on the quality of happiness itself, stating that happiness associated with the worldly life gives only a very brief feeling of joy and, owing to its transient nature, can never satiate. It is thus something which causes much sorrow instead of happiness, while spiritual happiness is everlasting:

> O man who is addicted to enjoyment [*zevk*] and pleasure [*lezzet*]! I am seventy-five years old, and I know with utter certainty from thousands of experiences, proofs, and events that true enjoyment, pain-free pleasure, grief-free joy, and life's happiness are only to be found in belief and in the sphere of the truths of belief. While a single worldly pleasure yields numerous pains; as though dealing ten slaps for a single grape, it drives away all life's pleasure.[62]

Permanence versus transience

While Nursi's understanding with regard to the ephemerality of worldly existence and the importance of spiritual happiness is in line with our Quranic typology, the Izutsian analysis, the exegetes and the Muslim thinkers covered earlier, he diverges from the group with respect to the existential necessity for transitoriness and transient beings. The Muslim thinkers seem for the most part to view the existence of ephemeral objects negatively, making what appears to be a neat divide between the material and spiritual worlds and emphasising that in order to have a happier life one should get rid of as many worldly possessions as possible.[63] Nursi approaches the futility of attachment to transient beings in a different way. He stresses that transience is in fact a necessary undesirable, since without it one would not be able to see it for what it really is:

> If you want permanence in this transitory world, permanence comes from transitoriness. Find transience with regard to your evil-commanding soul so that you may be enduring.
>
> Divest yourself of bad morals, the basis of the worship of this world. Be transitory! Sacrifice your goods and property in the way of the True Beloved. See the ends of beings, which point to non-existence, for the way leading to permanence in this world starts from transitoriness.[64]

Nursi points out the contradictory state of human beings who are obsessed with externals, but who are never satisfied by them, and in much of his work he highlights the important role of created beings as signposts which need to be read in the correct way, that is, pointing not to themselves but to the One who is not ephemeral. In this way, Nursi shows how he believes the creation should be read, stressing that it is in fact through recognising the impotence and transitoriness of created beings that one may find a way to permanence. The existence of created beings as symbols of, and pointers to, the Other is thus absolutely essential.

> O my ignorant soul! Know that the world and its beings are certainly ephemeral, but you may find a way leading to permanence in each ephemeral thing, and may see two flashes, two mysteries, of the manifestations of the Undying Beloved's Beauty.
>
> Yes, it is within the bounty that the bestowal is to be seen and the favour of the Most Merciful perceived. If you pass from bounty to bestowal, you will find the Bestower. Also, each work of the Eternally Besought One makes known the All-Glorious Maker's Names like a missive. If you pass from the decoration

> to the meaning, you will find the One signified by way of His Names. Since you can find the kernel, the essence, of these ephemeral beings, obtain it. Then without pity you can throw away their meaningless shells and externals onto the flood of ephemerality.[65]

According to Nursi, therefore, the 'book of creation' – the macrocosm – has to be read, but it has to be read in the correct way, namely in accordance with the criteria found in the revealed words of the Creator. The whole of the *Risale-i Nur* can thus be seen as a Nursian tool for understanding the Quranic interpretation of creation.

Nursi points to what he believes is the wrong belief held by some that the saints abandoned the world. He explains the subtle difference between being 'in the world' and being 'of the world', opining that neither the companions nor the saints abandoned the world, nor did they, through heedlessness look only to the transitory face of creation in order to satisfy their base animal desires; rather, they looked beyond externals and "loved the face of the world which looks to the hereafter", seeing all creatures as the mirrors of the Divine Names.[66]

Nursi refers to the Quranic story of Abraham and the existential dilemma of searching for eternal love within an ephemeral realm, culminating in the words: "I love not those that set".[67] By examining the nature of created beings, Abraham realises that the creator of the universe cannot be subject to the same conditions as His creature and that therefore He must be outside of the realm of existence:

> And [mention, O Muhammad], when Abraham said to his father Azar, "Do you take idols as deities? Indeed, I see you and your people to be in manifest error."
>
> And thus did We show Abraham the realm of the heavens and the earth that he would be among the certain [in faith].
>
> So when the night covered him [with darkness], he saw a star. He said, "This is my lord." But when it set, he said, "I like not those that disappear."
>
> And when he saw the moon rising, he said, "This is my lord." But when it set, he said, "Unless my Lord guides me, I will surely be among the people gone astray."
>
> And when he saw the sun rising, he said, "This is my lord; this is greater." But when it set, he said, "O my people, indeed I am free from what you associate with Allah.
>
> Indeed, I have turned my face toward He who created the heavens and the earth, inclining toward truth, and I am not of those who associate others with Allah."[68]

Nursi elaborates on this verse, explaining the futility of being attached to ephemeral beings and claiming that anyone who wants to be saved from the despair of transience needs the assistance of this phrase. The Sufi influence on Nursi's work is clear. Quoting from Jāmī (1414-1492),[69] he gives poetic expression to the notion that all beings proclaim the oneness of God in their own tongues, emphasising the imperative that humans, as vicegerents of God, have to detach from the 'metaphorical beloved' in order to reach the 'undying beloved':

> Want only One (the rest are not worth wanting).
>
> Call One (the others will not come to your assistance).
>
> Seek One (the rest are not worth it).
>
> See One (the others are not seen all the time; they hide themselves behind the veil of ephemerality).
>
> Know One (knowledge other than that which assists knowledge of Him is without benefit).
>
> Say One (words not concerning Him may be considered meaningless).[70]

Nursi states that it is this attachment to 'metaphorical beloveds', that is, the hopeless and wretched condition of human beings who expect permanence from a transient world, which brings about pain and suffering. He explains that the heart, which is created for eternal love, cannot truly love ephemeral beings, and therefore in order to avoid regret, sorrow and grief, one should not attach oneself to things which are 'lost on setting':

> It made me weep, the verse I love not those that set, which was uttered by Abraham (PBWH), and which announces the universe's passing and death.
>
> The eyes of my heart wept at it, pouring out bitter tear-drops. The verse causes others to weep, and it is as though it weeps itself. The following lines are my tear-drops: they are a sort of commentary of some words present within the Divine Word of God's Wise One, the Prophet Muhammad.
>
> A beloved who is hidden through setting is not beautiful, for those doomed to decline cannot be truly beautiful. They may not love with the heart, which is created for eternal love and is the mirror of the Eternally Besought One, and should not be loved with it.

As for a desired one who is doomed to be lost on setting, such a one is worthy of neither the heart's attachment nor the mind's preoccupation. He may not be the object of desires. He is not worthy of being regretted with the sorrow and grief that follows. So why should the heart worship such a one and be bound to him?[71]

Denial of death: sorrow due to misguidance, heedlessness and ungratefulness

Ernest Becker (1924-1974) in *The Denial of Death* explains that in a physical world where everything perishes, fear of death fuels the human tendency to attempt to transcend the dilemma of immortality by inventing some kind of 'immortality project' or *causa sui*. The desire for immortality pushes people to be part of something which symbolizes it. This may manifest as, *inter alia*, the wish for sons,[72] who will continue to carry their title, or the building of monuments and other structures, the size and grandeur of which are symptomatic of the desire for eternity. According to Becker, the failure to bring such projects to fruition leads either to severe depression or to the need for persistent self-medication:

Modern man is drinking and drugging himself out of awareness, or he spends his time shopping, which is the same thing. As awareness calls for types of heroic dedication that his culture no longer provides for him, society contrives to help him forget.[73]

For Becker, these so-called immortality projects are nothing but products of collective mendacity, emblemising the self-deception and delusion in which society enmeshes itself. But while Becker identifies the disease, he stops short of prescribing a clear solution for this most complex of ontological dilemmas.[74]

Nursi describes the ephemerality of the world and mankind's need for eternity in a way similar to that of Becker, with the main difference being that Nursi suggests a solution. The solution he offers is belief, which he sees as stemming from an understanding of the true nature of beings and an awareness of the importance of reading the creation as a collection of signs pointing not to themselves but to the Other. Addressing the caring professionals, he states that the only solution to overcome sadness lies in belief:

By analogy, the country is also a household, and the fatherland, the home of the national family. If belief in the hereafter rules in these broad homes, true respect, earnest compassion, disinterested love, mutual assistance, honest service

> and social relations, un-hypocritical charity, virtue, modest greatness, and excellence will all start to develop.
>
> It says to the children: "Give up messing around; there is Paradise to be won!", and teaches them self-control through instruction in the Qur'an.
>
> It says to the youth: "There is Hell-fire; give up your drunkenness!", and brings them to their senses.
>
> It says to the oppressor: "There is severe torment; you will receive a blow!", and makes them bow to justice.
>
> It says to the elderly: "Awaiting you is everlasting happiness in the hereafter far greater than all the happiness you have lost here, and immortal youth; try to win them!" It turns their tears into laughter.
>
> It shows its favourable effects in every group, particular and universal, and illuminates them. The sociologists and moralists, who are concerned with the social life of mankind, should take special note. If the rest of the thousands of benefits and advantages of belief in the hereafter are compared with the five or six we have alluded to, it will be understood that it is only belief that is the means of happiness in this world and the next, and in the lives of both.[75]

Nursi states that man views creation negatively whenever he is disconnected from the Creator, adding that he himself experienced such disconnection on various occasions as a result of heedlessness, until the light of belief rescued him:

> Then I saw within the animal world another grievous [*ḥazīn*] world which was swathed in darkness and would make anyone feel pity and in which young were struggling in their need and powerlessness. I was sorry I had looked through the eyes of the people of misguidance. Suddenly, belief gave me other spectacles and I saw the Name of All-Compassionate rise in the sign of clemency; it transformed and lit up that pitiful world in joyous and beautiful fashion, changing my tears of complaint and sorrow [*ḥüzün*] into tears of joy and thanks.[76]

The above quotation indicates that like the Izutsian, the Quranic, the exegetical and the Muslim intellectual analyses,[77] Nursi's findings acknowledge the fact that *ḥuzn* can be a means of guidance. Seen through the eyes of misguidance, the world became a bleak and cruel place for Nursi, but when he was able to see it through the eyes of belief, he was able to view the world differently. It is essential to point out here that although Nursi was experiencing what he himself described as the negative kind of *ḥuzn* – the kind connected to seeing the world with the eyes of misguidance – he did nevertheless see it as a means of test and guidance, for it gave him the opportunity to throw away what he called the 'spectacles of misguidance' and view the world with the 'eyes of belief'. Therefore, there is an indication here that the existence of negative *ḥuzn* may in fact not be negative if it does not endure, or if, through God's compassion, it is transformed to positive *ḥuzn*, for in this case it served as a means of guidance and had a positive outcome.

Also, in a manner not unlike that of Izutsu, Nursi connects unbelief (*kufr*) to heedlessness, misguidance and ungratefulness.[78] In the Izutsian analysis we saw that belief is related very closely to the concept of *shukr* (to give thanks), which is also connected to the meaning of being grateful, as well as its opposite, unbelief, which thus then becomes connected to the idea of ungratefulness.[79] In the above quote Nursi admits that he was looking at the world through the eyes of the people of misguidance, and that it was only by turning to God in submission and total impotence that God transformed the negative view of the world for him; understanding that God does not create anything without a reason, Nursi is then able to offer thanks (*shukr*).[80]

If 'worldly happiness' is nothing more than 'poisonous honey', as Nursi says it is,[81] then it can be understood that the fleeting sweet taste will no longer be enjoyable if there is awareness that the enjoyment will end. He explains further that through the eyes of misguidance, both the past and future are viewed as non-existent:

> those who have passed away have gone to non-existence, while the future for them and everyone around them is bleak, since without the concept of the hereafter, the future will also be seen as a journey towards non-existence.

Nursi states that when the past and future are viewed in this light, the whole universe becomes dark, resembling a kind of hell.[82] As discussed earlier, this is why Ernest Becker stresses that in order to survive death anxiety, people have to fashion immortality projects for themselves.[83] For Nursi, it is this view of creation – one that is seen through the eyes of misguidance – that cuts off the present from the past and future. The light of belief, on the other hand, connects the present to the past and future, giving the assurance that the manifestation of existence is everlasting, and in turn resulting in true and enduring happiness:

> For the people of misguidance, the world is full to overflowing with deaths, separations, and non-existence; for them, the universe becomes a sort of Hell. Having only a flash of existence, everything is surrounded by never-ending non-existence. The past and the future are filled with the darkness of non-existence;

> they may find a sad [*ḥazīn*] light of existence only in the fleeting present. While through the mystery of the Qur'an and the light of belief, a light of existence becomes apparent which shines from pre-eternity to post-eternity; they may become connected with that, and through it secure eternal happiness.[84]

Nursi explains further that in the realm of belief there is a kind of timelessness and a sense of permanence, whereas in the realm of misguidance and heedlessness, life has only a brief existence: its enjoyments are as insubstantial and as illusory as a dream, and thus will, on account of their inability to satisfy, result inevitably in regret and sorrow. Nursi thus reiterates that in order to satisfy one's needs for immortality, all one's actions should be performed solely for the sake of God:

> There is the famous saying: "A moment's separation lasts a year, and a year's union passes as swiftly as a moment." I say the complete opposite to this: a moment's union for God's sake within the bounds of the Enduring One of Glory's pleasure is a window of union, not of only a year, but a permanent window. While not one year, but perhaps a thousand years spent in heedlessness and misguidance are like a second.
>
> Since everyone strongly desires a long life and yearns for immortality; and since there is a means of transforming this fleeting life into perpetual life and it is possible to make it like a long life; for sure anyone who has not lost his humanity will seek out the means and try to transform the possibility into a reality and will act accordingly. Yes, the means is this: work for God's sake, meet with others for God's sake, labour for God's sake; act within the sphere of 'For God, for God's sake, on account of God.' Then all the moments of your life will become like years.[85]

Nursi also describes his own experience of sadness, caused by separation from his homeland and friends, particularly when he was in exile. He talks about five kinds of exile which he experienced personally, namely:

1. old age; loss of youth
2. sad sense of separation and exile due to attachment to things he loved
3. sadness due to separation from his native land and relations
4. lonesomeness of the night and the mountains
5. spiritual pain caused by exile

It is to Nursi's sense of alienation with regard to the above feelings of exile that we now turn.

Nursi states that the main reason he wrote the *Risale* was to serve as a guide and reminder that would acknowledge his impotence and address his own shortcomings.[86] The whole of the *Risale* is thus written in a reflective and confessional style, detailing his own personal experiences.

Nursi talks about the hardships and obstacles he had to endure, particularly on account of old age and separation from friends, together with the pain and loneliness he felt spiritually because of the treatment he received while imprisoned. He shares his own life experience with his readers in order to show that the pain and sorrow given to him by God had an evident purpose. For Nursi found that through recourse to belief, those experiences provided opportunities for him to receive and make use of divine guidance. He lists his experiences under various hopes linked to the main pillars of Islam. And so, while he associates his initial feelings with his description of the negative *ḥuzn*, he explains that through the light of belief his negative view changed as his sorrow and sense of alienation were transformed into the positive, 'light-scattering' and 'guidance-giving' *ḥuzn*.

> Respected elderly brothers and sisters who have reached the age of maturity! Like you, I am elderly. I am going to write the 'hopes' I have found in my old age and some of the things that have befallen me, out of the desire to share with you the lights of consolation they contain.[87]

Through the examples he gives of sixteen hopes linked to the main pillars of Islam, namely belief in the mercy of the Divine, the Prophet, the Quran, the hereafter and Divine Determining, Nursi explains how the light of belief changed his pessimistic view of the world and his difficult experiences into a positive one.[88] It is this light of belief given by the Merciful that enabled him to realise that his initial negative view was due to heedlessness and to accept that the difficulties and calamities he experienced were given by God for a reason, and therefore rather than feel sorry for his wretched state, he realised that the calamities which made him sad were there to serve as a means of guidance and thus he became thankful.[89]

The obviation of *ḥuzn* through belief in God's Mercy

Nursi blames the sorrow he experienced personally on his own heedlessness, while recognising the guidance he received as coming not from external causes but directly from divine mercy. Nursi shares his innermost feelings with his readers by describing not only his thoughts but also the circumstances that attended when these thoughts occurred. For example, he states that it was "at the time of the afternoon prayer" and during "late autumn" when he was standing on top of a mountain and viewing the world that he began to experience negative feelings with regard to his 'old age'.[90] The afternoon prayer appears to signify an end to the day, while autumn heralds the apparent death of life and the insignificance of everything, particularly when viewed from the top of a mountain. It was during this moment of 'heedlessness' that his mind began to fill with dark thoughts and feelings of sorrow. Nursi describes how grateful he was when, suddenly, Divine mercy made itself felt, transforming negative feelings of sadness and separation into a powerful sense of hope and reassurance:

> For I saw that I had become old. The day too had grown old, and so had the year; the world itself had aged. As the time of departure from the world and separation from those I loved drew ever closer, the realisation of my own old age shook me severely. But then all of a sudden, divine mercy unfolded in such a way that it transformed that plaintive sadness and separation into a powerful hope and shining light of solace.[91]

Nursi explains that God's mercy is manifested in all creation and open to all. But the only way that the veil of darkness can be drawn back is by acknowledging God as the All-Compassionate Lord and asking for His Mercy. Here Nursi explains that in order to build such a relationship with God, sincere belief is needed; belief also demands submission, such as the performance of the five daily prayers.

> To those who, like me, have grown old, I say this: the All-Compassionate Creator presents himself to us in a hundred places in the All-Wise Quran as the Most Merciful of the Merciful, and always sends His mercy to the assistance of living creatures on the face of the earth who seek it, and every year fills the spring with innumerable bounties and gifts from the Unseen, sending them to us who are needy for sustenance, and manifests His mercy in greater abundance relatively to our weakness and impotence. For us in our old age, therefore, His mercy is our greatest hope and most powerful light. It may be obtained by forming a relation with the Most Merciful One through belief, and performing the five daily prayers, by being obedient to Him.[92]

Again, it was during a period of exile, perched in a tree on top of a high mountain, that Nursi's extreme feelings of loneliness made themselves known. He expresses these feelings in terms of five kinds of exile, all of them intertwined: the spiritual pain due to his physical exile; the loss of the people whom he loved and who had now passed away; separation from his native land and friends; the stark loneliness of the mountains; and his separation from the world.[93] Feeling the pangs of these sorrowful exiles, Nursi searched for a light of hope. Gradually, through belief in God, his negative view of the world began to change:

> Elderly men and women! Since we have a Compassionate Creator, there can be no exile for us! Since He exists, everything exists for us. Since He exists, the angels exist too. The world is not empty. Lonely mountains and empty deserts are full of Almighty God's servants. Apart from His conscious servants, stones and trees also become like familiar friends when seen through His light and on His account. They may converse with us and give us enjoyment.[94]

> Yes, evidences and witnesses to the number of beings in the universe and to the number of the letters of this vast book of the world testify to the existence of our All-Compassionate, Munificent, Intimate, Loving Creator, Maker, and Protector; they show us His mercy to the number of living creatures' members, foods, and bounties, which may be the means to His compassion, mercy, and favour, and indicate His Court. The most acceptable intercessor at His Court is impotence and weakness. And precisely the time of impotence and weakness is old age. So one should not feel resentful at old age, which is thus an acceptable intercessor at a court, but love it.[95]

Through the light of belief, then, Nursi was able to feel a sense of oneness with the rest of the universe, seeing himself as connected even to stones and trees, simply by the virtue of the fact that they, like everything else in creation, are connected to God through their contingent and dependent existence, and are signs or mirrors manifesting His Names.

Nursi seems to imply that if God is the Protector of all creatures in the world who are dependent on Him for their existence, then it no longer makes sense to feel lonely and sad, or to be frightened of anything except Him; one has to trust that there is a reason for one's feelings of loneliness. In Nursi's case, the sorrow that he felt on account of his detachment was a means of guidance and an opportunity for him to realise his weakness and impotence, both of which acted as 'intercessors' for him in his old age. If old age helps one to realise one's impotence and to turn to God's court for mercy, Nursi says, then one should not be resentful about losing one's youth; rather, one should relish it.[96]

Returning to the definition Nursi provides for negative and positive kinds of *ḥuzn*,[97] if this feeling of loneliness Nursi experienced was indeed the means for him to realise his impotence, then one may argue that these negative feelings of isolation and disconnectedness cannot ultimately be a bad thing, for what may have started as a negative *ḥuzn* was, through the light of belief and Nursi's recognition of his own impotence, transformed into a wholly positive view of creation. This seems to imply that just as 'transitoriness' is necessary in order to be able to see existence for what it really is,[98] the state of apparently negative *ḥuzn* is also necessary in order for one to become aware of one's impotence, which affords one the opportunity to seek divine mercy.

Nursi shares with his readers his personal experience as prisoner-of-war in Kosturma in north-eastern Russia. He explains that due to his heedlessness, he felt a kind of spiritual sadness, with everything around him appearing dark and melancholic. And even though he was no older than forty, the war was making him feel old:

> And while I was forty years old, I felt myself to be eighty. In those long, dark nights and sorrowful exile and melancholic state, I despaired of life and of my homeland. I looked at my powerlessness and aloneness, and my hope failed.[99]

Here again, it is while Nursi is feeling physically impotent, admitting verbally that he is powerless and weak, and then pleading for forgiveness, that the light of the Quranic verse "*God is enough for us; and how excellent a guardian is He*"[100] comes to his aid, with his weakness and impotence acting as intercessors for him at the Divine Court.[101] He states later that it was through such Divine Mercy that he was able to escape the prisoner-of-war camp, finding his way through Poland and Austria until he reached Istanbul.[102] Nursi explains that in just the same way that infants receive God's sustenance on account of their impotence, the sustenance of the believing elderly will also be provided for them in ways which may appear miraculous:

> I have had experiences which have given me the absolutely certain conviction that just as the sustenance of infants is sent to them in wondrous fashion by Divine mercy on account of their impotence, being made to flow forth from the springs of breasts, so too the sustenance of believing elderly, who acquire innocence, is sent in the form of plenty.[103]

Nursi stresses that since so much Divine Mercy is open to older people on account of their frailty and neediness, old age should be therefore be appreciated and not compared with the fleeting pleasures of youth.

Nursi goes on to describe another occasion when, although comfortable on a material level, he was experiencing sadness on account of the disloyalty of a friend whom he had once considered faithful and also on account of his encroaching old age, heralded by the appearance of white hairs in his beard. Again, he links these feelings to 'heedlessness' resulting from attachment to the world of causes. Nursi's search for hope enabled him to re-examine his life and admit that not only philosophy but also the Islamic sciences had actually obstructed his spiritual growth; through God's mercy and munificence he was able to take guidance directly from the Quran, and in particular the verse "There is No god but He" [104] – the latter in order to exclude any causal factors or partnership in God's creation. This realisation that in fact he had been a 'student' of 'misguided philosophy' enabled him to enter into debate with his soul, resulting in what he called "the victory of my heart".[105] This victory of heart over intellect appears to imply that reasoning has its limits, and stands in need of revelation, which appeals to one's innate being through the heart. Before discussing why Nursi appears to be linking sadness to the dependence on causes and the 'line of philosophy', the role of the heart in affirming reality will be discussed.

The heart's journey of purification

Similar to those who favour the spiritual path towards knowledge of God enshrined in the Sufi tradition, Nursi appears to be stressing the importance of the heart's journey of purification in order to move beyond the mere knowledge of God and become a mirror for the manifestation of His names. According to Nursi, this journey is the key to conquering loneliness, for it enables one to become intimate with God and, as a result, to understand one's connection with the rest of creation and thus overcome one's solitariness.

> For such a person, true solace, intimacy and sweet pleasure are to be found in addressing his own heart in those distant places and desolate mountains and distressing valleys, in working it through remembrance of God and reflection. Calling on God Almighty, he may become intimate with Him in his heart, and by virtue of that intimacy think of the things around him, which were regarding him savagely, as smiling on him familiarly. He will say: "My Creator, whom I am recollecting, has innumerable servants here in my place of solitude, just as He has everywhere. I am not alone; loneliness has no meaning." Thanks to his faith, he receives pleasure from that sense of familiarity. He grasps the meaning of life's happiness, and he offers thanks to God.[106]

According to Ghazālī, the source of the light of pure knowledge (*ma'rīfa*) is channelled through the world of the unseen (*malakūt*) to the inner heart (*qalb*). However, effects of this knowledge such as happiness or fear – descend to the chest (*ṣadr*), which pertains to the intermediate realm (*jabarūt*). Unlike the visible, corporeal world (*mulk*), which can be perceived by the senses, the realm of *malakūt* can be perceived only through inner vision, since it is a realm where there is no gradation: it is the world of the 'preserved tablet', or the realm of Divine determining where God's decrees are recorded. Without revelation, therefore, the realm of the unseen (*malakūt*) cannot be fathomed, and although reason has the ability to accept it, owing to its limitation it cannot demonstrate it empirically in the corporeal world. The realm of *malakūt* is also a created realm but it is a different kind of creation to that of the realm of *mulk*, and so the same 'laws of God' (*sunnatullāh*) do not apply to it. There is also a correspondence between the two realms. Both

Ghazālī and Nursi describe *mulk* as the place of manifestation or the mirror where the *malakūt* is reflected.[107] Thus just as transient beings are necessary[108] and the abandonment of the visible world, advised by many Muslim thinkers, is proscribed, one may conclude that one of the wisdoms behind the existence of the physical world is that it is the means by which the *malakūt* or the inner meaning of creation can be comprehended.

While Nursi's approach to the purification of the heart may be redolent of the Sufi doctrine of self-annihilation, it is clear from his writings that he did not subscribe to any of the Sufi paths. For the Sufi mystics, the most important aim is the attainment of direct knowledge (*ma'rīfa*) from God and the ability to live one's life in such a way that this purpose will be served. This in turn requires asceticism, which is the journey of self-purification. Ghazālī believed that the Sufi method was, during his era, the soundest way to reach God, since the experiential journey of knowledge acquisition focuses on bringing about internal changes – in accordance with the saying attributed to Prophet Muhammad that "He who knows himself knows God" – rather than on looking for external shortcomings. In this way there is the potential to reach the highest station of being totally absorbed (*fanā*) in God.[109] Although there is much Sufi[110] influence in Nursi's work and the terminology he uses is very similar to that employed by Ghazālī, he is of the opinion that in this day and age the Sufi path is not the safest route for everyone, and recommends instead a more direct route through recourse to the Quran.[111]

Unlike the Muslim thinkers discussed in Chapter Four who make a neat divide between the transient world and the spiritual world or world of the 'intellect', Nursi advises his readers to 'be transitory'.[112] By this he means that rather than totally denounce possessions, one should foster a temporary sense of imaginary ownership in order to be able to understand that in fact one does not own anything. Self-annihilation can obtain only through the understanding of the self, or what Nursi calls the 'I'.

According to the *ḥadīth*, the reason for the existence of human beings and jinn is to know, love and worship God; this is also implied in many of the verses in the Quran.[113] In other words, the innate disposition of humankind is to be a mirror for the manifestation of God's Names. Nursi explains how this responsibility or trust (*amāna*) can be fulfilled in his discourse on the human 'I' (*ene*).

The 'trust': The human 'I'

In the Quran it is Adam who, by virtue of having been taught all the 'Names and Attributes' of God, was given the 'trust' in order to act consciously as God's vicegerent and display these Names in creation at the highest possible level. As is implied in the Quran, the angels had only a limited knowledge with regard to the Names of God, sufficient for their particular tasks and duties, whereas Adam was taught all the Names in their entirety:

> And He taught Adam the names – all of them. Then He showed them to the angels and said, "Inform Me of the names of these, if you are truthful.
>
> They said, "Exalted are You; we have no knowledge except what You have taught us. Indeed, it is You who is the Knowing, the Wise."[114]

Thus, Adam and, by extension, all human beings, are God's representatives on earth and are able potentially to display God's Names consciously. However, on account of one's possession of free choice (*ikhtiyār*) one can choose to deceive oneself and lay claim to those attributes, in which case instead of attaining the highest position of vicegerent, one may sink instead to the level of the 'lowest of the low'.[115] Unlike the Sufis and their emphasis on the 'annihilation of the self',[116] Nursi offers a different approach, stressing that the human 'I' is the key to the treasures of the universe and the riddle of creation, which the individual is to solve by resolving existential questions such as 'Where did I come from?', 'What is my purpose here?' and 'What is my destination?' Nursi states that the reason that the riddle of creation can be solved only through this immaterial 'I' is that 'indications' and 'samples' which hold the key to the knowledge of God's Names and attributes are contained within it:

> The All-Wise Maker gave to man as a Trust an 'I' which comprises indications and samples that show and cause to recognize the truths of the attributes and functions of His dominicality, so that the 'I' might be a unit of measurement and the attributes of dominicality and functions of Divinity might be known. However, it is not necessary for a unit of measurement to have actual existence; like hypothetical lines in geometry, a unit of measurement may be formed by hypothesis and supposition. It is not necessary for its actual existence to be established by concrete knowledge and proofs.
>
> For example, an endless light without darkness may not be known or perceived. But if a line of real or imaginary darkness is drawn, then it becomes known. Thus, since God Almighty's attributes like knowledge and power, and Names like All-Wise and All-Compassionate are all-encompassing, limitless, and without like, they may not be determined, and what they are may not be known or perceived. Therefore, since they do not have limits or an actual end, it is necessary to draw a hypothetical and imaginary limit. The 'I' does this. It imagines in itself a fictitious dominicality, ownership, power, and knowledge: it draws a line. By doing this it places an imaginary limit on the all-encompassing

> attributes, saying, "Up to here, mine, after that, His;" it makes a division. With the tiny units of measurement in itself, it slowly understands the true nature of the attributes.[117]

The 'I', therefore, being familiar with all the Names, is able to act as a 'measuring unit' and make comparisons; it is able to say things such as, "Just as I made this house and arranged it, so someone else must have made the universe and arranged it", and so on.[118] Therefore since human beings are created in the image of God and have been taught all the Names, they are able potentially to understand all of God's attributes. As discussed previously, just as Abraham was able to realise that all created beings are transient and dependent,[119] and that consequently there must be an Absolute Creator who is absolutely independent, all individuals have the potential to realise that human beings are ephemeral and that consequently all attributes such of perfection such as beauty, power, wisdom and the like belong in fact to God. Therefore, as Nursi states, once one has used the 'shell' – namely the measuring unit' – one is able to reach the 'kernel' and so abandon one's 'imaginary dominicality' and 'supposed ownership'.[120] Thus the Nursian method of 'purification of the soul' (*tazkiyya al-nafs*) begins firstly by owning and then disowning God's attributes, or returning them to Him. This is followed by what Nursi describes as the 'fourfold way', based on certain key themes in the Quran, namely impotence (*'ajz*), existential poverty (*faqr*), compassion (*shafaqa*) and reflection (*tafakkur*):

> The ways leading to Almighty God are truly numerous. While all true ways are taken from the Quran, some are shorter, safer and more general than others. Of these ways taken from the Quran is that of impotence (*'ajz*), poverty (*faqr*), compassion (*shafaqa*), and reflection (*tafakkur*), from which, with my defective understanding, I have benefited.
>
> Indeed, like ecstatic love, impotence is a path which, by way of worship, leads to winning God's love; but it is safer. Poverty too leads to the Divine Name of All-Merciful. And, like ecstatic love, compassion leads to the Name of All-Compassionate, but it is a swifter and broader path. Also like ecstatic love, reflection leads to the Name of All-Wise, but it is a richer, broader and more brilliant path. This path consists not of ten steps like the 'ten subtle faculties' of some of the Sufi paths employing silent recollection, nor of seven stages like the 'seven souls' of those practising public recitation, but of Four Steps. It is reality (*ḥaqīqa*), rather than a Sufi way (*ṭarīqa*). It is the path of Divine precepts.
>
> However, let it not be misunderstood. It means to see one's impotence, poverty and faults before Almighty God, not to fabricate them or display them to

> people. The method of this short path is to follow the Practices of the Prophet (PBWH), perform the religious obligations and give up serious sins. And it is especially to perform the prescribed prayers correctly and with attention, and following them to say the *tasbīḥāt*.[121]

Nursi's binary definition of both *ḥuzn* and happiness has a whole series of ramifications which are also pertinent to his use of other concept pairs in his writings. Table 3, below, helps to show the distinction Nursi makes between positive and negative *ḥuzn* as discussed so far; it can also be compared with the Izutsian analysis of 'belief' and 'unbelief', which together constituted one of the main semantic categories of *ḥuzn*.[122]

Table 3: *ḥuzn* as described by Nursi

Positive *ḥuzn*	**Negative *ḥuzn***	
Other-indicative (*ma'nā-i ḥarfī*)	Self-referential (*ma'nā-i ismī*)	*The Words*, p. 757
Separation from friends	Lack of friends	*The Words*, p. 771
Guidance-giving	Misguidance/heedlessness/stirs up desire	*The Words*, p. 424
Yearning/elevated sorrow	Woebegone sadness	*The Words*, pp. 771-72
Light scattering/ hopeful sorrow	Dark sorrow/without hope	*The Words*, p. 423-24
Divine power and will	Nature/blind force	*The Words*, p. 771
Elevated lover	Dejected mournfulness	*The Words*, p. 423
Sorrow of love, not of orphans	Motherless orphan	*The Words*, p. 772
Connected	Disconnected/no Owner	*The Words*, p. 771
Divine art	World seen as desolate wasteland/a 'cruel slaughterhouse'/ an 'awesome house of sorrows'	*The Words*, p. 771 *The Rays*, pp. 173-74
Enduring	Transient	*The Rays*, p. 91
True love/undying beloved	Metaphorical love	*The Flashes*, p. 325
Eagerness – spirit stimulated	Eagerness – Ego (*nafs*) stimulated	*The Words*, p. 772
Thankful	Ungrateful	*The Words*, p. 172
Pain-free pleasure	Poisonous honey	*The Words*, p. 158

The examples from Nursi's life and the hardships he experienced all show that when he looked at events through what he called the 'eyes of misguidance' he felt sad and alone, but when he tried to see those events from a Quranic perspective he was able to interpret them in a positive way. The question that arises here, of course, concerns the notion of good and evil: is everything that happens in the created realm innately good? And if the answer is in the affirmative, does this mean that the concept of evil is linked not to beings innately, but rather to human intention alone?

The obviation of *ḥuzn* through belief in revelation, prophethood, the hereafter and Divine determining

The Quranic thematic analysis showed that if human beings are not on what the Quran considers to be the right path, they will be in a state of loss and confusion.[123] This 'right path', which requires belief in one God, the revelation, the hereafter, and submission through prayer, is considered to be the only source of guidance and means of salvation.[124] As his approach to his own life experiences shows, Nursi agrees that creation has to be read in accordance with these criteria.

Nursi is also of the view that when creation is seen solely in terms of cause and effect or 'blind nature', that is, when its connection to the Divine is severed, it appears dark and meaningless. Such a vision inevitably brings confusion and anxiety. However, if everything is seen ultimately as good, and if all that human beings are required to do is to submit to the conditions in which they find themselves, the question which then arises is this: how does Nursi – and how do we – reconcile human free choice with the dictates of Divine sovereignty? The second question, of course, concerns evil, and whether, if all things are innately good, it can be said to have any meaningful kind of existence at all. In the following section, Nursi's stance on Divine Determining will be compared with those of the Jabriyya and the Mu'tazilites.

The Jabriyya and the Mu'tazīlites on Divine determining (*qadar*)

According to the Jabriyya, individuals do not have free will at all and therefore all their actions are predetermined. At the other end of the spectrum the Mu'tazīlites believed that individuals are free to act; consequently, they are also able to determine good and evil through the use of reason.[125] As discussed in Chapter Four, al-Kindī followed the Mu'tazilite line and therefore held individuals responsible for bringing about their own sorrow – something that he personally considered to be an evil.[126]

Following the Ash'arite line on the issue of Divine determining, Nursi occupies the middle ground; for him, therefore, not only is there no incompatibility between

Divine determining and human free will, there is in fact perfect harmony between the two. He describes Divine Determining as a 'plan' existing in God's knowledge, in much the same way that an architect would have a plan in mind before constructing a building. Therefore, all created beings, whether from the present, the past or future, come from the unseen realm of Divine knowledge and appear in the realm of external existence through Divine will and power. The concept of Divine unity and absoluteness is important here, for God is not within space and time and so the present, future and past are all the same for Him. But, Nursi argues, just because God is omniscient does not mean that individuals are coerced to carry out actions which they do not wish to do.[127] Individuals are given the choice to either cover the truth or to accept it, and it is this choice which gives them the potential to reach either the highest rank of *ahsan al-taqwīm* (the most excellent of patterns) as God's vicegerent on earth or the lowest rank of *asfal al-sāfilīn* (lowest of the low). However, as will be discussed below, Nursi's claim is that evil does not exist as a created state or being.

Insights into Nursi's theodicy

Many explanations of evil exist, mostly in the form of attempts to exempt God from creation of so-called 'evil'. One such theodicy is St. Augustine's (354-430) explanation of evil as *privatio boni* meaning that evil does not have an actual existence but is defined simply as the absence of goodness, in the same way as darkness is the absence of light. Seen from this view, then, all of creation is considered to be good and it is only human will (*improba voluntas*) that is responsible for evil.[128] The theodicy of Irenaeus, the second century philosopher and theologian, viewed suffering and evil as necessary since it enables human beings to develop and progress. Therefore, while Augustine believed that God did not create evil since (a) it was not part of His plan; and (b) its existence is purely due to human choice, Irenaeus believed that evil is part of God's plan and is necessary because it plays an important role in human moral development.[129]

Nursi also believed that evil does not have an external existence (*wujūd-i khāriji*), and that it is simply the absence of good, in the same way that darkness is the absence of light. One question that this poses however, is this: how can something which does not have a real existence be evil? According to Nursi, all creation is brought into existence by God and is therefore good; that which is evil is the intention of human beings to bring about evil, and it is on this account that they are punished. But in the Nursian scheme, human beings do not create evil. They do not create evil because, firstly, they do not create anything. And even if they were capable of creating something, evil would not be among their creations because evil does not have an external existence; it has an external reality (*ḥaqīqat-ı khāriji*), in much the same way that darkness – which is the absence of light – has an external reality but no external existence. On the creational level, human beings have only the potential to cover the light of truth, which is a state of denial, and it is God who brings into being the tangible results of human bad intentions. Moreover, while human intentions may be bad, God makes good of them, for He is incapable of being or creating evil. Thus, all occurrences in the created realm are ultimately good, even though it is at times difficult for humans to accept this.[130] Nursi thus concurs with the Quranic verse that:

> *it is possible that ye dislike a thing which is good for you, and that ye love a thing which is bad for you. But God knoweth, and ye know not.*[131]

While Irenean theodicy attributes evil to God on account of the positive role that it has to play, Nursi does not believe that in fact evil exists, as all existence in its creational sense is good. What Nursi means when he says that non-existence is pure evil is that the intention to cover the truth, or to bring about darkness and obfuscation, is itself evil. What Nursi has in common with Ireneus is the idea that evil plays a role in the moral development of human beings. However, for Nursi, evil does not have an external existence: human evil stems solely from the choice to do wrong, or to 'cover' the truth, and it is this free choice, given to man as part of the Divine plan, which affords him the potential for moral development. Human beings are therefore capable, in theory at least, of reaching higher stations than those occupied by the angels, simply by dint of the fact that they are able to choose not to cover the truth.

> The facts that all virtues and perfections return to existence and that the basis of all rebellion, calamities and defects is non-existence are a proof that existence is pure good and non-existence is pure evil. Since non-existence is pure evil, circumstances that either result in non-existence or give an inkling of it also comprise evil. Therefore life, the most brilliant light of existence, proceeding through different circumstances, finds strength; it encounters varying situations and is purified; it takes on numerous qualities and produces the desired results, and enters many stages and displays comprehensively the impresses of the Bestower of Life's Names. It is on account of this fact that certain things happen to living creatures in the form of griefs, calamities, difficulties and tribulations, whereby the lights of existence are renewed in their lives and the darkness of non-existence draws distant and their lives are purified.[132]

From the above it appears that Nursi's understanding of trial and tribulations (*balā*) is in line with the Izutsian analysis of the Quran, which located *ghamm*, meaning distress and anguish, in the semantic field of *ḥuzn*. While *ḥuzn* is more specific and is related to sorrow arising from loss of possessions and loved ones, *ghamm* was defined as a more general distress stemming from harm which has already taken place and which is often given by God in the form of *balā* (tribulation), a trial and temporary suffering as part of a test of faith. As well as being a test, *balā* is often linked to objects of attachment, providing an opportunity for guidance through recognition of the fact that God is the real Owner of all possessions.[133] One example of the *ḥuzn-ghamm* dynamic, given in Chapter Three, can be found in the Quranic story of Moses. Having entrusted her baby to God by casting him into the river, his mother is soon reunited with Moses in order, the Quran tells us, that she be spared grief (*ḥuzn*) over her loss. While it is *ghamm* that has the potential to occur *after* an action, in this particular example, *ḥuzn* is used to indicate the distress that might have happened if Moses's mother had not been given the opportunity to be a wet nurse for her son.[134] The Quranic analysis also showed that stress (*ghamm*) is given by God as a lesson teaching one not to have *ḥuzn*. The story of the Quraysh and the near loss at Uhud through negligence serves as an example.[135] It shows that *ghamm* given by God can serve as Divine mercy, for firstly the series of stresses (*ghamm*) given by God would serve to reduce the first great anxiety resulting from near defeat at Uhud; and secondly, it would serve as a lesson for them not to have *ḥuzn*. In other words, trust was asked of them in the same way that it was asked of Moses's mother, whom God rewarded by re-uniting her with her son and thus protecting her from *ḥuzn*.

The Muslim thinkers studied here appear generally to represent *ḥuzn* in a negative light only and never point directly to the positive role it may play as a test of faith or a means of guidance.[136] Al-Kindī, for example, argues that if the future actions of others are likely to result in *ḥuzn*, and those actions are such that one is powerless to prevent them from occurring, to feel sorrow before those actions have occurred is illogical; after all, they may not occur at all. Although he is in agreement with the Quran on this issue, namely that it is futile to agonise over something that may not happen, he does not discuss the possibility that the external reality of *ḥuzn* may indicate its possible utility.[137] Nursi, however, has shown in the previous quote that hardships and tribulations are not evil and, in fact, have a Divine purpose.[138] Nursi's recollection of his own life experiences has also shown that whenever heedlessness brought about 'negative *ḥuzn*', recourse to belief and revelation would, thanks to the mercy and compassion of God, be transformed into a means of guidance. This prompted Nursi to offer thanks for the apparently calamitous situations in which he found himself, realising as he did that calamities and disasters were occasioned through Divine determining as a remedies for despair and grief.[139] Nursi's positive outlook towards the trials and tribulations he suffered is very similar to the Sufi view of calamities and sorrow; Rumi in particular was someone who considered sorrow and tribulation to be positive, to the extent that he believed that they should be welcomed, not least because they are sent by God. According to Rumi, therefore, sorrow is not something to be endured patiently; it is something that one should love and be thankful for, since it is nothing but happiness disguised as agony:

> When new worries and calamities come to your heart, do not run away from either of them. Instead run toward them and welcome them as a dear guest. Thank God for sending them to you and say: "O my Creator, O God, protect me from the evil of the calamities you have given to me. Do not deprive me of the bounties that will come because of these calamities and make me attain them."[140]

Does Nursi's 'negative *ḥuzn*' have a positive role to play?

Horwitz and Wakefield state that in the contemporary era, sadness is viewed as a serious medical condition, or an abnormal state requiring medical treatment.[141] They point to the fact that treatment of depression in outpatient settings in the United States increased by three hundred percent between 1987 and 1997, while use of antidepressant drugs such as Prozac among adults almost tripled between 1988 and 2000. Also, according to the World Health Organization's projection, by 2020 depression will be 'the second leading cause of disability'.[142] Although the above authors agree that depression is a widespread phenomenon, they disagree that 'normal sadness' that is causal in origin, and associated usually with experiences of painful loss, should be lumped together with sadness that lacks an apparent cause, such as *melancholia*. The authors oppose the DSM's inclusion, under the category 'Major Depressive Disorder (MDD)', of conditions which, unlike endogenous depression, are simply normal reactions to sad or painful external events,[143] which, they state, need to be distinguished carefully from one another.[144]

As discussed in Chapter Four, Abū Zayd al-Balkhī, who is possibly the first to have made a clear differentiation between neuroses and psychoses, expressed similar sentiments, indicating that reactive depression needs a different approach to endogenous depression.[145]

According to Horwitz and Wakefield, 'normal sadness', which is due to social problems such as loss, is a natural reaction and therefore therapy and medication are not appropriate treatments.[146] They conclude that there must be a reason for the intense sadness that human beings feel from time to time, and that the experience of transient, non-enduring sadness is not a medical condition; instead, therefore, of masking the symptoms it presents with medication, therapists should explore whether this sadness has a positive role to play, for it may well have reparative functions that are still not understood.[147] As discussed previously, Nursi also addresses the caring professionals, warning that a temporary salve does not address the root of the problem. This approach has huge implications for therapists and social workers, whose efforts consist traditionally in integrating those who are reactively depressed back into the very society from which they wished to escape in the first place.[148]

Shuman and Meador also question authors such as Koenig,[149] who appears to be in competition with his secular compeers by offering 'belief' as an alternative treatment for sadness.[150] They agree that it is natural to desire good physical and mental health and that in order to maintain and restore health, religion has an important role to play. What they object to, it seems, is the desiring for health and happiness for their own sake, which they describe as 'subjective', 'instrumental', 'reductive' and 'utilitarian'.[151] Similar to Nursi, who defines positive *ḥuzn*[152] as the outcome of one's longing for one's true home, Shuman and Meador also believe that complete satisfaction cannot be obtained in this transient world, and that all our longings are ultimately longings for God and thus loving things, including health and happiness, for their own sake, is not only wrong but also a kind of 'idolatry' and 'injustice'.[153] According to Horwitz and Wakefield, then, sadness stemming from loss may well have a positive role to play, while for Shuman and Meador, one's longing for God cannot be satiated totally in the material realm and therefore it is wrong to try.

As we have seen,[154] Nursi is also of the opinion that loss stemming from calamity and disaster has a positive role to play. What needs to be questioned, however, is whether, negative *ḥuzn* as defined by Nursi also has a positive role to play. In the narratives of his personal life, while Nursi often points to those feelings of sadness and isolation he experiences on account of momentary disconnectedness from the Creator as a negative kind of *ḥuzn*, it is clear that he believes that the creation of the events which produce those feelings is pure good, for those events serve as a test of faith and a means for self-awareness and spiritual growth. Moreover, such events also provide him with the opportunity to seek God's mercy and guidance, resulting in the realisation that ultimately all situations are created by God and should not be attributed to causes.[155] These 'negative' episodes which Nursi experienced seem to culminate in a kind of breakthrough, generated by feelings of impotence, in which Divine mercy comes to rescue him from negativity. It is, he says, only through the recognition of his own sheer and utter impotence that, by the grace of God, he realises that the surface of things is not the true reality. In response to the question posed by Horwitz and Wakefield, therefore, it appears that sadness does indeed have a positive role to play.

We have seen that Nursi attributed the negative kind of *ḥuzn* he experienced to his own state of heedlessness and misguidance.[156] But since *ḥuzn* and its opposite are given directly by God, then those particular experiences and the feelings that they engendered, however apparently negative, must have had a positive role to play. If those negative experiences were given in order to be fought against, thus culminating in a positive experience, then from the perspective of their existence they were not in fact negative; rather, they were necessary obstacles, put there simply in order to be surmounted. In other words, it is possible that the obstacle and the surmounting of the obstacle are both part of the Divine plan.

The idea that *ḥuzn* is given by God is not too dissimilar to the notion of the 'happy fault' (*felix culpa*) discussed earlier.[157] This phrase, used by St. Augustine, refers to the belief that Adam and Eve were created in a perfect state, but, having being tempted by Satan to eat the forbidden fruit, fell from paradise. Their disobedience to God resulted in the origin of sin, not only for Adam and Eve but also for the entire human race. Their sin was considered to be a 'happy fault', for without it meaningful redemption would not be possible.[158] John Hick (1922-2012)[159] is of the opinion that God created humankind with the ability to sin and that temptations are necessary in order that they may be overcome.[160] According to Hick, if the inclination to sin had not been given to Adam and Eve, they would not have been able to sin. However, he states that although the inclination to sin is given by God, it is created beings who are responsible for actualising evil.[161]

Similarly, one could conclude that Nursi's experiences of negative *ḥuzn* were in fact 'positive' as they served as a means of guidance. In other words, they were there to be fought against. Similar to Abraham's journey through creation and also the fall of Adam, these experiences were possibly necessary as a test of faith and a means of guidance. Thus, unlike al-Kindī, who appears to attribute the creation of happiness to God and the creation of sorrow to individuals themselves,[162] the Quranic understanding indicates that the apparently negative feelings of sadness are there to serve a purpose and can be a means for guidance. For example, if Nursi had not witnessed his village in ruins, or had not experienced the emptiness and sense of alienation he felt, his utter impotence may have gone unnoticed and he may not have taken refuge in God's mercy.

In the same way that the Quran often uses binary opposites – belief and unbelief, light and darkness and so on – to explain itself,[163] Nursi also uses conceptual binaries to elucidate certain Quranic concepts. With regard to the concept of *ḥuzn*, the *ma'nā-i ismī/ ma'nā-i ḥarfī* binary is used, with Nursi associating the negative *ḥuzn* with an overtly *ismī* interpretation of the world, in which things are seen as referring only to themselves, unlike the *ḥarfī* interpretation, in which things are seen as indicating other than themselves, namely, their Creator. [164] While the *ismī* attitude obscures the connection to the transcendent, giving rise to the state of "weeping orphans" and "powerlessness" that Nursi describes,[165] the *ḥarfī* attitude opens the door, as it were, offering one the opportunity to detach oneself from "the metaphorical beloved" in order to reach the "undying beloved."[166] However, just as without apparent darkness there could be no understanding of light, or, as Nursi asserts, just as without the understanding of transitoriness there could be no understanding of permanence, or without the imaginary ownership of the 'I' one could not conclude that all beings belong to God, one may also conclude that without the experience of apparently negative *ḥuzn*, the concept of true happiness remains indiscernible.

Edinger's (1922-1998)[167] emphasis on the necessity of a sense of alienation for the realisation of one's impotence, which is a *sine qua non* of self-development, can be compared to Nursi's approach to alienation, discussed previously.[168] Edinger points to the importance of the ego's becoming at one with the self[169] and alludes to the necessity of the sense of alienation as a means of becoming aware of one's impotence:

> The classic symbol of alienation is the image of the wilderness. And it is here, characteristically, that some manifestation of God is encountered. When the wanderer lost in the desert is about to perish, a source of divine nourishment appears. The Israelites in the wilderness are fed by manna from heaven (Exodus 16:4) [Picture 9]. Elijah in the wilderness is fed by ravens (Kings 17: 2-6) [Picture 10]. According to the legend, the desert hermit St. Paul was likewise fed by a raven [Picture 11]. Psychologically this means that the experience of the supporting aspect of the archetypal psyche is most likely to occur when the ego has exhausted its own resources and is aware of its essential impotence by itself. "Man's extremity is God's opportunity.[170]"

It can be understood therefore, that the negative *ḥuzn* and all of its definitions as shown in Table 3 [171] serve, as Nursi opines, as a 'shell' for understanding the 'kernel'. Since it has a reality, it cannot be negative *per se*, and so long as it does not endure, it provides the perfect opportunity for one to seek the truth. It can be concluded therefore that all that God sends to his servants as trials and tribulations, together with feelings of sadness, are actually positive since they can serve as means of guidance.

This leads us conveniently to the discussion about the experiences of the Prophets, most of whom, visited by such trials and tribulations, were also exhorted not to be sad.[172]

The sadness of the Prophets

The exegetes studied in Chapter Four appeared generally to be unable to unpack to any meaningful degree the negative *ḥuzn* of the prophets. And they were certainly unable to link the prophetic experiences to 'heedlessness' – no doubt because to posit heedlessness on the part of the prophets would be tantamount to questioning their fallibility. However, the fact that God exhorts the prophets not to have *ḥuzn* is an argument in favour of the notion that prophets can indeed lapse. For if prophets were perfect or infallible, why would they be chastised on account of negative sadness? Also, when prophet Muhammad was commanded by God to be patient, does this not imply a lack, a fault or a lapse?

The concept of the 'fall' (*hubūṭ*) began with the first prophet, Adam. But the Quran makes an important distinction between the fall of Iblīs[173] and the fall of Adam.[174] While Adam was in a state of forgetfulness when he tasted the forbidden fruit and consequently fell from heaven, Iblīs relied on his own limited reasoning to disobey God, stating that he was superior to man since he was made from fire, while man was made of mere clay.[175] Furthermore, while Adam repented for his momentary lapse, Iblīs remained proud and failed to submit to God's will. Although both Adam – and, by extension, all human beings – and Iblīs fell from heaven, Adam through his repentance was given the potential to rise consciously to the highest level in creation, whereas Iblīs continued to rely on his own judgement/self (*anā*).[176]

When talking about prophets and messengers in anything but a totally positive light, it is perhaps understandable that the question of prophetic infallibility should raise its head; after all, is emotional lability not a lack, a deficit? Here, a very brief discussion on the issue of the alleged faultlessness of the prophets and messengers is not without relevance.

The doctrine of prophetic infallibility (*'iṣma*) came to the fore mainly out of the discussions between Sunni and Shi'ite scholars, the earliest having been recorded in Kulayni's (864-941) *al-Kāfī*.[177] Fakhr al-Dīn al-Rāzī (1149-1209), a prominent Sunni theologian from the Ash'arite school, has dealt in detail with the controversy over the question of the infallibility of prophets from the perspective of different schools, a summary of which is provided below.[178]

According to al-Rāzī, the disputes regarding the putative infallibility of the prophets centre on belief, mission and personal character. With regard to belief, the general consensus is that prophets are immune from unbelief (*kufr*) and heretical innovation (*bid'a*). As far as mission is concerned, there are different opinions as to whether prophets are immune from error. And with regard to personal character, again there are different opinions regarding prophetic immunity from sin, whether minor or major. The extreme Sunni *Hashwiyya* [179] owing to their emphasis on a literal understanding of the Quran, believe that prophets are immune from neither minor nor major sins. By contrast, the majority view among the Mu'tazilites was that prophets are able potentially to commit very minor sins but not major ones. Exceptions to this stance include 'Alī Muḥammad Jubbā'i (849-916), a tenth century Persian Mu'tazīlite theologian and philosopher, who believed that although prophets can err in their interpretation of the Quran, they cannot commit either major or minor sins;[180] and Ibrāhīm ibn Sayyār al-Naẓẓām[181] (775-845), another Mu'tazīlite theologian, who held a slightly different view, agreeing that prophets cannot commit major or minor sins, either deliberately or by mistake, but that it is possible for them to slip obliviously into error. The Shi'ite belief is that prophets are completely infallible; they cannot commit major or minor sins, be they deliberate or unintended. Having taken all of these opinions into account, al-Rāzī concludes that the general orthodox opinion is that although prophets are immune from major and minor sins committed deliberately, they may commit sins or make mistakes inadvertently.[182]

Despite the orthodox opinion that prophets are, outwith their prophetic mission, not immune from inadvertent errors in their day-to-day lives as ordinary men, the exegetes covered in our study tend to shy away from stating overtly that prophets are not immune from momentary, unintentional lapses. This reluctance on their part may stem from their fear of being accused of imputing weakness to the character of the prophets. As for the Shi'ites, belief in the inerrancy of the prophets prevents them from criticising prophetic actions. Ironically, however, it is the Shi'ite exegete Ṭabāṭabā'ī who interprets 10:65 – when Muhammad is told 'Let not their speech grieve thee' – as a case of "sympathetic chastisement".[183] The question that poses itself here is why, if he is infallible, should Muhammad be reprimanded at all? In 18:6, Muhammad is so upset that people are not heeding his message that a verse is revealed to him not only as a consolation and guidance but also, as Ṭabāṭabā'ī puts it, as a kind of gentle chastisement: Muhammad is being warned that if he does not put an end to his sorrow, he may eventually put an end to himself:

> *Thou wouldst only, perchance, fret thyself to death, following after them, in grief, if they believe not in this message.*[184]

When Muhammad sees his followers going hungry on account of trade sanctions while other, unbelieving tribes were enjoying luxuries,[185] he receives guidance and reassurance from God, who reminds him that he must accept divine determining (*qadar*) and truly internalise the fact that the task of a prophet is to deliver the message without any expectation.[186] In 5:44 it is explained to Muhammad that if people choose to ignore God's signs – in this case tribulation that is sent as a warning – then they do not deserve to be guided and so God will not purify their hearts:

> *If any one's trial [fītna] is intended by God, thou hast no authority in the least for him against God. For such – it is not God's will to purify their hearts. For them there is disgrace in this world, and in the Hereafter a heavy punishment.*[187]

The above verse appears to confirm that trials and tribulations are sent as a test and a form of guidance; the hearts of those who choose to ignore God's signs will not be purified, in which case Muhammad must accept God's decree and not agonise over their unbelief.

A similar situation can be seen in 12:85, where Jacob is warned that if he does not get Joseph out of his mind he will grieve himself to death:

> *They said: "By Allah! [never] wilt thou cease to remember Joseph until thou reach the last extremity of illness, or until thou die!"*[188]

These verses show that sadness, especially when taken to the extent that it causes problems for one's physical and mental health, is not desired, and that indeed God warns against it. The paradox, however, is that sadness is actually given by God in order to remind us of our impotence; it is, in fact, a means of guidance.[189] We know that Jacob was well aware of this, for he spoke openly about his weakness, stating that he was making a complaint to his Lord alone and to no-one else. Thus, Jacob was careful not to attribute his difficult circumstances to causes, having realised that the situation was given to him as a test of faith, occasioned in this particular case by his attachment to Joseph.

Joseph himself also experienced many trials and tribulations: separation from his family at a young age; abandonment in a dark well; and years of enslavement and incarceration in Egypt. And yet when he rises to a high position and is finally reunited with his family at what must have been the happiest time of his life, he confesses his longing to return to his true home.

> *Take my soul [at death] as one submitting to Your will [as a Muslim], and unite me with the righteous.*[190]

According to Nursi, despite his worldly happiness, Joseph is now ready to face death for he is aware that the happiness of the next world is far greater than any happiness in this world could be. This state of awareness appears to be how Nursi defines the positive *ḥuzn*, that is, not feeling totally detached – as one would, perhaps, in an 'orphan-like' state – yet having a profound desire to return to the One beyond the material realm:

> That is to say, there is beyond the grave a happiness and joy greater than the pleasurable happiness of this world, so that while in that most pleasurable worldly situation, a truth-seeing person like Joseph (Upon whom be peace) wished for bitter death, so as to receive that other happiness.
>
> So see this eloquence of the All-Wise Qur'an; in what way it announces the end of the story of Joseph. It causes not sorrow and regret to those listening to it, but gives good tidings and adds further joy. It also gives guidance, saying: Work for beyond the grave, for it is there that true happiness and pleasure will be found. It also points out Joseph's exalted veraciousness, saying: even the most brilliant and joyful situation of this world did not cause him to become heedless; it did not captivate him; he still wanted the hereafter.[191]

It can be understood therefore that the 'calamities' and 'sorrows' Joseph experienced in his life were necessary steps for him on the path of spiritual development – the path to a state of realisation in which one becomes totally aware that in this transitory world, one's needs can never be fulfilled, and that true contentment can obtain only when one has reached one's 'true home'. One can conclude therefore that like the *felix culpa*, the blessing in disguise that was the 'happy fall', the apparently negative *ḥuzn* is a test which much be faced if one is to develop spiritually, and thus is wholly positive. Without the calamities and sorrows that the prophets experienced, they would never have been able to reach the highest level of manifestation of God's names and attributes.

Thus, just as the fall of Adam was necessary in order to for him to manifest consciously the names of God, in a sense the forbidden fruit – or, in Nursi's terminology, the shell – has to be eaten if the kernel is to be reached. In the same way that darkness is necessary in order for us to be able to conceptualize light, Nursi's conceptual binaries help us to understand the positive aspect of *ḥuzn* and to discourage the denigration of the prophets by placing them on par with angels when in fact their apparent lapses were the means whereby they were able to transcend the stations of the angels and attain such high levels of belief.

Conclusion

The findings from the typology, and from Izutsu and the exegetes, all show that *ḥuzn* has the potential to be a means of guidance or misguidance, depending on which path one follows – belief or unbelief. Nursi appears to agree with these findings, but what he adds to the discussion is his postulation that there are two kinds of *ḥuzn* from the outset: one positive and the other negative. Most of the Muslim thinkers in this study however, appear to define *ḥuzn* as negative only, emphasizing that through the employment of reasoning and the training of one's thought processes, *ḥuzn* must be eliminated.[192] While Nursi does not reject the importance of human reason, unlike some of the Muslim thinkers he bases his arguments directly on the verses in the Quran, which he considers as the only salve for all spiritual illnesses.[193]

The differentiation that Nursi makes between negative and positive *ḥuzn* is very subtle, for while both kinds appear to be similar, in fact they are polar opposites in the manner of belief and unbelief.[194] The 'orphan-like' state associated with the negative kind of *ḥuzn* is linked to the state of unbelief, or the grief brought about by disconnecting creation from its Creator. Nursi refers to the negative sorrow connected to the moral decadence of 'literature from Europe' as 'worldly sorrow', while he describes the positive *ḥuzn* produced by revelation as the 'sorrow of love'.[195]

Nursi's definition of positive *ḥuzn* seems to imply that although there is a sense of separation as opposed to total disconnectedness, and while the sorrow is one of love rather than total dejectedness, the truth remains that total happiness cannot be obtained in this transient world. His explanation of the story of Joseph, who, despite being happily reunited with his family after all of the trials and tribulations he suffered, still longed for the world of permanence, serves to support this idea. Nursi's definition of positive happiness, which, he states, can be attained only by preparing the subtle faculties for the 'eternal abode', also implies that complete happiness is unattainable in this world.[196]

Nursi links negative sorrow to the 'literature of civilization' that grew out of Enlightenment ideas, which limit human knowledge to knowledge of the sensible world only. Apart from its apparent 'glamour', modern civilization's biggest deception in Nursi's eyes is its false claim to 'scientific advancement', which is usually contrasted with the 'backwardness' of religion.[197] Nursi opines that it is the 'literature of Europe', which attributes creation to 'deaf and blind' nature, that is responsible for this sense of alienation and disconnectedness; without an ultimate purpose, post-Enlightenment civilization opens up the way to heedlessness and misguidance.

Another thinker who, like Nursi, avers that the quest for happiness cannot be found in the physical realm is Ernest Becker (1924-74). Becker also points to the existential dilemma occasioned by the disconnect between the ephemerality of the physical world and the universal human desire for immortality.[198] He stresses that the desire for immortality is so great that people deceive themselves by creating 'immortality projects', while those who are unable to achieve this false status suffer badly as a result.[199] It is important to question here, as Nursi does,[200] whether the professionals and institutions which give social support that is not based on belief are merely offering another form of 'immortality project'. However, while Becker concurs with Nursi, Muslim thinkers and the exegetes in portraying the transient nature of this world as one which cannot satisfy the human need for permanence, he does not offer any precisely delineated solutions as to how and where permanence may be obtained. Nursi addresses this dilemma by stressing the importance of understanding the nature of the human 'I' (*anā*), for it holds the key, he believes, to the 'treasures of the universe'. He explains that because human beings have 'samples' of all of God's attributes within them, they are potentially able to manifest them at the highest possible level. However, while Becker implies that all human problems stem from their falsely laying claim to those attributes, he does not unpack this adequately and thus falls short of offering the solution that Nursi offers, namely that the key to happiness is the use of the human 'I' as a unit of measurement for understanding God's Names. It is only with the realisation of one's own ephemerality, Nursi claims, that one is able to give up one's imaginary ownership and dominicality.

Through revisiting his own personal experiences, Nursi demonstrates the difference between concept pairs such as *ma'nā-i ismī* (self-referential) and *ma'nā-i ḥarfī* (Other-indicative),[201] *mulk* (corporeal or visible realm) and *malakūt* (the hidden realm).[202] He blames his temporary lapses on viewing the world in a negative way, and on his own 'heedlessness' and 'ungratefulness' which stemmed from his failure to examine his feelings in an 'Other-indicative' manner. However, he says that his terrifying and grievous state during these instances of negligence enabled him inevitably to gain awareness of his own impotence and existential poverty, thus pushing him to seek God's mercy. Nursi's experiences accord with the discussion of Edinger, who argues that alienation has a positive role to play, since it serves as a means whereby one is able to realie one's impotence, thus providing the perfect state for seeking the One who is not impotent.[203]

Nursi explains that it is because of Divine compassion that his sense of loneliness and detachment from the world changed, to the extent that the petrifying images he beheld suddenly disappeared, allowing him once again to feel connected to everything around him, including apparent lifeless objects such as stones, for he was now able to see everything in creation as signs pointing to their Creator. Nursi's remedy for the obviation of *ḥuzn* is thus four-fold: to submit to one's impotence; to acknowledge one's existential poverty; to view the cosmos in terms of Divine compassion; and to be engaged in constant reflection and self-examination.[204]

As has been discussed, Nursi attributes the negative kind of *ḥuzn* he experienced to his own heedlessness. However, if *ḥuzn* is given directly by God, then it must ultimately have a positive role to play. In Nursi's case, by following the four-fold way he recommends for the obviation of *ḥuzn*, his negative feelings culminated in a positive experience. The notion that life's obstacles and the solutions that one finds to surmount them are part of the divine plan is comparable to the notion of the fall of Adam being understood as a blessing in disguise – a *felix culpa*, without which man's moral development would have been impossible.

Nursi's concept pairs have served as an excellent means of uncovering the hypothetical nature of negative *ḥuzn*. This has facilitated our understanding that since the apparently negative *ḥuzn* is given by God, it must serve some purpose. This purpose, we have seen, is guidance.

Conclusion

The main aim of this study has been to explore the concept of *ḥuzn* from the point of view of the modern Muslim theologian, Said Nursi. The Quranic typology and the study of the interpretations of *ḥuzn* by a number of key Quranic exegetes and Muslim philosophers which constitute the first section of this book have identified important points of convergence and divergence in how this concept has been understood and approached. An exploration of Nursi's interpretation of *ḥuzn* has facilitated what is hopefully a novel and coherent synthesis of understandings and approaches, adding a new dimension to the Muslim discourse on the nature of sorrow and its cognates.

The textual analysis of the Quranic verses provided a picture of *ḥuzn* as a feeling related strongly to grief as a result of loss, be it loss of possessions or of loved ones. The findings of the typology indicate that in order to avoid *ḥuzn*, submission to, as well as belief in, God is necessary. This much is demonstrated by the words 'submission of one's whole self',[1] which necessitates belief in the hereafter, following God's guidance, carrying out righteous acts, and spending one's substance (*amwāl*) in the cause of God.

The thematic analysis revealed the fact that although all believers, including prophets, are commanded not to be sad, with sadness seen as a quality associated with a lack of hope and trust, and thus seemingly negative, sadness also has a positive aspect, since it serves as a form of trial and Divine guidance and offers a real opportunity for moral development. The conclusion of the thematic analysis was that although we are commanded not to be in a state of *ḥuzn*, the experience of sadness itself can serve as a reminder that all possessions, including loved ones, belong ultimately to God, and that the obviation of *ḥuzn* can happen only through trust and acceptance of this fact.

The Izutsian method proved to be an excellent tool for the analytical study of the concept of *ḥuzn*. It began with the selection of all the verses in which *ḥuzn* was mentioned. The verses were gathered, compared and contrasted with each other, as well as with other verses where synonyms and antonyms of this word were mentioned, in order to obtain what Izutsu describes as a 'word-thing' interpretation as opposed to a word-for-word reading. In this way, some of the main concepts which had a strong relational meaning with the term *ḥuzn* were identified, enabling a more contextual understanding of the meaning of the concept and revealing why people become sad and how sadness may be obviated. The objective of the analysis was to provide us with the 'story of ḥuzn' from the perspective of the Quran, the *Weltanschauung* of which forms the foundation stone upon which the whole of Nursi's worldview is constructed.

By examining the synonyms and antonyms of the word *ḥuzn* it was shown that it has a strong connection with the concept pair of 'belief' (*īmān*) and 'unbelief' (*kufr*). These concepts, in turn, were related to a large number of other strings of concept pairs. For example, it was found that, Quranically, the concept of belief appears to be almost synonymous with the concept of gratefulness (*shukr*), which is connected to the state of happiness as opposed to the state of ingratitude (*kufr* from the verb *kafara* meaning to 'cover the truth'), which is connected to the state of loss and unhappiness.[2]The Izutsian analysis showed that those who refuse to accept God's guidance and who choose instead to show their ingratitude by covering the truth (*kāfir*) through open rebellion (*fāsiq*) against it, will in the end be seen as *ẓālimūn* ('wrong-doers'), since through their own choice they remain in darkness. Thus, the key to the obviation of *ḥuzn* and the attainment of true happiness is sincere belief (*īmān*), which translates into: belief in only one God, with no ascription of 'partners' to Him; fear of, and trust in, Him alone; following His guidance only, as laid down in the Quran; carrying out acts of righteousness purely for His sake; and showing patience and perseverance in times of hardship.

The 'story of *ḥuzn*' from an exegetical angle revealed a general consensus with regard to the meanings of *ḥuzn* and *khawf*, interpreting the former as loss, in terms of both possessions and loved ones, and the latter as fear relating to the future generally and to the hereafter in particular.

All of the exegetes studied agree that the obviation of *ḥuzn* and *khawf* necessitates belief in God, belief in the hereafter, the performance of good deeds, and giving in charity with total sincerity. An act performed with total sincerity is defined as something that is done purely for the sake of God and in accordance with the doctrine of *tawḥīd* and the laws of jurisprudence.

The thematic analysis of the concept of *ḥuzn* has also shown that all of the exegetes agree that *ḥuzn* given by God serves as a test, as punishment or as guidance. With the exception of Ṭabāṭabā'ī, they also concur that the three categories of believer mentioned in the Quran, namely: "he who wrongs himself"; "he who is moderate" and the third category "he who is foremost in good deeds by permission of Allah",[3] are potentially able to obviate *ḥuzn* in a manner commensurate with their different degrees of understanding and submission. According to Ṭabāṭabā'ī, however, the removal of sorrow does not have any relevance to the third category, since believers in this category do not have any sins in their book to be grieved about in the first place.

All of the exegetes concur that *ḥuzn* is linked to loss and, as such, can have a positive aspect, that is, by serving as a test and a means of guidance and reassurance. And while, unlike the Shi'ite Ṭabāṭabā'ī, the Sunni exegetes make no overt reference to prophetic infallibility (*'iṣma*), they do appear to try somehow to justify the extent of the prophets' sorrow, which implies that they tend to regard *ḥuzn* in something of a negative light when it comes to God's messengers, reluctant as the exegetes are to ascribe the slightest deficit, momentary lapse or even fleeting instance of forgetfulness to those tasked with delivering the Divine message.

In Chapter Four al-Kindī's understanding of *ḥuzn* was compared with a selection of Muslim thinkers who have specifically written about this topic, the aim being to capture the philosophical aspect of the notion of *ḥuzn* as conveyed by the generality of Muslim thinkers. Although al-Kindī's epistle is considered to be based on ideas and analogies attributed to the Stoics, the analysis of his work has shown that he has engaged with and developed only those ideas which accord with the Islamic revelation.

Al-Kindī's definition of *ḥuzn* as "psychological pain occurring on account of the loss of an object of love or the missing of things desired"[4] is in line with the Quranic definition offered by the exegetes, as well as that given by most of the Muslim thinkers. There is also support among the exegetes and Muslim thinkers for al-Kindī's idea that the inclination towards permanence is a natural disposition, as well as for his description of this world as one of 'generation and corruption.'[5] Although al-Kindī does not refer directly to revelation, he argues that to become attached to what is ephemeral is bound to lead to disappointment, and therefore one must think logically and seek what is permanent, namely the soul.

Al-Kindī identifies attachment to this world as being responsible for the tarnishing of souls, and offers ten remedies for the denormalisation of one's immoral habits and the rectification of one's character. While the Quranic analysis shows that *ḥuzn* is ultimately from God and can play a positive role as a source of direction, guidance and remembrance,[6] al-Kindī, together with most of the Muslim thinkers studied here, do not seem to consider this aspect of *ḥuzn*. There is also some ambiguity in Al-Kindī's argument, for while on the one hand he suggests that *ḥuzn* is a universal condition, on the other he stresses that it is a negative, self-inflicted attribute which is not part of human nature.[7] Moreover, in contradistinction to the Quranic analysis, which showed that the feeling of sadness is ultimately given by God and thus offers the opportunity for guidance and purification of the soul, al-Kindī appears to attribute sadness to human beings, seeming thus to indicate that it is not God-given and therefore serves no purpose.[8]

The Quranic analysis of *ḥuzn* has shown, however, that its source is ultimately God, and that since it may serve as a reminder and guidance, it can have a positive role to play. However, although the Muslim thinkers agree with the Quranic analysis that the obviation of *ḥuzn* can be realised only by detaching oneself from the worldly life, and despite the fact that they offer logical reasons and ways of training the mind and body to accept this fact, there is no discourse on why sorrow exists in the first place or whether, ontologically, it has a positive role to play.

In Chapter Five an account of Nursi's life and works was given, thus providing a contextual backdrop for his teachings and also for Chapter Six, which focuses on the concept of *ḥuzn* in Nursi's work.

The downfall of the Ottoman Empire and the rise of the secular regime of Mustafa Kemal Ataturk concerned Nursi greatly. On the one hand he was not totally satisfied with the teachings of the religious schools, which focused mainly on the externals of religion, and on the other hand, he was alarmed that many young people were being attracted to western secularism and the association of Islam with 'backwardness'. Nursi felt strongly that it was necessary to respond to these new materialistic trends through educational reform. However, plans for such reform did not come to fruition and, discontented with political life, he experienced profound spiritual turmoil, which led eventually to his transformation from the 'Old Said' to the 'New Said'. Despite the fact that Nursi avoided politics and stayed away from all disputes and confrontations, throughout his life he suffered considerably at the hands of the authorities. Nursi being Nursi, however, he blamed himself for the suffering he experienced and later related how, through taking refuge in the Quran and acknowledging his impotence, these apparently negative experiences were transformed into a most positive means of guidance.

The 'New Said' now believed that the only way in which society might be influenced towards change would be through the exposition of Quranic truths. This inspired him to write his magnum opus, The *Risale-i Nur*, a modern commentary on the Quran, which he claimed would serve as an antidote for what he believed were the sicknesses of today's so-called civilised societies.

The Quranic typology and the Izutsian analysis of the concept of *ḥuzn* in the Quran have shown that sadness has the potential of being a source of guidance or misguidance, depending on whether the path of belief or unbelief is followed. Most of the Muslim thinkers analysed in this study appear to define *ḥuzn* as negative only, emphasizing that through human reasoning and the training of one's thought processes, it has to be eliminated. While the exegetes generally agree that although *ḥuzn* is essentially a sign of lack or absence, it nevertheless offers the opportunity for guidance, they seem to be reluctant to attach this apparently negative attribute to prophets. That which distinguishes Nursi from other expositors of *ḥuzn* right from the outset is his binary definition of *ḥuzn*.

Nursi describes the first kind of sorrow in terms of 'lack of friends' or 'having no owner' and accuses what he calls the 'literature of civilization', which deceptively misguides its readers into attributing everything to nature rather than to the Divine, of engendering feelings of alienation and heedlessness.

Nursi describes the second kind of *ḥuzn* as an 'elevated sorrow': a "guidance-giving", "light-scattering" sorrow which is produced by the Quran[9] and which acknowledges that friends exist and that it is only their absence which causes this "sorrowful yearning" (*ḥüzn-ü müştakane*). This second definition of *ḥuzn* seems to resonate with the Sufi understanding of the concept, which welcomes all forms of sorrow as totally positive experiences, since they provide the means for union with God.[10] Therefore while Nursi makes a clear distinction between *ḥuzn* as an outcome of heedlessness caused by disconnection from belief, and *ḥuzn* as an outcome of the yearning for permanence, this distinction is absent in classical Sufism, which appears to consider all forms of sorrow to be positive.

Nursi points to an example of this 'yearning sorrow' in the Quranic story of Joseph, who, after all of the difficult trials he has experienced in his life, asks to be united with God, and this a time when he is no longer experiencing any great difficulties. Joseph was no longer separated from his family and he enjoyed a high position in the Egyptian elite, yet he declared himself ready to return to his 'true home'. Nursi explains that Joseph's understanding and belief were such that he realised that this ephemeral world could never satiate his need for permanence, and that this is why he asked to be reunited with his Lord.[11]

According to Nursi, then, total happiness is not possible in this world, since sadness, be it negative or positive [12] is inevitable where there is ephemerality. It may be argued that the whole of the *Risale* is devoted to the notion of belief and submission to One God, the outcome of which would be the positive kind of *ḥuzn*, whereas attachment to the ephemeral world would result in the kind of alienation Nursi describes in terms of the first kind of sadness. Nursi therefore agrees with al-Kindī's description of this ephemeral world as one of 'generation and corruption'. He also confirms the innate human need for permanence, which is corroborated also by the typology, the exegetes and the Izutsian analysis. At first glance, Nursi's description of negative *ḥuzn* appears to accord with the Muslim thinkers, since both link the sense of alienation and hopelessness to attachment to the world rather than seeing the world as a collection of signs that point to the One who is not ephemeral. However, while it appears initially that Nursi's depiction of his first kind of *ḥuzn* is at one with the description of this concept given by the Muslim thinkers, namely as something attributable to individuals' own heedlessness and thus something which must be avoided, further analysis reveals that Nursi adds another important dimension to the understanding of this apparently negative *ḥuzn*. Nursi explains that it is the attachment to 'metaphorical beloveds' which are unable to satiate the desire for permanence that is responsible for the pain and suffering of human beings.[13] Nursi's conclusion is in fact similar to the findings of the Quranic analysis, for he attributes heedlessness, misguidance and ungratefulness to unbelief (*kufr*), and gives examples of his own painful experiences in this regard. However, while he associates his initial sorrowful state with the negative *ḥuzn*, he goes on to describe how the light of belief transformed his sorrow and sense of alienation into the positive, 'light-scattering' and 'guidance-giving' *ḥuzn*.[14] Thus Nursi's remedy for the transformation of negative *ḥuzn* into positive *ḥuzn* is reconnection with the

Creator by reading the creation in a *ma'nā-i ḥarfī* ('Other-indicative') rather than a *ma'nā-i ismī* ('self-referential') way. It is only by reading the creation in this way that one is able to recognise one's impotence, acknowledge one's existential poverty, view the cosmos in terms of Divine Compassion, and be engaged in constant reflection and self-examination.[15]

However, while the Muslim thinkers appear in the main to make a neat divide between the material and spiritual worlds, recommending that in order to decrease the likelihood of sorrow one should rid oneself of as many worldly possessions as possible, Nursi stresses that permanence, in fact, 'comes from transitoriness'.[16] Nursi also talks about the correspondence between the unseen realm (*malakūt*) and the corporeal world (*mulk*), stressing that without the existence of the physical world it would be impossible to comprehend the inner meaning of creation. Thus, unlike some of the Muslim thinkers studied here, who appear to denounce possessions altogether, Nursi believes that an initial sense of imaginary ownership is necessary in order to foster the realisation that one does not in fact own anything at all. He points to the human 'I' or *anā* (*ene* in Turkish), which he claims holds the key to the riddle of creation, since without it, it would not be possible to know God.[17] The human 'I' is therefore posited as the immaterial entity through which samples of reflections of all Divine attributes, deposited within the inner being of all individuals, may be understood. The 'I' does not have a real existence as such but rather serves as a unit of measurement for the understanding of God's attributes. Similar to the Abrahamic journey through creation, from Abraham's initial attribution of God's attributes to causes until his realisation that the Creator of all ephemeral beings must be absolute, the Nursian path of purification of the self (*nafs*) also begins by first owning and then disowning God's attributes. It serves therefore as an important measuring unit, without which it would be impossible to abandon one's 'imaginary dominicality' and 'supposed ownership'.[18]

Thus, in a manner similar to Edinger, who emphasizes the necessity of a sense of alienation as a means of becoming aware of one's impotence,[19] Nursi blames his personal experiences of *ḥuzn* and the sense of alienation he feels on his own heedlessness. However, Nursi also acknowledges that these feelings were necessary for him, for without them he would not have been able to recognize his impotence and seek guidance.[20]

This study has shown that the typology, the Izutsian analysis, the Muslim thinkers, the exegetes and Nursi himself all place *ḥuzn* in the category of reactive depression and that *ḥuzn* is a result of how one interprets events in one's life. They also agree that the mind can be trained to see things differently.

While most of the Muslim thinkers appear to define *ḥuzn* in only a negative sense, and offer devices for its denormalization, the Quranic analysis shows that *ḥuzn* can offer an opportunity for guidance, therefore indicating that its existence is necessary. However, the position of the exegetes is affected by a paradox. The paradox is that although *ḥuzn* is given to believers – the prophets in particular – as a means of test and guidance, they are commanded by God not to have *ḥuzn*, since it is associated with a state of ungratefulness. Whereas, the Sufi understanding is that all forms of sorrow, including *ḥuzn*, should be welcomed, as they represent signals of God's attention to His servants. What the Sufi explanation fails to explain clearly, however, is how and why, as well as being linked to guidance, *ḥuzn* is also linked to unbelief and the rest of the negative words in its semantic category.

Nursi alludes to the fact that complete happiness cannot be obtained in this world in his positing of two kinds of sorrow: a positive sorrow and an apparently negative one, with the former representing a state of grateful yearning for the Beloved and the latter indicating a state of alienation and loss resulting from a disconnection from the Creator. A closer analysis of Nursi's arguments, however, reveals his emphasis, similar to that of Ghazālī, that imperfection is necessary in order that perfection may be known;[21] just as darkness is necessary to for the concept of light to become clear, Nursi stresses, one cannot understand permanence without first recognizing the ephemeral and transient nature of creation. The apparently negative *ḥuzn*, then, is in effect a *felix culpa*, for it is the means whereby man may be tested and guided; as a necessary step in the journey of spiritual development, it cannot in fact be anything but ultimately positive. Hence just as the fall of Adam was necessary in order for the names of God to be manifested consciously, the sorrow experienced by the prophets was also necessary in order for them to be able to manifest God's names and attributes at the very highest levels. Nursi's binary classification of Quranic concepts has helped us to understand the positive aspect of *ḥuzn* and thus discourage this tendency on the part of believers to denigrate – albeit unwittingly the status of prophets by placing them on a par with angels, when in fact their apparent shortcomings were actually the means by which they reached such elevated levels of belief.[22]

The analysis of Nursi's work has shown that *ḥuzn* is inevitable; consequently it is something that has to be not obliterated but, rather, changed or transformed into positive *ḥuzn* through the attribution of God's Names to their rightful Owner (*ma'nā-i ḥarfī* 'Other-indicative') rather than to oneself or to nature (*ma'nā-i ismī* 'self-referential').[23] In other words, Nursi's whole argument is that it is important to understand the nature of 'the mirror' – itself ephemeral and insubstantial – in order to be able to love the One whose reflection is visible in it.

The discussions on *ḥuzn* in this book, particularly with regard to Said Nursi's arguments on the importance of understanding the nature of transitoriness in order to understand permanence, have hopefully served to show that without the apparently negative *ḥuzn*, and without its transformation to positive *ḥuzn*, personal development is impossible. It is hoped that the conclusions of our research will encourage a model of care for Muslims suffering from reactive depression that incorporates the idea that, ultimately, everything in creation has a purpose. Although a full discussion of this would require further work, the path revealed by our findings here will be compatible with a model of care that is not dismissive of experiences of *ḥuzn*, and which aims to transform those experiences in a positive direction.

As Nursi has shown through his own life experiences, everything that happens to human beings is a test, a form of guidance from God, a sign to be read and interpreted in accordance with the criteria provided by the Quran. Nursi found the antidote for all of his misfortunes in the different verses in the Quran, and applied them as a salve in order to cure his spiritual injuries. This research paves the way to a new approach – one which uses Quranic antidotes in order to empower individuals so that they may see beyond the material world (*mulk*) and into the realms of the supra-material and the spiritual (*malakūt*). It is hoped therefore that the conclusions reached here will encourage further research on how to apply this understanding of *ḥuzn* to behaviour change techniques from a Muslim perspective.

Appendix

Ibn Sina's (Avicenna) manuscript on *ḥuzn* in Arabic

فصل في الحزن واسبابه من كلام الشيخ الرئيس

Ibn Sina's (Avicenna) original manuscript: *Rīsāla fī al-ḥuzn*. Arabic PDF obtained on line from: http://www.muslimphilosophy.com/sina/
On 15 April 2014

Translation of manuscript

Ibn Sina – Above manuscript rough translation into English – with the help of Abed Al-Zuweiri 18 March 2014

We verify what is *Al-ḥuzn* and its reasons, so that it will be known. Then we say grief is a psychological pain (*nafsanī*). It happens because of the loss of the things one loves and also not obtaining 'what one wishes' (*talab*). There is no one who does not have these reasons and no one can be found that does not lose the things that they like or desire. If human beings want the things in this world which is subject to loss and not fixed, both their worldly attachments and the things that they seek for the hereafter, will be obliterated. Contrary to that, the things related to the intellect ('*aql*) are fixed and persist and cannot be lost, since no hand can touch them, nor can they be touched by any harmful things. This is Contrary to worldly matters which cannot be protected and their corruption (*fīsad*) cannot be prevented. There should be no fear of losing the things related to the intellect (*'aql*). This applies to the person who does not want grief to touch him. This person must imagine his worldly things which he loves in this life and his immediate wishes, to be as they really are, that is, they may come to an end, or be corrupted or be lost. Therefore, one must not expect things one loves to behave contrary to their nature. If you keep this idea in your mind that these things have the innate nature of being lost, changed and corrupted, you will not find it strange when you see how they become corrupted. In this way, you will not despair (*ya's*) for not obtaining what you would like nor will you grieve for not getting what you wish for. Instead, you will take what is essential, and when they are lost, you will keep yourself occupied, without making extreme effort to regain them. The mind should not be preoccupied with this loss. If anyone follows this guide, then this is indeed, from the morals of the kings (*muluk*). The kings do not give importance to what comes to them, and they don't care about what they lose. And against this example, is the morals of the common people (*'ām*), who become very happy gaining things and sad when they lose them. Also it is important for people to imagine (keep in mind) that they should never be sad for anything that they love and that sadness (grief) will never be continuous. This is because it is impossible during one's life not to lose anything that one likes, or obtain whatever one wishes. Therefore one should be satisfied with all situations in order to be safe from the pain of grief.

Notes

Chapter 1

1 Quran, 44:38. See also 21:16-17.
2 See Allan V. Horwitz and Jerome C. Wakefield, *The Loss of Sadness: How Psychiatry Transformed Normal Sorrow into Depressive Disorder* (New York: Oxford University Press, 2007), 59.
3 The works of Ya'qūb ibn Ishāq al-Kindī and Abū Zayd al-Balkhī, along with those of other Muslim thinkers, will be discussed in detail in Chapter Four.
4 Horwitz and Wakefield, 9-10.
5 The reason that Nursi's work has been included in this study will be explained presently.
6 See Malik Badri, *Abū Zayd al-Balkhī's Sustenance of the Soul: The Cognitive Behaviour Therapy of a Ninth Century Physician* (London: International Institute of Islamic Thought, 2013), 21.
7 See Jerome C. Wakefield, 'The Concept of Mental Disorder: Diagnostic Implications of the Harmful Dysfunction', *World Psychiatry,* 6 (2007), 153; Allen Frances, 'The New Crisis of Confidence in Psychiatric Diagnosis', *Ann Intern Med.* (2013) 159 (3), 221-222; and Horwitz and Wakefield, *The Loss of Sadness*, who have criticised the *DSM-5* Manual for not making a clear distinction between 'depressive disorders' and 'normal sadness'.
8 Ibid., 6.
9 Christopher J.L. Murray and Alan D. Lopez,' Evidence-Based Health Policy: Lessons from the Global Burden of Disease Study', *Science*, (New Series), 274, no. 5288, (November, 1996), 740-743.
10 For a discussion of the *DSM*'s definition of major depression, see Horwitz and Wakefield, 8-26.
11 Wahiba Abu-Ras, Ali Gheith and Francine Cournos, 'The Imam's Role in Mental Health Promotion: A Study at 22 Mosques in New York City's Muslim Community', *Journal of Muslim Mental Health*, (2008) 3:2, 155-176.
12 Ibid.
13 For a discussion on the meaning of extrinsic and intrinsic religion and the exoteric (external) versus the esoteric (experiential) expressions of religion, see Charles Topper, *Spirituality in Pastoral Counseling and the Community Helping Professionals* (New York: Haworth Press, 2003), 9.
14 For a discussion on the traditional roles of imams, see Ahmed Nezar Kobeisy,' Faith-Based Practice: An Introduction', *Journal of Muslim Mental Health*, (2006), 57-63.
15 See Sophie Gilliat-Ray, 'From "Visiting Minister" to "Muslim chaplain": The Growth of Muslim Chaplaincy in Britain, 1970-2007', in Eileen Barker (ed.), *The Centrality of Religion in Social Life: Essays in Honour of James A. Beckford* (Aldershot: Ashgate, 2008), 145-160.
16 See: F. Rahman, *Avicenna's Psychology,* (London: Oxford University Press, 1952), 1, and George N. Atiyeh, *Al-Kindi: The Philosopher of the Arabs* (India: Nice Printing Press, 2006), 88.
17 See Seyyed Hossein Nasr, *A History of Islamic Philosophy*, in Seyyed Hossein Nasr and Oliver Leaman (Eds.), *History of Islamic Philosophy*, 21.
18 Ibid, 22.

19 See Quran, 3:153, 35:34, 28:8, 36:76 and 10:65.

20 See: Rachel L. Seddon, Edgard Jones and Neil Greenberg, 'The Role of Chaplains in Maintaining the Psychological Health of Military Personnel: An Historical and Contemporary Perspective' in *Military Medicine*, 176, 12:1357 (2011).

21 For more information on Muslim chaplaincy see Sophie Gilliat-Ray Mansur Ali and Stephen Pattison, *Understanding Muslim Chaplaincy*, (England: Ashgate, 2013).

22 See: James Woodward and Stephen Pattison, *The Blackwell Reader in Pastoral and Practical Theology*, (USA: Blackwell, 2000), 5.

23 Ibid, 10-11.

24 Colin Turner, *The Qur'an Revealed: A Critical Analysis of Said Nursi's Epistles of Light* (Berlin: Gerlach Press, 2013), 4.

25 For example, see Nursi, *The Letters*, trans. Şukran Vahide (Istanbul: Sözler Neşriyat, 1994), 44, where he refers to Jalāl-al-Dīn Rūmī, Sufi poet of the thirteenth century, as one of his "masters."

26 For a discussion on Nursi's concepts of *ḥarfī* and *ismī*, see Chapter Six.

27 See, 'Abd al-Ḥusayn Zarrinkūb, *Sirr-i Nay: A Critical Analysis and Commentary of Masnavi* (Tehran: Eṭṭelā'āt, 1388), V1, 340-43.

28 Rumi, Mathnawī, IV 97-100 translated by William C. Chittick, in William C. Chittick, *The Sufi Path of Love,* 236-245.

29 Nasrin Rouzati, *Trial and Tribulation in the Quran: A Mystical Theodicy* (Berlin: Gerlach Press, 2015).

30 Abū Ḥāmid al-Ghazālī, *Mīzān al-ʿamal*, trans. by Akbar Kasmāī (Tehran: Soroosh, 1974), 151-153.

31 Ibid.

32 For a discussion on Ghazālī's 'best of all possible worlds' see Eric Linn Ormsby, *Theodicy in Islamic Thought: Dispute over Al-Ghazali's "Best of All Possible Worlds* (Princeton, N.J.: Princeton Legacy Library, 1984).

33 Abū Ḥāmid al-Ghazālī, *Kitāb al-tawḥīd wa al-tawakkul*, trans. as *Faith in Divine Unity and Trust in Divine Providence* by David Burrell (Louisville, KY: Fons Vitae, 2001), 46.

34 Nursi believed that the *Risale* offers a shorter and safer way to belief by eliminating the need to follow a *murshid* (spiritual guide), blind emulation of whom runs the risk of divergence from Quranic principles. See Turner, *The Qur'an Revealed*, 349.

35 Toshihiko Izutsu (1914-1993) was a professor at Keio University in Japan and author of many books on Islam and other religions.

36 On the difference between the exoteric and esoteric in the Quran, see Mahmoud Ayoub, *The Quran and Its Interpreters*, 1 (Albany, NY: State University of New York Press, 1984), 21-40.

37 Ghada Jayyusi-Lehn, 'The Epistle of Ya'qu'b ībn Isha'q al-Kīndī: On the Device for Dispelling Sorrows', *British Journal of Middle Eastern Studies*, 29, 2 (2002), 121-135.

38 Ibid., 236-245.

39 Chittick, *The Sufi Path of Love,* 237-238.

40 By the term 'no owner' here, Nursi means a hopeless feeling of not belonging to anyone. For further discussion on Nursi's description of 'ownerlessness', see Chapter Six.

41 Nursi, *The Words*, 424.

Chapter 2

1 Nursi, *The Letters*, 41.

2 Nursi's major works will be discussed briefly in Chapter Five.

3 These constitute of all the verses which point to how *ḥuzn* can be obviated. These verses have been grouped together for separate discussion and semantic analysis. The rest of the verses which are

not linked directly to the obviation of *ḥuzn* have been used for a thematic analysis of the concept. For a further explanation, see Chapter One.

4 http://corpus.quran.com/translation

5 Murtaḍā Mutahharī, Understanding the Uniqueness of the Quran, translated from the Persian by Mahliqa Qara'i, *Al-Tawḥīd*, 1 (*Muharram – Rajab* 1404 AH), http://www.alseraj.net/maktaba/kotob/english/women/Womenin/al-tawhid/default.htm [accessed 29 October 2013].

6 For example, see verses 2:62 and 5:51. Also, for a greater elaboration on this subject, see Muttaharī, *Understanding the Uniqueness of the Qur'an*. See also 'Alī al-Awsī, *Al-Ṭabāṭabā'ī wa manhajuhu fītafsīrihi al-Mīzān*, (Tehran: Mu'āwiniyyat al-Riyasa lil 'Alaqat al-Dawliyyah, 1985), 125.

7 Amina Wadud, 'Towards a Quranic Hermeneutics of Social Justice: Race, Class and Gender', *The Journal of Law and Religion* 12, 1 (1995-1996), 37-50.

8 Quran, 46:13.

9 Quran, 29:64.

10 There are many references in the Quran which invite the reader to look at creation for proof of the unity of God; hence the creation itself is a source of guidance. But creation by itself is not enough; the book of guidance, namely the Quran, is also needed to interpret the created realm. Furthermore, the prerequisite of obtaining guidance is to listen to 'the guide', namely Muhammad, who was entrusted with the mission to guide humankind "from every kind of darkness into light…." See Quran: 14:1, 2:2, 31:10-11.

11 Or examples of verses in the Quran which show the necessary correlation between belief (*īmān*) and submission (*islām*), please refer to verses 3:52, 43:69, 5:111 and 3:84.

12 Quran, 29:64.

13 Quran, 2:112.

14 Quran, 2:62.

15 Quran, 10:62.

16 Quran, 7:44-49.

17 Quran, 43:68.

18 Edward William Lane, *An Arabic English Lexicon*, Part 6 (Beirut: Libraire du Liban, 1968), 1935.

19 Quran, 3:169-170.

20 Quran, 2:262 and 2:274.

21 Quran, 8:29.

22 Quran, 7:35.

23 Quran, 6:48.

24 Quran, 95:5.

25 Quran, 95:4.

26 Quran, 51:56.

27 Quran, 2:153.

28 Quran, 2:155.

29 For more information about the Quraysh and the Battle of Badr and Uhud, see Colin Turner, *Islam the Basics*, 2nd ed. (Oxon: Routledge 2011), 20-22.

30 Quran, 3:153.

31 Quran, 9:92.

32 For more information on Satan's role, see Quran, 15:36-42, 7:16-18 and 14:22.

33 Quran, 58:10.

34 Quran, 35:34.

35 Quran, 28:8.

36 Quran, 33:51.

37 See Quran, 3:176.

38 Quran, 36:76.

39 Quran, 10:65.

40 Quran, 3:176.

41 'Abdul Mannān 'Omar, *Dictionary of the Holy Quran*, 3rd ed. (United States & Germany: Noor Foundation 2005), 489.
42 Abdulkader Tayob, 'An analytical survey of al-Tabari's exegesis of the cultural symbolic contstruct of *fitna*', in *Approaches to the Qur'an*, ed. by G. R. Hawting and Abdul-Kader A Shareef (NY and London: Routledge, 2013),158-59.
43 Quran: 5:44.
44 Quran, 6:34.
45 Quran, 6:35.
46 Quran, 6:33.
47 The noun *ḍayq* means 'tightness', from the verb *ḍāqa* (to become narrow, restricted, troubled). See 'Omar, *Dictionary of the Holy Quran*, 336.
48 Quran, 16:127.
49 *yaḍīqū*' is the imperfect third person masculine singular from the verba ḍāqa, meaning to 'become narrow, straightened, troubled, distressed'.
50 'Omar, *Dictionary of the Holy Quran*, 336.
51 Quran, 15:97, 15:92 and 15:95.
52 Turner, *Islam the Basics*, 22.
53 Quran, 652, footnotes 2009-10.
54 Quran, 15:88.
55 Quran, 29:33.
56 Quran, 3:54.
57 Quran, 27:70.
58 Quran, 9:40.
59 Quran, 19:24.
60 Quran, 30:39.
61 Quran, 28:7.
62 Quran, 41:30.
63 Quran, 31:23.
64 Quran, 103:1-3.
65 Quran, 4:136.
66 Quran, 46:13.
67 See Quran, Chapter 12.
68 Quran, 12:13.
69 Quran, 12:84.
70 Quran, 12:86.
71 Quran, 37:99-110.
72 Quran, 28:13.
73 Quran, 20:40.
74 Toshihiko Izutsu, *Ethico Religious Concepts in the Quran* (Montreal: McGill-Queen's University Press, 2007), 3.
75 Ibid.
76 Ibid., 4.
77 Ibid., 9.
78 Ibid., 8.
79 Toshihiko Izutsu, *God and Man in the Koran: Studies of the Qur'anic Weltanschauung* (Tokyo: Keio Institute of Cultural and Linguistic Studies, 1964), 11.
80 Izutsu, *Ethico Relgious Concepts in the Quran*, 25.
81 Ibid., 14.
82 Stephen Ullmann, *Semantics: An Introduction to the Science of Meaning* (NY: Barnes & Noble, 1962), 7. See also Ferdinand de Saussure, *Course in General Linguistics* (NY: Philosophical Library, 1959), and Izutsu, *Ethico-religious concepts in the Qur'ān*, 7.

83 Izutsu, *God and Man in the Koran*, 40-42.
84 Ibid., 45.
85 Izutsu, *God and Man in the Koran*, 20.
86 Ibid., 25.
87 Izutsu, *Ethico-Religious Concepts in the Quran*, 20-21.
88 For more on the five values/rulings in Islam, see Kemal Faruki, "Al-Aḥkām al-Khamsah: The Five Values", *Islamic Studies*, 5(1), March 1966, 43-98.
89 Ibid.
90 Ibid., 22.
91 William Montgomery Watt, 'Review of God and Man in the Koran and the Concept of Belief in Islamic Theology', *Journal of Semitic Studies*, 12, 1 (Spring 1967), 155-57.
92 Fazlur Rahman, 'Review of Izutsu's Book: God and Man in the Koran', *Islamic Studies* (June 1966) 5, 2, 221-224.
93 Norman Calder, 'Tafsir from Tabari to Ibn Kathir', in *Approaches to the Quran*, ed. by G.R. Hawting and Abdul-Kader A. Shareef (London: Routledge, 1993), 105.
94 Fazlur Rahman, 'Review of Izutsu's Book', 221-24.
95 Izutsu, *God and Man in the Koran*, 25-26.
96 Izutusu, *Ethico Relgious concepts in the Quran*, 26.
97 Ibid., 14.
98 Ibid., 37.
99 Ibid., 37-41.
100 Colin Turner, *Islam: The Basics*, 51.
101 Neal Robinson, *Discovering the Quran, A Contemporary Approach to a Veiled Text* (London: SCM Press, 2003), 62.
102 Jane Dammen McAuliffe, *The Cambridge Companion to the Quran* (NY: Cambridge University Press, 2006), 32-33.
103 Turner, *Islam: The Basics*, 49-50.
104 See Neal Robinson, *Discovering the Quran.*
105 'Omar, *Dictionary of the Holy Quran*, 296.
106 Quran, 16:127.
107 Quran, 11:77.
108 Quran, 29:33.
109 Quran, 20:124.
110 Quran, 3:153.
111 Quran, 2:155-156.
112 Quran, 3:154.
113 Quran, 7:150.
114 Lane, *An Arabic-English Lexicon*, 158.
115 Quran, 18:6.
116 Quran, 26:3.
117 See also translations of the Quran for this verse by Pickthall, Shakir, Muhammad Sarwar and Mohsin Khan at: http://corpus.quran.com/translation.
118 Quran, 18:6.
119 Quran, 26:3.
120 'Omar, *Dictionary of the Holy Quran*, 487.
121 Quran, 12:84, 16:58, 43:17, 3:134, 40:18, 68:48.
122 Quran, 12:85.
123 http://corpus.quran.com/qurandictionary.jsp?q=xwf
124 http://corpus.quran.com/qurandictionary.jsp?q=rhb#.
125 'Omar, *Dictionary of the Holy Quran*, 618.

126 See various translations of the Quran, on-line version at: http://corpus.quran.com/translation.jsp?chapter=7&verse=35.
127 Quran, 7:35.
128 Quran, 2:21.
129 Quran, 2:177.
130 See verses: 23:32 and 5:8.
131 See Quran: 2:194; 2:112; 5:2; and 58:9.
132 Quran, 33:39. See also verses: 9:13, 9:18, 20:44, 21:49, 24:52, 31:33 and 33:37.
133 See Quran, 2:38.
134 Quran, 2:3; 2:4; and 2:5.
135 Quran, 3:200.
136 Quran, 2:120.
137 Quran, 2:272.
138 Quran: 2:272.
139 Quran, 2:38.
140 Quran, 2:98 and 2:99.
141 Quran, 2:272.
142 Ibid.
143 Quran, 2:2-5.
144 Quran, 2:272.
145 Quran, 2:98 and 2:99.
146 Quran, 3:200.
147 Quran, 3:139.
148 Quran, 2:25 and 2:26 and 3:200 and 6:154.
149 Quran, 2:26.
150 Quran, 5:44.
151 Quran, 5:45.
152 Quran, 5:47.
153 Quran, 2:26.
154 Quran, 33:43 and 103-1-3.
155 Izutsu, *God and Man in the Koran*, 22.
156 Quran, 14:7.
157 Quran, 27:40.
158 Quran, 31:12.
159 Quran, 39:7.
160 Izutsu, *God and Man in the Koran*, 22.
161 See Chapter Two, Part Two.
162 Quran, 39:66.
163 Quran, 4:147.
164 Quran, 14:5.
165 'Omar, *Dictionary of the Holy Quran*, 420.
166 See Quran: 3:120, 3:188, 6:44, 9:81 and 13:26.
167 Quran, 10:22.
168 Quran, 10:23.
169 See Chapter Two, Part Two.
170 'Omar, *Dictionary of the Holy Quran*, 258.
171 See Chapter Two, Part Two.
172 'Omar, *Dictionary of the Holy Quran*, 255.
173 Although there is a relationship between derived forms of Arabic verbal roots, in certain cases derived forms may have totally different meanings. See Ziadeh, Farhat J and Winder R. Bayly, *An Introduction to Modern Arabic* (New York: Dover Publications, 2003), 21.

174 See Quran, 35:8.
175 See Table 2 in Chapter Two.

Chapter 3

1 Mahmoud Ayoub, *The Quran and its interpreters*, 2 vols. (State University of New York Press, Albany 1984), I, 22.
2 See Quran, 2:185.
3 See Quran, 3:7.
4 Ayoub, *The Quran and its interpreters*, 18.
5 For further discussion on *muḥkam* and *mutashābih* verses see Abū Ja'far Muḥammad ibn Jarīr al-Ṭabarī, *Jāmī al-bayān fī tafsīr al-Qur'ān* (Beirut: Dār al-Ma'rifa, 1986), 3:115-6; al-Ḥusayn ibn Mas'ūd al-Farrā al-Baghawī, *Ma'alīm al-tanzīl*, ed. by Khālīd 'Abd al-Raḥmān al'Akk and Marwān Suwār (Beirut: Dār al-Ma'rīfa, 1986), 1:279; Muḥammad ibn al-Ḥasan al-Ṭūsī,*al-Tibyān fī tafsīr al-Qur'ān*, ed. by Aḥmad Shawqī al-Amīn and Aḥmad Ḥabīb Qasīr (Najaf: Maktabat al-Amīn, 1957), 2:395.
6 Ayoub, *The Quran and its Interpreters,* 20.
7 McAuliffe, *The Cambridge Companion to the Quran,* 196-197.
8 Sahl b. 'Abd Allāh al-Tustarī, *Tafsīr al-Tustarī, Great Commentaries on the Holy Quran,* trans. by Annabel Keeler and Ali Keeler (Jordan: Royal Aal al-Bayt Institute for Islamic Thought, 2011).
9 See Quran, 25:33.
10 'Omar, *Dictionary of the Holy Quran*, 427.
11 For further information on the early developments of *tafsīr* (exegesis) see Abdullah Saeed, *Interpreting the Quran, towards a contemporary approach* (New York: Routledge, 2006) 1; *The Koran, Critical Concepts in Islamic Studies*, ed. by Colin Turner, 4 vols. (New York: Routledge, 2004), IV.
12 Abū Ja'far Muhammad b. Jarīr Al-Ṭabarī, *The Commentary on the Quran*, abridged English trans. by John Cooper (Oxford University Press, 1989) xiii.
13 For more discussion on textualist and contextualist approach see Abdullah Saeed, *Interpreting the Quran.*
14 Quoted in Ayoub, *Quran and its interpreters*, 4.
15 Ibid., 4.
16 Ibid.
17 See Norman Calder,'Tafsīr from Ṭabarī to Ibn Kathīr: Problems in the Description of a Genre, Illustrated with Reference to the Story of Abraham', in G.R. Hawting and Abdul-Kader, A. Shareef eds, *Approaches to the Quran* (London: Routledge, 1993), 124.
18 Al-Qurayshī al-Dimishqī 'Imad al-Dīn Abī al-Fidā Ismā'īl Ibn Kathīr, *Tafsīr al-Quran al-'aẓīm*, 7 vols. (Beirut: Dār al-Fikr, 1970) on-line English version [accessed 1 May 2015 – 22 July 2015] http://www.quranwebsite.com/tafsir%20ibn%20kathir/tafsir_ibn_kathir.html
19 Sahl b. 'Abd Allāh al-Tustarī, *Tafsīr al-Tustarī, Great Commentaries on the Holy Quran,* tans. by Annabel Keeler and Ali Keeler (Royal Aal al-Bayt Institute for Islamic Thought: Fons Vitae, 2011).
20 Jane Dammen McAuliffe, *The Cambridge Companion to the Quran* (Cambridge University Press: 2006), 194.
21 Gerhard Bowering, *The Mystical Vision of Existence in Classical Islam: The Quranic Hermeneutics of the Sūfī Sahl at-Tustarī* (Berlin: De Gruyter, 2010).
22 See Sayyid Abul A'lā Mawdūdī, *Towards Understanding the Qur'ān: Abridged Version of Tafhīm al-Quran*, trans. by Zafar Ishaq Ansarī (Leicester: Islamic Foundation,1988); Encyclopedia of the Quran, 6 vols, ed. by Jane Dammen McAuliffe, (Boston: Brill, 2002) II.

23 Muḥammad Ḥusayn Ṭabāṭabā'ī, *al-Mizān fī l-tafsīr al-Quran*, 20 vols (Beirut: Mu'assasat al-A'lamī lil-Maṭbū'āt, 1974), trans. by Noor Foundation into Persian [on DVD].
24 See Jane Dammen McAuliffe, *The Cambridge Companion to the Quran*, 39.
25 Quran, 2:38.
26 Ibn Kathīr, *Tafsīr al-Qurān al-'aẓīm*, http://www.qtafsir.com/index.php?option=com_content&task=view&id=395#1
27 Abū Ja'far Muḥammad b. Jarīr al-Ṭabarī, *The Commentary on the Qur'an,* introduction and notes by J. Cooper, ed. by W.F. Madelung and A. Jones (Oxford: Oxford University Press, 1987), 267.
28 Ibid., pp. 262-268.
29 Ṭabāṭabā'ī, *al-Mizān,* English translation accessed on 1 May 2015: http://www.almizan.org/.
30 Ibid.
31 Ibid.
32 Ibn Kathīr, *Tafsīr al-Qurān al-'aẓīm*, http://www.qtafsir.com/index.php?option=com_content&task=view&id=371
33 Quran, 3:85.
34 Ṭabāṭabā'ī, *al-Mizān,* English translation, [accessed 1 May 2015]: http://www.almizan.org/
35 Ayoub, *The Quran and its Interpreters*, 20.
36 For further discussion on the concept of abrogation, see: David S. Powers, 'On the Abrogation of the Bequest Verses' in *Arabica* (BRILL, 1982), 246-295 URL: http://www.jstor.org/stable/4056186, accessed: 14 September 2013; also see *The Quran: An Encyclopedia*, ed. by Oliver Leaman (London: Routledge, 2006), 2.
37 Mawdūdī, *Tafhīm al-Quran,* on line version [accessed 1 May 2015 – 22 July 2015] http://www.englishtafsir.com/Quran/2/index.html#sdfootnote80sym
38 Ṭabarī, *The Commentary on the Qur'an,* 356.
39 Quran, 2:112.
40 Ibn Kathīr, *Tafsīr al-Qurān al-'aẓīm*, http://www.qtafsir.com/index.php?option=com_content&task=view&id=325
41 Tustarī, *Tafsīr al-Tustarī,* 22.
42 Ṭabāṭabā'ī, *al-Mizān,* http://www.almizan.org/
43 Quran, 2:262.
44 Ibn Kathīr, *Tafsīr al-Qurān al-'aẓīm*, http://www.qtafsir.com/index.php?option=com_content&task=view&id=132#1
45 Ṭabāṭabā'ī, *al-Mizān,* http://www.almizan.org/
46 Ibn Kathīr, *Tafsīr al-Qurān al-'aẓīm*, http://www.qtafsir.com/index.php?option=com_content&task=view&id=122#1
47 Quran, 2:277.
48 Ṭabāṭabā'ī, *al-Mizān,* http://www.almizan.org/
49 Ibid.
50 Quran, 3:170.
51 Ibn Kathīr, *Tafsīr al-Qurān al-'aẓīm*, http://www.qtafsir.com/index.php?option=com_content&task=view&id=477&Itemid=46#2
52 Ṭabāṭabā'ī, *al-Mīzān,* http://www.almizan.org/
53 Mawdūdī, *Tafhīm al-Quran,* http://www.englishtafsir.com/Quran/3/index.html#sdfootnote122sym
54 The words in brackets are added by Ṭabāṭabā'ī.
55 Ibn Kathīr, *Tafsīr al-Qurān al-'aẓīm*, http://www.qtafsir.com/index.php?option=com_content&task=view&id=755&Itemid=60#1
56 Ṭabāṭabā'ī, *al-Mizān,* http://www.almizan.org/
57 See Mohsin Khan's on-line translation of the Quran. Other versions of the translation of the Quran such as Yusuf Ali and Sahih International and Arberry do translate this word as 'amend' or 'reforms'. http://corpus.quran.com/translation.jsp?chapter=68&verse=48

58 http://corpus.quran.com/qurandictionary.jsp?q=SlH
59 Ibn Kathīr, *Tafsīr al-Qurān al-'aẓīm*, http://www.qtafsir.com/index.php?option=com_content&task=view&id=1009&Itemid=61#1
60 Quran, 6:48.
61 Ṭabāṭabā'ī, *al-Mizān*.
62 For explanation of how the Quran itself defines the word *taqwā* please refer to Chapter Two.
63 See also verse 39:61.
64 Ibn Kathīr, *Tafsīr al-Qurān al-'aẓīm*, http://www.qtafsir.com/index.php?option=com_content&task=view&id=1252&Itemid=62#1
65 Quran, 10:62.
66 Ibid.
67 Ibn Kathīr, *Tafsīr al-Qurān al-'aẓīm*, http://www.qtafsir.com/index.php?option=com_content&task=view&id=2611&Itemid=65
68 Tustarī, *Tafsīr al-Tustarī*, 89.
69 Meaning: those in conformity with God's Will.
70 Ṭabāṭabā'ī, *al-Mizān*, 10, 130.
71 Ibid.
72 See for example verses: 3:176; 5:44; 6:33; 10:65; 15:88; 16:127 and 29:33.
73 Abū Bakr a-Siddīq ('Abdullāh ibn Abi Quḥāfa) also known as Abū Bakr (d. 13/634) was a companion and the father-in-law of Muhammad. He became the first Muslim caliph after the death of Muhammad. For further information on Abū Bakr and the Muslim Caliphate see Encyclopedia of the Quran, 1, ed. by Jane Dammen McAuliffe.
74 Ibn Kathīr, *Tafsīr al-Qurān al-'aẓīm*, file:///G:/Quran%20Surah%20(Sura)%20Fussilat%20(Ha%20Mim%20Sajda)%20Tafsir%20Ibn%20Kathir.htm#إِنَّ
75 Tustarī, *Tafsīr al-Tustarī*, 89.
76 Mawdūdī, *Tafhīm al-Quran*, http://www.englishtafsir.com/Quran/9/index.html#sdfootnote94anc
77 Ibn Kathīr, *Tafsīr al-Qurān al-'aẓīm*, file:///G:/Quran%20Surah%20(Sura)%20Zukhruf%20Tafsir%20Ibn%20Kathir.htm#هَلْ
78 Tustarī, *Tafsīr al-Tustarī*, 184.
79 Ṭabāṭabā'ī, *al-Mizān*, 18, 183.
80 Ibn Kathīr, *Tafsīr al-Qurān al-'aẓīm*, http://www.alim.org/library/quran/AlQuran-tafsir/TIK/46/10
81 Ṭabāṭabā'ī, *al-Mizān*, 18, 299.
82 For more information about the battle of Uhud see: Colin Turner, *Islam the Basics*, 21; Shabbir Akhtar, *The Quran and the Secular Mind, A Philosophy of Islam* (New York: Routledge, 2008), 20; Fred M. Donner, *The Cambridge Companion to the Quran*, ed. by Jane Dammen McAuliffe (Cambridge: Cambridge University Press, 2006), 28.
83 Ibn Kathīr, *Tafsīr al-Qurān al-'aẓīm*, http://www.quran4u.com/Tafsir%20Ibn%20Kathir/003%20Imran.htm#عِدْ
84 Ṭabāṭabā'ī, *al-Mizān*, 4, 69.
85 Mawdūdī, *Tafhīm al-Quran*, http://www.englishtafsir.com/Quran/3/index.html#sdfootnote112sym
86 Ṭabarī, *Jam 'al-Bayān*, 3, 649.
87 Mawdūdī, *Tafhīm al-Quran*, http://www.englishtafsir.com/Quran/9/index.html#sdfootnote93sym
88 Ṭabāṭabā'ī, *al-Mizān*, 9, 490.
89 Quran, 35:32.
90 Quran, 35:33.
91 Quran, 35:34.
92 For more information on Zamakhsharī and Fakh al-Dīn al-Rāzī see Ayoub, *The Quran and Its Interpreters*.

93 Mawdūdī, *Tafhīm al-Quran,* http://www.englishtafsir.com/Quran/35/index.html#sdfootnote 56sym
94 Tustarī, *Tafsīr al-Tustarī,* 162.
95 Ibn Kathīr, *Tafsīr al-Qurān al-'aẓīm,* http://www.quran4u.com/Tafsir%20Ibn%20Kathir/035%20 Fatir.htm#أوْزر
96 Ibid.
97 Ṭabāṭabā'ī, *al-Mizān,* 17, 67.
98 12:84.
99 12:85.
100 12:86.
101 Tabarī, *Jam 'al-Bayān,* 3, 99.
102 See verse 12:84.
103 See verse 12:85.
104 See verse 12:86.
105 Ibn Kathīr, *Tafsīr al-Qurān al-'aẓīm,* http://www.quran4u.com/Tafsir%20Ibn%20Kathir/012%20 Yusuf.htm#بَلْ
106 See verse 12:86.
107 Tustarī, *Tafsīr al-Tustarī,* 97-98.
108 See Annabel Keeler, *Encyclopaedia Iranica,* XV. Fasc.1, 34-41.
109 See verse 12:84.
110 See verse 12:86.
111 Ṭabāṭabā'ī, *al-Mizān,* 11, 317.
112 28:8.
113 28:10.
114 28:13.
115 Ibn Kathīr, *Tafsīr al-Qurān al-'aẓīm,* http://www.alim.org/library/quran/AlQuran-tafsir/ TIK/28/7
116 Tustarī, *Tafsīr al-Tustarī,* 147.
117 Mawdūdī, *Tafhīm al-Quran,* http://www.englishtafsir.com/Quran/28/index.html#sdfootnote 11sym
118 Ṭabāṭabā'ī, *al-Mizān,* 16, 13.
119 Ibid.
120 Quran: 36:76
121 Ibn Kathīr, *Tafsīr al-Qurān al-'aẓīm,* file:///G:/Quran%20Surah%20(Sura)%20Yasin%20 (Yaseen)%20Tafsir%20Ibn%20Kathir.htm#اتَّخَذُوا
122 Ṭabāṭabā'ī, *al-Mizān,* 17,165.
123 Mawdūdī, *Tafhīm al-Quran,* http://www.englishtafsir.com/Quran/36/index.html#sdfootnote 63sym
124 Ibn Kathīr, *Tafsīr al-Qurān al-'aẓīm,* http://www.quran4u.com/Tafsir%20Ibn%20Kathir/010%20 Yunus.htm#وَلَا
125 Ṭabāṭabā'ī, *al-Mizān,* 10, 137.
126 Quran, 5:41.
127 Ibn Kathīr, *Tafsīr al-Qurān al-'aẓīm,* file:///G:/Quran%20Surah%20(Sura)%20Maida%20 (Ma'ida)%20%20Ch%205%20Tafsir%20Ibn%20Kathirwnload.htm#ول
128 Ṭabāṭabā'ī, *al-Mizān,* 5, 554.
129 Mawdūdī, *Tafhīm al-Quran,* http://www.englishtafsir.com/Quran/5/index.html#sdfootnote 63sym
130 Quran, 6:33.
131 Ibn Kathīr, *Tafsīr al-Qurān al-'aẓīm,* file:///G:/Ibn%20Kathir%20-%20Chapter%20Six.htm#نَع
132 Ṭabāṭabā'ī, *al-Mizān,* 7, 87.

133 Mawdūdī, *Tafhīm al-Quran,* http://www.englishtafsir.com/Quran/6/index.html#sdfootnote21sym
134 Quran, 19:24.
135 Quran, 19:25.
136 Ibn Kathīr, *Tafsīr al-Qurān al-'aẓīm,* file:///G:/Quran,%20Tafsir%20Ibn%20Kathir%20Sura%20Maryam.htm#فَن
137 Ṭabāṭabā'ī, *al-Mizān,* 14, 55.
138 Ṭabarī, *Jam 'al-Bayān,* 4, 980.
139 Mawdūdī, *Tafhīm al-Quran,* http://www.englishtafsir.com/Quran/19/index.html#sdfootnote18sym
140 Quran: 9:40.
141 Ibn Kathīr, *Tafsīr al-Qurān al-'aẓīm,* file:///G:/Quran,%20Surah%20Tawbah,%20Tafsir%20Ibn%20Kathir.htm#تَن
142 Ṭabarī, *Jam 'al-Bayān,* 3, 648.
143 Ṭabāṭabā'ī, *al-Mizān,* 9, 374.
144 Mawdūdī, *Tafhīm al-Quran,* http://www.englishtafsir.com/Quran/9/index.html#sdfootnote43sym
145 See Quran, 2:38.
146 See previous discussion in Chapter Three.
147 See Quran 41:30, 46:13 and 2:112.
148 See Quran, 2:262.
149 Quran, 3:170.
150 See previous discussion in Chapter Three.
151 Ibid.
152 Ibid.
153 See Quran, 7:35.
154 See previous discussion in Chapter Three.
155 Ibid.
156 Ibid.
157 Ibid.
158 Quran, 43:68.
159 See earlier discussion in Chapter Three.
160 Ibid.
161 Ibid.
162 Ibid.
163 First category: "he who wrongs himself", second category: "he who is moderate" and the third category: "He who is foremost in good deeds by permission of Allah". See Quran, 35:32, 35:33 and 35:34.
164 See earlier discussion in Chapter Three, *Fear and sadness given as a test.*
165 See Chapter Two, Conclusion.
166 See Chapter Three, *Fear and sadness due to loss and separation.*
167 See Quran, 12:86.
168 See Chapter Three, *Fear and sadness due to loss and separation.*
169 See Quran, 12:88.
170 See Quran, 12:84-86.
171 See Chapter Three, *Fear and sadness due to loss and separation.*
172 Ibid.
173 Ibid.
174 Ibid.
175 Ibid.
176 See Chapter Three, *The reassurance and comforting of Prophets.*

177 Ibid.
178 Ibid.
179 Ibid.
180 Ibid.
181 See discussion in Chapter Three.
182 See Chapter Three, *The reassurance and comforting of Prophets.*
183 See discussion in Chapter Three.
184 Ibid.
185 I will return to this question in Chapter Six.
186 Ibid.

Chapter 4

1 David, B. Baker, 'History of Psychology' in *The Oxford Handbook of the History of Psychology: Global Perspectives* (London: Oxford University Press, 2012), 443.
2 For more information on metaphysics see Charles Genequand, 'Metaphysics', in Seyyed Hossein Nasr and Oliver Leaman (Eds.), *History of Islamic Philosophy*, Part II (London and New York: Routledge 1996), 783-798.
3 Amber Haque, 'Psychology from Islamic Perspective: Contributions of Early Muslim Scholars and Challenges to Contemporary Muslim Psychologists', *Journal of Religion and Health*, 43, 4 (2004), 359.
4 For more information on the Mu'tazīlites, see Mariam al-Attar, *Islamic Ethics: Divine Command Theory in Arabo-Islamic thought* (New York: Routledge, 2010), 44-62; Majid Fakhry, *A History of Islamic Philosophy* (New York: Columbia University Press, 2004), 45-66.
5 Ibid.
6 Ibid.
7 Quran, 14:4.
8 For further discussion on the Mu'tazīlite concept of justice and free will, see Hammond Kassem & Elias Crim, *The Ideas of Justice in Islamic Philosophy* (1st September 1972), on-line version downloaded 25 August 2014: http://dio.sagepub.com/content/20/79/81.citation.
9 See for example Quran 13:39.
10 For further information on the Jabrīyya school of theology, see B. Lewis, C.H. Pellat and J. Schacht (Eds.), *Encyclopaedia of Islam* (Leiden: Brill, 1991), II, 365.
11 See Peter, S. Groff, 'Al-Kindi and Nietzsche on the stoic Art of Banishing Sorrow', *The Journal of Nietzsche Studies*, Issue 28 (2004), 139-173; and 'Epictetus', *The Stanford Encyclopaedia of Philosophy* (2013), accessed on line: 20 December 2013. URL = <http://plato.stanford.edu/archives/spr2013/entries/epictetus/>.
12 See Daniel H. Frank, 'Ethics' in Seyyed Hossein Nasr and Oliver Leaman (Eds.), *History of Islamic Philosophy* (London: Routledge, 1996), Part II, 959-968.
13 See Mariam al-Attar, *Islamic Ethics*, 2-3.
14 Plato, *The Apology*, trans. Benjamin Jowett, URL: http://www2.hn.psu.edu/faculty/jmanis/plato/apology.pdf (Pennsylvania University 1998-2013). Accessed on 16 December 2013.
15 A.A. Long, *Hellenistic Philosophy*, 107-152.
16 Ibid.
17 Christopher Gill (Ed.), *The Discourses of Epictetus* (London: J.M. Dent, 1995).
18 Epictetus, *Stanford Encyclopaedia of Philosophy*, URL: http://plato.stanford.edu/entries/epictetus/ Accessed: 20 December 2013.
19 Ibid.
20 Ibid.

21 Ibid.
22 For a discussion on God's absolute existence as opposed to contingent beings, see Colin Turner, *The Qur'an Revealed*, 9-54.
23 'Epictetus', *Stanford Encyclopaedia of Philosophy*.
24 Ibid.
25 Peter Adamson, *Al-Kindī* (New York: Oxford University Press, 2007), 150.
26 Al-Kindī was a direct descendant of al-Ash'ath b. Qays, the king of Kinda and a companion of he Prophet. See Adamson, *Al-Kindī*, 4.
27 Ibid.
28 Ibid. 5.
29 Ibid. 7.
30 S. Hamarneh, 'Al-Kindi, a Ninth-century physician, Philosopher and Scholar', *Medical History Journal*, 9, 4, October 1965, 328-342.
31 Ibid., 336.
32 For further discussion on al-Kindī's metaphysics see Adamson, 64-73, and Fakhry, *A History of Islamic Philosophy*, 67-95.
33 George N. Atiyeh, *Al-Kindi: The Philosopher of the Arabs.*
34 Ibid.
35 Fakhry, *A History of Islamic Philosophy,* 69.
36 Thérèse-Anne Druart, 'Al-Kindīs's Ethics', *The Review of Metaphysics, a Philosophical Quarterly*, 47, 2 (Dec., 1993), 329-357.
37 See Atiyeh, *Al-Kindī*, 16.
38 Ibid., 113.
39 See Arthur Still and Windy Dryden, 'Ellis and Epictetus: Dialogue vs. Method in Psychotherapy', *Journal of Rational-Emotive & Cognitive-Behaviour Therapy*, 21, 1 (2003), 43-44.
40 On the discussion between the primacy of religion or philosophy, see Atiyeh, *Al-Kindī,* 16-36.
41 Ibid., 112.
42 For a discussion on the division of the parts of this epistle, see Charles E. Butterworth, 'Al-Kindi and the Beginnings of Islamic Political Philosophy' in Charles E. Butterworth (Ed.), *The Political Aspects of Islamic Philosophy, Essays in Honor of Muhsin S. Mahdi* (Cambridge: Harvard University Press, 1992), 35-40.
43 Ghada Jayyusi-Lehn, 121-135.
44 See Chapter Two, Part Two.
45 See Chapter Three, Conclusion.
46 Ghada Jayyusi-Lehn, 122.
47 Ibid.
48 Ibid. Al-Kindī is using the general term for sadness here, i.e. *shaqī* rather than the word *ḥuzn*. The Quranic use of the word *shaqī* refers to 'turning away from God and His guidance' (see verses 11:105 and 20:2). Al-Attas also opines that this word refers to 'those who have lost their souls in this world by being overwhelmed by worldly pleasures leading them astray and making them fall into error'. See Syed Muhammad Naquib al-Attas, *Prolegomena to the Metaphysics of Islam* (Kuala Lumpur: International Institute of Islamic Thought & Civilisation, 1995), 102-103.
49 Note that the Arabic word al-Kindī uses for 'meanness of spirit' is *istīghnā*, the Quranic meaning of which is 'considering one-self as self-sufficient or free from need'. See Quran, 64:6; 80:5; 92:8; 96:7 and 2:267.
50 Jayyusi-Lehn, 123.
51 Ibid.
52 *Shāṭir* means 'villain' or 'brigand'. The *shuṭṭār* (pl.) were outlaws from Baghdad and al-Karkh who kidnapped people, including women and boys, and created much havoc and fear among people. See: Jayyusi-Lehn, 123-125.
53 Ibid., 124.

54 Charles Butterworth (born 1938) is a Professor of Political Philosophy, with special interest in Arabic and Islamic Civilization. His publications include translations of treatises and books by Averroes (Ibn Rushd), Al-Farabi and Al-Razi.
55 Butterworth, 'Al-Kindi and the Beginnings of Islamic Political Philosophy', ed. by E.C. Butterworth, 42.
56 Jayyusi-Lehn, 124.
57 See Groff, *The Journal of Nietzsche Studies*, 146.
58 See Chapter Three.
59 For further elaboration of the Quranic concept of self-reform, see William C. Chittick, *The Sufi Path of Knowledge* (Albany: Suny Press, 1989), 21-22.
60 'Omar 'Abdul Mannān, *Dictionary of The Holy Qur'ān* (United States: Noor Foundation, 2005), 197.
61 Jayyusi-Lehn, 124-25.
62 Ibid.
63 Butterworth, *The Political Aspects of Islamic Philosophy*, 42.
64 The trilateral root for these two words is *kh-l-q* meaning to create; *khuluq* meaning moral character or inner qualities, *takhalluq* meaning rectification. Also from the same verbal root are the words *akhlāq* (ethics) and *khalq* (creation). See William Lane dictionary on-line: http://www.tyndalearchive.com/tabs/lane/
65 It is by accepting one's own servitude and God's Mastership that one is potentially able to realise that one does not own anything. For a discussion on 'ownership' see Chapter Six, Nursi on Divine Unity.
66 Jayyusi-Lehn, 126.
67 See Quran, 28:8 and 35:34. Also see Textual Exegesis of the Quran, by Muhammad Baqīr Behbūdī, *The Quran, A New Interpretation,* trans. by Colin Turner (Surrey: Curzon Press, 1997), 37.
68 Ibid.
69 Ibid.
70 Ibid.
71 See Chapter Three.
72 For the Iztusian analysis of the word *ḥuzn*, see Chapter Two.
73 See Chapter Three.
74 For example, see Quran, 36:76, 10:65, 3:176, 5:44, 6:33, 16:127, 15:88, 12:13 and 12:84.
75 Jayyusi-Lehn, 126.
76 See Chapter Two.
77 Jayyusi-Lehn, 127.
78 Ibid.
79 Ibid.
80 See: 'Epictetus' in *The Stanford Encyclopaedia of Philosophy*, downloaded 20/12/2013 http://plato.stanford.edu/entries/epictetus, section 4.8.
81 See, for example: Quran, 2:245, 5:11-12, 57:18 and 64:17.
82 Butterworth, *The Political Aspects of Islamic Philosophy*, 46.
83 Ibid.
84 Jayyusi-Lehn, 127.
85 Capital L is used for Lender here, as my analysis of al-Kindī's analogy shows that by Lender, he is referring to God.
86 See Chapter Two, Part Two.
87 Jayyusi-Lehn, 128.
88 See Quran, 2:34, 15:32, 17:61, 18:50 and 38:74.
89 For a discussion on İblīs's downfall, see Anna Maria Martelli, *Islamic Images and Ideas: Essays on Sacred Symbolism* (North Carolina: McFarland & Company Inc., 2014), 70.
90 See Quran, 28:10.

91 See Chapter Two.
92 Jayyusi-Lehn, 130-133.
93 Ibid., 129.
94 Ibid.
95 Ibid., 130.
96 Ibid.
97 See Adamson, *Al-Kindī*, 151.
98 Jayyusi-Lehn, 130-132.
99 Ibid., 132.
100 Butterworth, *The Political Aspects of Islamic Philosophy*, 39.
101 See Chapter Two.
102 Turner, *The Quran Revealed*, 9-10.
103 Butterworth, *The Political Aspects of Islamic Philosophy*, 48-49.
104 There are many verses in the Quran where the words 'truth' (*ḥaqq*) and the 'home of the hereafter' (*al-dār al-ākhira*) occur in juxtaposition with 'the worldly life' (*al-ḥayāt al-dunyā*). For example, see Quran, 31:33, 35:5, 6:32, 12:109, 16:30 and 28:77.
105 Jayyusi-Lehn, 132-133.
106 Ibid.
107 Ibid.
108 Ibid., 133-134.
109 Ibid.
110 For a discussion on the word *shukr* see Chapter Two.
111 Quran, 27:40.
112 Jayyusi-Lehn, 134.
113 Quran, 2:245, 57:11, 57:18 and 73:20.
114 See Chapter Two.
115 Quran, 12:84.
116 Quran, 37:102-110.
117 Quran, 28:13.
118 See Chapter Three.
119 Jayyusi-Lehn, 134.
120 For the different states or levels of the soul (*nafs*), see Quran 12:53, 75:2 and 89:27-28. For the Quranic meaning of *shahwa*, see Quran, 3:14 and 4:27.
121 Malik Badri, *Abū Zayd al-Balkhī's Sustenance of the Soul, The Cognitive Behaviour Therapy of a Ninth Century Physician* (London: International Institute of Islamic Thought, 2013),1-7.
122 Ibid., 4.
123 Ibid., 5.
124 Oliver Leaman, 'Al-Balkhi, Abu Zayd' in *The Biographical Encyclopedia of Islamic Philosophy* (London: Bloomsbury Publishing PLC, 2006), 48-49.
125 Ibid., 30.
126 *Nafs* can be described as the inward spiritual state of the 'self'. For more information on the *nafs* see William C. Chittick, 'The Perfect Man as the Prototype of the Self in the Sufism of Jāmī', *Studia Islamica*, Maisonneuve & Larose, 49 (1979), 135-157.
127 Badri, *Sustenance of the Soul*, 29.
128 Ibid., 13-14.
129 Ibid., 28.
130 Ibid., 30-33.
131 Ghada Jayyusi-Lehn, 122.
132 Badri, *Sustenance of the Soul*, 31.
133 Ibid., 32.
134 Ibid., 33.

135 Ibid., 34.
136 For more information on '*nafs*' see Chittick, *The Perfect Man*, 135-157.
137 Badri, *Sustenance of the Soul*, 34.
138 The Principle of Opposites appeared originally in Plato's Phaedo (Phd. 70E). For a discussion on Plato's and Socrates' ontology of The Principle of Opposites, see Julie Staton, '*The Immortality of the Soul*' in Plato's Phaedo, Philosophy Honors Theses, Paper 2, Trinity University, accessed on line on 9 December 2015: http://digitalcommons.trinity.edu/cgi/viewcontent.cgi?article=1002&context=phil_honors
139 See Abū Ḥāmid Muḥammad al-Ghazāli, *Ihyā' 'ulūm al-dīn*, trans. by Fazl-ul-Karim (Karachi: Darul-Ishaat, 1993), 3,199.
140 Badri, *Sustenance of the Soul*, 36.
141 Ibid., 35.
142 Ibid., 36-39.
143 Ibid., 39-44.
144 Ibid., 44-49.
145 Ibid., 49-54.
146 Ibid., 54-71.
147 Badri, *Sustenance of the Soul*, 50.
148 Ghada Jayyusi-Lehn, 127.
149 See Badri, *Sustenance of the Soul*, 50-51. According to Badri, here Balkhī is classifying depression as reactive mood disorder which has a known reason and endogenous depression which has no known reason and is a result of organic malfunction. While Balkhī recommends psychotherapy for the former, he states that the latter also requires physical treatment.
150 Badri, *Sustenance of the Soul*, 51.
151 Ibid., 52.
152 Ibid.
153 Ibid., 52, footnote 23.
154 Ibid., 4.
155 Ghada Jayyusi-Lehn, 126-127.
156 Badri, *Sustenance of the Soul,* 52.
157 Ibid., 53.
158 Ibid.
159 Ghada Jayyusi-Lehn, 125.
160 Ibid., 32-33.
161 Ibid., 53-54.
162 Ibid., 54.
163 Ghada Jayyusi-Lehn, 127.
164 Ibid.
165 See Badri, *Sustenance of the Soul,* 21.
166 Ibid., 19.
167 See Badri, *Sustenance of the Soul,* 50, where he quotes Chapter 2:38 directly from the Quran.
168 Ibid.
169 See Chapter Four.
170 Lenn E. Goodman, *Avicenna* (Ithaca: Cornell University Press, 2006), 32.
171 For more information on Avicenna's life and works see Soheil M. Afnan, *Avicenna, His Life and Works* (London: George Allen & Unwin Ltd., 1958).
172 Ibid., 109-112.
173 See translation of Avicenna's manuscript on *ḥuzn* in the Appendix.
174 Lenn E. Goodman, 155.
175 See: Stanford Encyclopaedia of Philosophy accessed on line: http://plato.stanford.edu/entries/descartes-epistemology/ on 26 June 2014.

176 Jayyusi-Lehn, 128.
177 For further information on Avicenna's ideas concerning the soul, see F. Rahman, *Avicenna's Psychology*. For further discussion on Avicenna's 'floating man' argument for the existence of the soul, see Lenn E. Goodman, 155.
178 See translation of Avicenna's manuscript on *ḥuzn* in the Appendix.
179 Jayyusi-Lehn, 127.
180 Ibid.
181 Ibid., 133.
182 See Faruk Karaca, *Modern Thanatological Researches and Ibn Sina (Avicenna)*, Conference paper, 1-5, downloaded on 24 July 2014. https://www.inter-disciplinary.net/ptb/mso/dd/dd3/karaca%20paper.pdf
183 Ibid.
184 Jayyusi-Lehn, 135.
185 Karaca, 1-5.
186 Jayyusi-Lehn, 129-130.
187 Karaca, 1-5.
188 For a discussion on al-Kindī's distinction between 'sensible' and 'intelligible objects' see Adamson, *Al-Kindī*, 151-153.
189 Idris Zakaria, 'Ibn Sina on Pleasure and Happiness', *Advances in Natural and Applied Sciences*, 6, 8 (2012), 1285.
190 See the translation of Avicenna's manuscript on *ḥuzn* in Appendix.
191 Jayyusi-Lehn, 123.
192 Ibid., 132.
193 Aḥmad ibn Muḥammad Miskawayh, *The Refinement of Character*, trans. by Constantine K. Zurayk (Beirut: Heidelber Press, 1968).
194 For a discussion on Plato's influence on Miskawayah, see Majid Fakhry, 'The Platonism of Miskawayh and Its Implications for His Ethics', *Studia Islamica*, 42 (1975), 39-57.
195 Miskawayh, *The Refinement of Character*, 157-196.
196 Miskawayh, *The Refinement of Character*, 72.
197 Ibid., 73.
198 Ibid.
199 Ibid., 74.
200 Ibid., 77.
201 Ibid.
202 See Chapter Two.
203 Deal W. Hudson, *Happiness and the Limits of Satisfaction* (Maryland: Rowman & Littlefield, 1996), 138.
204 Although the terms soul (*nafs*) and spirit (*rūḥ*) tend to be used interchangeably, al-Kindī, Avicenna and Miskawayh distinguish it from spirit, as the spirit is not subject to change, whereas the *nafs* can remain at the animal level or reach the highest point of perfection. For further insight into the difference between *nafs* and *rūḥ*, see Golam Dastgir, 'Contextual Analysis of the Concept of Nafs', *Copula*, V. 16 (1999).
205 Miskawayh, *The Refinement of Character*, 157-158.
206 Ibid., 159.
207 Jayyusi-Lehn, 129.
208 Ibid., 128-129.
209 Miskawayh, *The Refinement of Character*, 157.
210 Ibid., 159.
211 Ibid., 161.
212 Ibid., 163.
213 Jayyusi-Lehn, 123. See also the translation of Avicenna's manuscript on *ḥuzn* in the Appendix.

214 Miskawayh, *The Refinement of Character*, 162-163.
215 Ibid., 166.
216 Miskawayh, *The Refinement of Character*, 174.
217 Ibid., 170.
218 Ibid., 166.
219 Ibid., 167.
220 Ibid., 168.
221 Ibid.
222 Ibid., 169.
223 Ibid., 170.
224 For further discussion on the Platonic and Aristotelian influences on Miskawayh's ideas of virtue, see Majid Fakhry, *A History of Islamic Philosophy*, 194-195; and Oliver Leaman, in Seyyed Hossein Nasr and Oliver Leaman, *History of Islamic Philosophy*, 254.
225 For further understanding of Miskawayh's ideas on justice, see Miskawayh, *The Refinement of Character*, Fourth Discourse; and Y. Mohamed, 'Greek Theory in Arabic Ethics: Miskawayh's Theory of Justice', *Phronimon*, 2 (2000), 242.
226 Oliver Leaman in *History of Islamic Philosophy*, 254.
227 Fakhry, *History of Islamic Philosophy*, 191-196.
228 See Chapter Three.
229 See Chapter Two, Part two and Chapter Three, *Thematic categorization of the concept of ḥuzn.*
230 Miskawayh, *The Refinement of Character*, 172.
231 See Chapter Two, *The relational meaning of khawf with ḥuzn.*
232 See discussion in Chapter Three.
233 Miskawayh, 183.
234 Jayyusi-Lehn, 125.
235 Miskawayh, 184.
236 Ibid., 185-192.
237 Ibid., 188.
238 See Chapter Four, *Detachment from worldly possessions.*
239 Jayyusi-Lehn, 133.
240 Miskawayh, 188.
241 Jayyusi-Lehn, 187.
242 Miskawayh, 190.
243 See Chapter Three, *'Avoidance of fear and grief by those who are killed in the cause of God'.*
244 Jayyusi-Lehn, 134.
245 Miskawayh, 191
246 The Sufi saying attributed to the Prophet, 'Die before you die', exemplifies this state of self-annihilation. For a discussion on Sufism and detachment, see Reynold A. Nicholson, *The Mystics of Islam* (London: Arkana, 1989) 36-39 and Chittick, *The Sufi Path of Knowledge*, 232.
247 Leaman, *History of Islamic Philosophy*, 256.
248 Richard Walzer, *Greek into Arabic: Essays on Islamic Philosophy*, edited by S.M. Stern and R. Walzer (Oxford: Bruno Cassirer Ltd., 1962), 232.
249 Miskawayh, 194-196.
250 Ibid., 192.
251 Ibid.
252 Ibid., 193.
253 Jayyusi-Lehn, 123-124.
254 Miskawayh, 193.
255 Ibid., 194.
256 Miskawayh, 194.

257 Al-Ghazālī, *Incoherence of the Philosophers*, trans. by Michael E. Marmura (Utah: Brigham Young University Press, 2000), 7-9.
258 Averroes *(Ibn Rushd)*, *Tahāfut-al-tahāfut* (The Incoherence of the Incoherence), trans. by Simon Van Den Bergh, E-text, conversion by Muhammad Hozien, accessed on line on 29th July 2014, URL: http://www.newbanner.com/Philosophy/IbnRushd/Tahafut_al-Tahafut_en.pdf
259 See Mehdi Mohaghegh, 'Notes on the Spiritual Physic of Al-Rāzī', *Studia Islamica*, 26 (1967), 6.
260 See the introduction to *The Spiritual Physick of Rhazes*, trans. by Arthur J. Arberry (London: Butler & Tanner Ltd., 1950), 10.
261 Ibid., 8-9.
262 Paul E. Walker, 'The Political implications of Al-Razi's Philosophy' in Butterworth, *The Political Aspects of Islamic Philosophy*, 86-87.
263 Ibid., 89-92.
264 Ibid., 91-92.
265 See the introduction to *The Spiritual Physick of Rhazes*, 10-11.
266 Paul E. Walker, 'The Political Implications of Al-Razi's Philosophy', 75.
267 *The Spiritual Physick of Rhazes*, 27.
268 Mehdi Mohaghegh, 'Notes on the Spiritual Physic of Al-Razi', 7.
269 *The Spiritual Physick of Rhazes*, 22.
270 Ibid., 39.
271 Ibid., 40.
272 Ibid., 25.
273 Ibid., 27.
274 Ibid., 28.
275 Jayyusi-Lehn, 128.
276 Ibid., 129.
277 See Paul E. Walker, 'Political Implications of Al-Razi's Philosophy', 77.
278 *The Spiritual Physick of Rhazes*, 68.
279 Ibid., 69.
280 Ibid., 68.
281 Jayyusi-Lehn, 127.
282 *The Spiritual Physick of Rhazes*, 69.
283 Ibid., 70.
284 Jayyusi-Lehn, 128.
285 *The Spiritual Physick of Rhazes*, 70-71.
286 Ibid., 71.
287 *The Spiritual Physick of Rhazes*, 72.
288 Ibid.
289 Jayyusi-Lehn, 135.
290 Paul E. Walker, 'Political Implications of Al-Razi's Philosophy', 81.
291 Jayyusi-Lehn, 126.
292 Paul E. Walker, 'Political Implications of Al-Razi's Philosophy', 79.
293 For example, see Butterworth, *The Political Aspects of Islamic Philosophy*, 39.
294 Ghada Jayyusi-Lehn, 122.
295 *The Spiritual Physick of Rhazes*, 68.
296 Ghada Jayyusi-Lehn, 126.
297 Ibid., 127.
298 Ibid., 124.
299 Chittick, *The Sufi Path of Knowledge*, 21-22.
300 Ghada Jayyusi-Lehn, 130-133.
301 Ibid.
302 Ibid., 125-127.

303 See Chapter Two, *The reassurance and comforting of Prophets.*
304 Jayyusi-Lehn, 126-127.
305 Ibid., 127.
306 See Chapter Two, *Semantic field of ḥuzn* and Chapter Three, *Thematic categorization of the concept of ḥuzn.*
307 *The Spiritual Physick of Rhazes*, 40.
308 See Nicholson, *The Mystics of Islam*, 232.
309 Ibid.
310 See Chapter Two, *The reassurance and comforting of the Prophets and The reassurance and comforting of the faithful.*
311 Jayyusi-Lehn, 135.
312 See Chapter Four, *Detachment from worldly possessions.*
313 See Chapter Four, *The concept of happiness according to Miskawayh.*
314 See Chapter Four, *The manner in which grief may be repelled or lessened.*
315 See Chapter Four, *The concept of happiness according to Miskawayh.*
316 See Chapter Three, *Characteristics demonstrated by those who will not experience ḥuzn and khawf* and discussion in Chapter Four, Conclusion.
317 Ibid.
318 Ibid.
319 Nursi, *The Flashes*, 266-285.

Chapter 5

1 These tensions will be discussed in Chapter Six.
2 Şerif Mardin, *Religion and Social Change in Modern Turkey: The Case of Bediuzzaman Said Nursi* (Albany: State University of New York Press, 1989), 23.
3 For more information on the Ottoman Empire see Daniel Goffman, *The Ottoman Empire and Early Modern Europe : New Approaches to European History* (Cambridge: Cambridge University Press, 2002).
4 Ibid.
5 Şükran Vahide, *The Author of the Risale-i Nur: Bediuzzaman Said Nursi* (Istanbul: Sőzler Neeler N, 2000), 33-37.
6 Ibid., 53.
7 The CUP (Committee of Union and Progress) were a secret organization who opposed Sultan Abdulhamid's regime and were in favour of a constitutional government. For more information on the CUP see Feroz Ahmad, *The Young Turks: The Committee of Union & Progress in Turkish Politics 1908-1914* (Oxford: Clarendon Press, 1973).
8 See Erik J. Zurcher, *Turkey: A Modern History* (London: I.B. Tauris, 1998), 103-104.
9 Şükran Vahide, *Islam in Modern Turkey: An Intellectual Biography of Bediuzzaman Said Nursi* (State University of New York Press: Albany, 2005), 71-72.
10 Colin Turner and Hasan Horkuc, *Said Nursi* (Oxford University Press: Oxford, 2009), 23.
11 For more information on the Naqshbandi Order, of which the Khālidiyya is a branch, see Hamid Algar, 'A Brief History of Naqshbandi Order' in Marc Gaborieau, Alexandre Popovic & Thierry Zarcone eds., *Varia Turcica XVIII – Naqshbandis* (Istanbul: Editions Isis, 1990), 117-46.
12 Vahide, *Islam in Modern Turkey*, 4.
13 Ibid., 5-8.
14 Ibid., 11.
15 Vahide, *Islam in Modern Turkey*, 27-29.

16 Shihāb al-Dīn Yaḥyā ibn Ḥabash ibn Amīrak of Suhraward (d. 1191) is considered to be the founder of the Illuminationist School. Although he followed the Peripatetic philosophy developed by Ibn Sīnā, he had his own fundamental philosophy according to which all creatures are said to emanate from the 'pure and immaterial light' (*nūr-al-anwār*). The Ishrāqiyyūn, unlike other mystical orders, have no *murshid* (spiritual guide) other than the 'Angel of knowledge' and invisible master or interior guide that guides towards self knowledge. For more information on the Illuminationist school, see E. J. Jurji, *Illumination in Islamic Mysticism* (Princeton N.J: University Press, 1938), 14; W.M. Thackston, 'Introduction', in W.M. Thackston (trans.), *The Mystical and Visionary Treatises of Shihabuddin Yahya Suhrawardi* (London: The Octagon Press, 1982), 5; and H. Corbin, *Avicenna and the Visionary Recital,* trans. by W.R. Trask, Bollingen Series LXVI (Princeton N.J: University Press, 1988), 73.
17 Vahide, *Islam in Modern Turkey,* 11.
18 Ibid., 28.
19 Ibid., 29.
20 Hamid Algar, 'Sufism and *Tarikat in the Life and Works of Bediuzzaman Said Nursi', Journal of the History of Sufism,* 3 (2001), 200-04.
21 Said Nursi, *The Letters,* 85.
22 Turner and Horkuc, *Said Nursi,* 17.
23 Vahide, *Islam in Modern Turkey,* 23.
24 Ibid., 46.
25 Ibid., 45.
26 Nursi, *The Reasonings: A Key to Understanding the Qur'an's Eloquence,* trans. by Hūseyin Akarsu (Tughra Books: New Jersey, 2008), 4.
27 Vahide, *Islam in Modern Turkey,* 46.
28 Ibid., 43.
29 Ibid., 43-44.
30 Ibid., 51.
31 Ibid., 36-37.
32 Ibid., 107.
33 Turner and Horkuc, *Said Nursi,* 14.
34 Vahide, *Islam in Modern Turkey,* 21.
35 For a discussion on Nursi's arguments that democracy is in perfect harmony with the spirit of the *shari'a* see Mucahit Bilici, '*Islam and Christian-Muslim Relations, Said Nursi's Moral Philosophy*', published on-line http://www.tandfonline.com/loi/cicm20 on 21 September 2010.
36 Vahide, *The Author of the Rīsale-ī Nur Bediuzzaman Said Nursi,* 99.
37 Turner and Horkuc, *Said Nursi,* 21.
38 Ibid., 22.
39 Ibid.
40 Vahide, *The Author of the Rīsale-ī Nur,* 197.
41 Ibid., 153.
42 Ibid., 84-89.
43 Nursi, *The Damascus Sermon* (Sőzler Publications: Istanbul, 1996) 26-27.
44 Ibid.
45 'Externals of religion' here denotes the periphery rather than the core, or emphasis on rituals with little reference to belief.
46 Vahide, *The Author of the Rīsale-ī Nur,* 162-63.
47 Ibid., 158-59.
48 Vahide, *Islam in Modern Turkey,* 163-164.
49 Ibid., 167.
50 Ibid., 165.
51 Ibid., 166.

52 Vahide, *Islam in Modern Turkey*, 166.
53 Ibid., 177.
54 Ibrahim M. Abu-Rabi, *Islam at the Crossroads: On the Life and Thought of Bediuzzaman Said Nursi* (New York: State University of New York Press, Albany, 2003), 73-74.
55 Nursi, *The Flashes*, 161.
56 See Abu-Rabi, *Islam at the Crossroads,* 78.
57 Vahide, *Islam in Modern Turkey*, 189-192.
58 Gavin D. Brockett, 'Collective Action and the Turkish Revolution: Towards a Framework for the Social History of the Ataturk Era, 1923-38', Middle Eastern Studies, 34, 4, (Oct., 1998), 44-66.
59 Vahide, *Islam in Modern Turkey*, 193.
60 Al-Attas, *Prolegomena to the Metaphysics of Islam,* 81.
61 Nursi's discussion on 'literature of civilization' will be studied in greater detail in Chapter Six.
62 Vahide, *Islam in Modern Turkey*, 185.
63 Ibid., 189.
64 Ibid., 189.
65 Nursi, *The Letters*, 67.
66 Said Nursi, *The Rays* (Sözler Neşriyat: Turkey, 1998), trans. by Şūkran Vahide.
67 Ibid., 123-198.
68 Ibid., 123.
69 Ibid., 153.
70 Ibid., 162-63.
71 Ibid., 97-102.
72 Ibid., 213-289.
73 Nursi, *The Rays*, 222.
74 Vahide, *Islam in Modern Turkey,* 266.
75 Ibid., 44.
76 Ibid., 285-90.
77 Nursi, *The Flashes*, 315.
78 Nursi, *The Flashes*, 317.
79 For a discussion on some of Nursi's sense of exile and alienation, see Chapter Six.
80 Ibid.
81 Abu-Rabi, *Islam at the Crossroads*, 71.
82 Vahide, *Islam in Modern Turkey,* 305.
83 Ibid., 345.
84 Ibid., 334.

Chapter 6

1 See Chapter Two, *Quranic key terms in history.*
2 See Chapter Three, *Avoidance of sadness and fear by those who recognise God as their Lord and remain on the straight path.*
3 See Chapter Two.
4 Ibid.
5 Ibid.
6 Ibid.
7 See Chapter Three.
8 See Chapter Four, Conclusion.
9 Ibid.
10 See Chapter Four.

11 Ibid.
12 See Nursi, *The Words*, 106.
13 See Al-Attas, *Prolegomena to the Metaphysics of Islam*, 121-122.
14 See Chapter Two.
15 Ibid.
16 Al-Attas, 133.
17 Quran 96:1.
18 See Chapter Five.
19 This Nursian concept pair *ma'nā-i ismī* and *ma'nā-i ḥarfī* represent two opposing hermeneutical positions. The former interprets the cosmic narrative as a sign pointing to the Creator of the cosmos, while the latter cuts off that connection by pointing only to its material existence. See Nursi, *The Words*, 757.
20 See Chapter Two.
21 See Chapter Four.
22 See Nursi, *The Words*, 96-97 and 101.
23 See Al-Ghazālī, *The Incoherence of the Philosophers*, trans. M.E. Marmura (Utah: Brigham Young University Press, 2000).
24 For discussion on limitation of reason and the two concept pairs of *mulk* and *malakūt* see Turner, *The Quran Revealed*, 84-94.
25 Nursi, *The Words*, 424.
26 Nursi, *The Words*, 770-771.
27 Ibid., 771.
28 Ibid., 772.
29 Ibid.
30 Ibid., 771.
31 Ibid.
32 Nursi, *The Words*, 248.
33 Ibid., 364.
34 Ibid., 265, 268, 329, 339 and 442.
35 For further discussion on Divine Unity see Syed Muhammad Naquib al-Attas, *Prolegomena to the Metaphysics of Islam*, 12 and Fazlur Rahman, *Major Themes of the Quran* (Chicago & London: The University of Chicago Press, 1980), 1-12.
36 Nursi, *The Letters*, 41.
37 Ibid., 41.
38 Nursi, *The Rays*, 23.
39 Ibid., 614.
40 Ibid., 23.
41 See Chapter Six.
42 Nursi, *The Words*, 466.
43 See Chapters Two and Three.
44 Nursi, *The Words*, 322.
45 Ibid., 158.
46 Ibid.
47 Nursi, *The Flashes*, 652.
48 Darrin, M. McMahon, 'What Does the Ideal of Happiness Mean?', *Social Research*, 77, 2 (2010), 476.
49 Ibid.
50 Ibid., 480.
51 For a more detailed discussion on Rousseau's concept of happiness see Stephen, G. Salkever, *Rousseau and the Concept of Happiness*, Polity, 11, 1 (1978), 32-45.
52 Ibid.

53 Nursi, *The Words*, 247.
54 See Chapter Four, *Precautions against the occurrence of grief.*
55 Nursi, *The Words*, 424.
56 Ibid., 229.
57 See Chapter Four, Section Three.
58 Nursi, *The Letters*, 41.
59 For a discussion on al-Kindī's distinction between 'sensible' and 'intelligible objects' see Adamson, *Al-Kindī*, 151-153.
60 See Chapter Four, *Detachment from worldly possessions.*
61 See Chapter Four, *The concept of happiness according to Miskawayh.*
62 Nursi, *The Words*, 163.
63 See Chapter Four.
64 Nursi, *The Words*, 229.
65 Ibid.
66 Ibid., 510.
67 Ibid., 229.
68 See Quran, 6: 74-79.
69 For more information on Nūr ad-Dīn 'Abd ar-Rahmān Jāmī, famous Persian fifteenth century poet and historian see Hamid Algar, Jāmī and Sufism, *Encyclopaedia Iranica* (2008), XIV, 5, 475-479.
70 See Nursi, *The Words*, 230. (The words in brackets are Nursi's explanation).
71 Nursi, *The Words*, 228.
72 This analogy of 'sons' and 'wealth' with the wish for eternity is also mentioned in the Quran. See 3:14, 9:24 and 26:88
73 Ernest Becker, *The Denial of Death* (New York: Free Press, 1973), 47-66.
74 For a discussion on Becker's 'immortality project' see Becker, *The Denial of Death* and C.Turner, 'Wealth as an Immortality Symbol in the Quran: A Reconsideration of the *māl/amwāl* Verses', *Journal of Quranic Studies*, 8, 58-83.
75 Nursi, *The Rays*, 247.
76 Nursi, *The Rays*, 641.
77 See Chapters Two and Three.
78 Ibid.
79 See Chapter Two, Part Two.
80 Nursi, *The Rays*, 641.
81 Nursi, *The Words*, 158.
82 Nursi, *The Letters*, 351.
83 See Chapter Six, *Denial of death.*
84 Nursi, *The Letters*, 351.
85 Nursi, *The Flashes*, 33.
86 See Turner, *The Quran Revealed*, 470.
87 Nursi, *The Flashes*, 287.
88 Ibid., 286-288.
89 Ibid.
90 Ibid., 287.
91 Nursi, *The Flashes*, 287.
92 Ibid., 287-288.
93 Nursi, *The Flashes*, 292.
94 Ibid.
95 Ibid., 292-293.
96 Ibid.
97 Nursi, *The Words*, 424.

98 Ibid., 229.
99 Nursi, *The Flashes*, 300.
100 Quran, 3:173.
101 Nursi, *The Flashes*, 300.
102 Ibid.
103 Ibid., 301.
104 Nursi, *The Letters*, 42-44.
105 Nursi, *The Flashes*, 306.
106 Nursi, *The Letters,* 507-08.
107 See Kojiro Nakamura, 'Imām Ghazālī's Cosmology Reconsidered with Special Reference to the Concept of "Jabarūt"', *Studia Islamica*, 80 (1994) 32.
108 See Chapter Six, *Permanence versus transience.*
109 See Abū Ḥamīd Muḥammad al-Ghazālī, *The Alchemy of Happiness* (New York: M.E. Sharpe, Inc., 1991) xxx.
110 For a discussion on Sufism see Eric Geoffroy, *Introduction to Sufism: The Inner Path of Islam* (Indiana: World Wisdom, 2010), 4-5; and Colin Turner, *The Quran Revealed*, 338-349.
111 For a discussion on Nursi's evaluation of Susfism see Bilal Kuşpinar, *Nursi's Evaluation of Sufism*. Paper delivered at the Third International Symposium of Bediuzzaman Said Nursi. Paper downloaded on 6 November 2015: http://www.iikv.org/academy/index.php/sympeng/article/view/902/1229.
112 Nursi, *The Words*, 229.
113 See Nursi, *Signs of Miraculousness*, 23-24.
114 See Quran, 2:31-2.
115 Ibid.
116 See Fakhry, *A History of Islamic Philosophy*, 263-64.
117 Nursi, *The Words*, 558.
118 Ibid., 558-59.
119 See Chapter Six, *Permanence versus transience.*
120 Nursi, *The Words*, 559.
121 Nursi, *The Letters*, 536. The *tasbīhat* are the supererogatory invocations offered after each canonical prayer.
122 See Table 2 in Chapter Two.
123 See Chapter Two, Part One.
124 See Chapter Two, Part Two.
125 For a discussion on the Jabrī and Mu'tazīlite view on free will see James Pavlin in Nasr and Leaman, *History of Islamic Philosophy*, 108-109 and 131-35.
126 See Chapter Four, *Al-Kindī on ethics.*
127 Nursi, *The Words*, 481-487.
128 For further discussion on theodicy see John Hick, *Evil and the God of Love* (New York: Palgrave Macmillan, 2007) and Walter, E. Wyman, Jr., 'Rethinking the Christian Doctrine of Sin: Friedrich Schleiermacher and Hick's "Irenaean Type"', *The Journal of Religion*, 74, 2 (1994), 199-217.
129 Ibid.
130 Nursi, *The Words*, 487.
131 Quran, 12:1-2.
132 Nursi, *The Words*, 487.
133 See verses 76:2; 89:15; 11:7; 18:7 5:48 for *balā* as test. Also Chittick, *The Sufi Path of Love: The Spiritual Teachings of Rumi*, 238 for a discussion on Rumi's views on the necessity of *balā* for detachment from worldly life and purification of the heart.
134 See Chapter Two, *Ḥuzn due to separation and loss.*
135 See Chapter Two, *Fear and sadness given as a test.*
136 See Chapter Four.

137 Ibid.
138 See Chapter Six, *Insights into Nursi's theodicy.*
139 Nursi, *The Words*, 478.
140 For a discussion on Rumi's perspective on sorrow and calamities see Şefik Can, Fundamentals of Rumi's thought: A Mevlevi Sufi Perspective (New Jersey, USA: The Light, Inc., 2005), 212-216.
141 Alan V. Horwitz and Jerome C. Wakefield, *The Loss of Sadness, How Psychiatry Transformed Normal Sorrow Into Depressive Disorder* (New York: Oxford University Press, 2007), 3.
142 Ibid., 4-5.
143 For a definition of reactive and endogenous depression see Jamsari Alias and others, 'Managing Bipolar Disorder and Manic-Depressive Psychosis (MDP) According to Western and Islamic Approaches', *Research Journal of Applied Sciences*, 7, 7 (2012), 329-333.
144 Horwitz and Wakefield, *The Loss of Sadness*, 6-18.
145 See Badri, *Sustenance of the Soul*, 50-51.
146 Horwitz and Wakefield, *The Loss of Sadness*, 20-25.
147 Ibid., 51-52.
148 For a discussion on the social control function of psychotherapists and social workers see Stephen Joseph, Agents of Control, *The British Psychological Society*, July 2007, V20, 429-431.
149 See H.G. Koenig, *Faith and Mental Health Religious Resources for Healing* (Philadelphia and London: Templeton Foundation Press, 2005), 43-81.
150 J.J. Shuman and K.G. Meador, *Heal Thyself, Spirituality, Medicine, and the Distortion of Christianity* (New York: Oxford University Press, 2003), 34.
151 Ibid., 33, 36.
152 Nursi, *The Words*, 424.
153 Shuman and Meador, *Heal Thyself*, 12-14.
154 See Chapter Six, *Insights into Nursi's theodicy.*
155 Nursi, *The Words*, 478.
156 Nursi, *The Rays*, 641.
157 See Wyman, *Rethinking the Christian Doctrine of Sin*, 199-217.
158 Ibid.
159 John Hick was a twentieth century British philosopher of religion and theology. For more information on his life and works, see Encyclopedia of Philosophy http://www.rep.utm.edu/hick/ accessed 23 April 2015.
160 See 'Dr. Hick and the Problem of Evil', 413, http://jts.oxfordjournals.org/ downloaded 20 April 2015.
161 See Wyman, *Rethinking the Christian Doctrine of Sin*, 412.
162 See Ghada Jayyusi-Lehn, 127.
163 See Table 2, in Chapter Two.
164 See Table 3, in Chapter Six.
165 Nursi, *The Flashes*, 652.
166 Table 3, in Chapter Six.
167 Edward F. Edinger (1922-1998) was a supervising psychiatrist at Rockland State hospital in New York and later became a founding member of the C.G. Jung Foundation.
168 See Chapter Six, *Does Nursi's 'negative ḥuzn' have a positive role to play?*
169 For more information on Edinger's discussion on the relation of the ego with the self, see Edward F. Edinger, *Ego and Archetype, Individuation and the Religious Function of the Psyche* (Boston: Shamhala, 1992), 48-50.
170 Ibid., 50.
171 See Table 3, in Chapter Six.
172 See for example Quran: 36:76 and 5:41.
173 See Quran, 7:11-18.
174 See Quran, 7: 18-25.

175 See Quran, 7:12.
176 The Nursian concept of *ana* (the human 'I') has been discussed in Chapter Six.
177 See Ahmad Hasan, The Concept of Infallibility in Islam, *Islamic Studies*, 11, 1 (1972), 1-11.
178 For a detailed discussion on the Infallibility of the Prophets see: Mohammad Saeedimehr, The Infallibility of Prophets from the Viewpoint of Fakhr al-Din al-Razi, *Philosophical Investigations*, 6, 17,125-143.
179 The literal meaning of Hashwiyah is 'stuffers'. It is a derisive term used for radical Sunni traditionalists who preferred to dismiss reason and take a literal understanding of the Quran which resulted in an anthropomorphic interpretation. For more information on the roots of Hashwiyah see Karim Douglas Crow, *Roots of Sunni Traditionalism, Fear of Reason and the Hashwiyah* (Singapore: S. Rajaratnam School of International Studies, 2008), 1-55.
180 For more information on al-Jubbā'i see Encyclopedia of Islam 1999 (Leiden: Brill), Islamic Philosophy online: www.muslimphilosophy.com/ei2/Jubai.htm).
181 For further information on Al-Nazzām see Mir Valiuddin, Mu'tazilīsm, in M.M. Sharif, A History of Muslim Philosophy, Book Three, Chapter Ten, *Islamic Philosophy on-line* (2004), accessed 9 May 2015 http://www.muslimphilosophy.com/hmp/index.html
182 See Ahmad Hasan, *The Concept of Infallibility in Islam*, 5.
183 See Chapter Three, *Comforting, consoling and reassuring the prophets and the faithful in times of ḥuzn.*
184 Quran, 18:6.
185 See Turner, *Islam the Basics*, 20-21.
186 Quran, 15:88.
187 Quran, 5:44.
188 Quran, 12:85.
189 See discussion in Conclusion of Chapter Two.
190 Quran, 12:101.
191 Nursi, *The Letters*, 335.
192 See Chapter Four.
193 Nursi, *The Letters*, 41.
194 See Table 2 in Chapter Two and Table 3 in Chapter Six.
195 See Chapter Six, *ḥuzn due to the 'literature of civilization'.*
196 See Chapter Six, *Nursi's definition of happiness.*
197 See Chapter Six, *ḥuzn due to the 'literature of civilization'.*
198 Ibid.
199 See Chapter Six, *Denial of Death.*
200 See Nursi, *The Rays*, 247.
201 Nursi, *The Words*, 757.
202 For discussion on limitation of reason and the two concept pairs of *mulk* and *malakūt* see Turner, *The Quran Revealed*, 84-94.
203 Edinger, *Ego and Archetype*, 48-50.
204 Nursi, *The Letters,* 536.

Conclusion

1 See Quran, 2:272.
2 See Table 2 in Chapter Two.
3 See Quran, 35:32, 35:33 and 35:34.
4 Ghada Jayyusi-Lehn, 122.
5 Ibid., 127.
6 See Chapter Two.

7 Ghada Jayyusi-Lehn, 126-127.
8 Ibid., 127.
9 See Chapter Six, *The Nursian concept of sadness.*
10 See Chapter One.
11 See Quran, 12:101 and discussion on *The sadness of the Prophets* in Chapter Six.
12 It should be noted that 'positive' and 'negative' *ḥuzn* are my terms and not Nursi's, which are used for easy reference to Nursi's categories.
13 See Chapter Six, *Permanence versus transience.*
14 See Chapter Six, *Denial of death.*
15 See Chapter Six, *The 'trust'.*
16 See Chapter Six, *Permanence versus transience.*
17 For a discussion on Nursi's concept of 'I-ness' see Chapter Six, *The 'trust'.*
18 Ibid.
19 See Edinger, *Ego and Archetype,* 50.
20 See Chapter Six, *Insights into Nursi's theodicy.*
21 See Al-Ghazālī, *Kitāb Al-Tawhīd Wa' L-Tawakkul,* 46
22 Human beings as God's vicegerents on earth have the potential to reach a higher rank in belief than both jinn and angels. See Quran, 95:4.
23 See Table 3 in Chapter Six.

Bibliography

Abu-Rabi, Ibrahim, M., *Islam at the Crossroads: On the Life and Thought of Bediuzzaman Said Nursi* (New York: State University of New York Press, 2003), 73-74

Abu-Ras, Wahiba, Ali Gheith, and Francine Cournos, 'The Imam's Role in Mental Health Promotion: A Study at 22 Mosques in New York City's Muslim Community', *Journal of Muslim Mental Health* (2008), 155-176

Adamson, Peter, *Al-Kīndī* (New York: Oxford University Press, 2007), 150

Ahmad, Feroz, *The Young Turks, The Committee of Union & Progress in Turkish Politics 1908-1914* (Oxford: Clarendon Press, 1973)

Akhtar, Shabbir, *The Quran and the Secular Mind: A Philosophy of Islam* (New York: Routledge, 2008), 20

Al-Attar, Mariam, *Islamic Ethics: Divine Command Theory in Arabo-Islamic Thought* (New York: Routledge, 2010), 44-62

Al-Attas, Syed Muhammad Naquib, *Prolegomena to the Metaphysics of Islam* (Kuala Lumpur: International Institute of Islamic Thought & Civilisation, 1955), 102-103

Al-Baghawī, Al-Ḥusayn ībn Mas'ūd al-Farrā, '*ma'alīm al-tanzīl*', ed. by Khālīd 'Abd al-Raḥmān al'Akk and Marwān Suwār (Beirut: Dār al-Ma'rīfa, 1986)

Algar, Hamid, 'A Brief History of Naqshbandi Order' in Marc Gaborieau, Alexandre Popovic and Thierry Zarcone eds. *Varia Turcica XVIII – Naqshbandis* (Istanbul: Editions Isis, 1990),117-46

Algar, Hamid, 'Sufism and *Tarikat* in the Life and Works of Bediuzzaman Said Nursi', *Journal of the History of Sufism*, 3 (2001), 200-04

Algar, Hamid, Jāmī and Sufism, *Encyclopaedia Iranica* (2008), XIV, 5, 475-479

Al-Ghazzali, Abu Hamid, *Mīzān al-'Amāl*, trans. by Akbar Kasmāī (Tehran: Soroosh, 1974), 151-153

Al-Ghazzali, Abu Hamid, 'Faith in Divine Unity and Trust in Divine Providen *Kitāb Al-Tawhīd Wa' L-Tawakkul*', trans. by David Burrell (Louisville, KY: Fons Vitae, 2001), 46

Al-Ghazzali, Abu Hamid, *Incoherence of the Philosophers*, trans. by Michael E. Marmura (Utah: Brigham Young University Press, 2000)

Al-Ghazzali, Abu Hamid, *Ihyā' 'ulūm al-Dīn*, trans. by Fazl-ul-Karim (Darul-Ishaat: Karachi, 1993), 3, 199

Al-Ghazzali, Abu Hamid, *The Alchemy of Happiness*, trans. by Claud Field (New York: M.E. Sharpe, 1991)

Alias Jamsari and others, 'Managing Bipolar Disorder and Manic-Depressive Psychosis (MDP) According to Western and Islamic approaches', *Research Journal of Applied Sciences*, 7, 7 (2012), 329-333

Al-Rāzī, Abū Bakr Muhammad ibn Zakarāyā, *The Spiritual Physick of Rhazes,* trans. by Arthur J. Arberry (London: Butler and Tanner Ltd., 1950), 10

Al-Tabarī, Abū Ja'far Muhammad B. Jarīr, *'A Commentary on the Quran: An abridged translation of Jāmi' al-bayān 'an ta'wīl āy al-Qur'ān,* with an introduction and notes by John Cooper (Oxford: Oxford University Press, 1987)

Al-Tūsī, Muḥammad ibn al-Ḥassan, *al-Tībyān fī tafsīr al-Qurān,* ed. Aḥmad Shawqī al-Amīn and Aḥmad Ḥabīb Qaṣīr (Najaf: Maktabat al-Amīn, 1957)

Al-Tustarī, Sahl b. 'Abd Allāh, *Tafsīr al-Tustarī, Great Commentaries on the Holy Quran,* Trans. by Annabel Keeler and Ali Keeler (Jordan: Royal Aal al-Bayt Institute for Islamic Thought, 2011)

Atiyeh, N. George, *Al-Kindī: The Philosopher of the Arabs* (India: Nice Printing Press, 2006)

Ayoub, Mahmoud, *The Quran and its Interpreters,* 2 vols (Albany: State University of New York Press, 1984), 1, 21-40.

Badri, Malik, *Abū Zayd al-Balkhī's Sustenance of the Soul, The Cognitive Behaviour Therapy of a Ninth Century Physician* (London: International Institute of Islamic Thought, 2013),1-7

Baker, B. David ed.*The Oxford Handbook of the History of Psychology: Global Perspectives* (London: Oxford University Press, 2012), 443

Becker, Ernest, *The Denial of Death* (New York: Free Press, 1973) 47-66

Behbūdi, Muhammad Baqīr, *The Quran, A New Interpretation,* trans. by Colin Turner (Surrey: Curzon Press, 1997) 37

Bilici, Mucahit, *Islam and Christian-Muslim Relations, Said Nursi's Moral Philosophy*, published on-line http://www.tandfonline.com/loi/cicm20 on 21 September 2010

Bowering, Gerhard, *The mystical vision of existence in classical Islam: The Quranic hermeneutics of the Sūfī Sahl at-Tustarī* (Berlin: De Gruyter, 2010)

Brockett, D. Gavin, 'Collective Action and the Turkish Revolution: Towards a Framework for the for the Social History of the Ataturk Era, 1923-38', *Middle Eastern Studies*, 34, 4, (1998) 44-66

Butterworth, E. Charles, *Al-Kindi and the Beginnings of Islamic Political Philosophy,* in 'The Political Aspects of Islamic Philosophy, Essays in Honor of Muhsin S. Mahdi' (Cambridge: Harvard University Press, 1992) 35-40

Calder, Norman, 'Tafsir from Tabari to Ibn Kathir', in *Approaches to the Quran,* G.R. Hawting and Abdul-Kader A. Shareef ed. (London: Routledge, 1993), 105 and 124

Can, Şefik, *Fundamentals of Rumi's thought: A Mevlevi Sufi Perspective* (New Jersey, USA: The Light, 2005), 212-216

Chittick, C. William, 'The Perfect Man as the Prototype of the Self in the Sufism of Jāmī', *Studia Islamica,* Maisonneuve & Larose, 49 (1979), 135-157

Chittick, C. William, *The Sufi Path of Knowledge* (Albany: Sunny Press, 1989), 21-22

Chittick, C. William, *The Sufi Path of Love: The Spiritual Teachings of Rumi* (Albany: University of New York Press, 1983), 236-245

Corbin, Henry, '*Avicenna and the Visionary Recital*', trans. by W.R. Trask, Bollingen Series LXVI (Princeton N.J: Princeton University Press, 1988), 73

Crow, K. Douglas, *Roots of Sunni Traditionalism, Fear of Reason and the Hashwiyah* (Singapore: S. Rajaratnam School of International Studies, 2008), 1-55

Dastgir, Golam, 'Contextual Analysis of the Concept of Nafs' in *Copula*, 16 (1999)

De Saussure, Ferdinand, *Course in General Linguistics*, ed. by Charles Baily and Albert Sechehaye in collaboration with Albert Reidlinger, trans. by Wade Baskin (New York: Philosophical Library, 1959)

Donner, M. Fred, '*The Cambridge Companion to the Quran*', ed. by J.D. McAuliffe (Cambridge University Press: Cambridge, 2006), 28.

Druart, T. 'Al-Kīndīs's Ethics' in *The Review of Metaphysics, a Philosophical Quarterly*, 47, 2 (December, 1993), 329-357

Edinger, F. Edward, *Ego and Archetype, Individuation and the Religious Function of the Psyche* (Boston: Shamhala, 1992), 48-50

Encyclopedia of Islam, 1999, Al-Jubbāī, Islamic Philosophy online: www.muslimphilosophy.com/ei2/Jubai.htm)

Epictetus, *The Stanford Encyclopaedia of Philosophy* (2008), accessed online: http://plato.standford.edu/entries/epictetus/ 20 December 2013

Fakhry, Majid, 'The Platonism of Miskawayh and Its Implications for His Ethics' in*Studia Islamica*, 42 (1975), 39-57

Fakhry, Majid, *A History of Islamic Philosophy* (New York: Columbia University Press, 2004), 45-66

Faruki, Kemal, 'Al-Aḥkām al-Khamsah: the Five Values', *Islamic Studies*, 5, 1, March 1966, 43-98

Frances, Allen, 'The New Crisis of Confidence in Psychiatric Diagnosis', *Ann Intern Med.* (2013), 159, 3, 221-222

Frank, H. Daniel, 'Ethics' in Seyyed Hossein Nasr and Oliver Leaman eds., *History of Islamic Philosophy* (London: Routledge, 1996), 959-968

Genequand, Charles, 'Metaphysics', in Seyyed Hossein Nasr and Oliver Leaman eds., *History of Islamic Philosophy* (London and New York: Routledge 1996), 783-798

Geoffroy, Eric, *Introduction to Sufism: The Inner Path of Islam* (Indiana: World Wisdom, 2010), 4-5

Gianotti, J. Timothy, *Al-Ghazālī's Unspeakable Doctrine of the Soul: Unveiling the Esoteric Psychology and Eschatology of the Iḥyā* (Leiden: Brill, 2001)

Gill, Christopher, *The Discourses of Epictetus* (London: J.M. Dent, 1995)

Gilliat-Ray, Sophie, 'From "visiting minister" to "Muslim chaplain": the Growth of Muslim Chaplaincy in Britain, 1970-2007', in Eileen Barker ed., *The Centrality of Religion in Social Life: Essays in Honour of James A. Beckford* (Aldershot: Ashgate, 2008), 145-160

Goffman, Daniel, *The Ottoman Empire and Early Modern Europe: New Approaches to European History* (Cambridge: Cambridge University Press, 2002)

Goodman, E. Lenn, *Avicenna* (Ithaca: Cornell University Press, 2006), 155

Groff, Peter, 'Al-Kindi and Nietzsche on the stoic Art of Banishing Sorrow' in *The Journal of Nietzsche Studies*, 28 (2004), 139-173

Hamarneh, S., 'Al-Kindi, a Ninth-century physician, Philosopher and Scholar' in *Medical History Journal*, 9, 4, October 1965, 328-342

Haque, Amber, 'Psychology from Islamic Perspective: Contributions of Early Muslim Scholars and Challenges to Contemporary Muslim Psychologists', *Journal of Religion and Health*, 43, 4 (2004), 359

Hasan, Ahmad, 'The Concept of Infallibility in Islam', *Islamic Studies*, 11, 1 (1972), 1-11

Hick, John, *Evil and the God of Love* (New York: Palgrave Macmillan, 2007)

Horwitz, V. Allan and Wakefield, C. Jerome, *The Loss of Sadness: How Psychiatry Transformed Normal Sorrow into Depressive Disorder* (New York: Oxford University Press, 2007) 59

Hudson, W. Deal, *Happiness and the Limits of Satisfaction* (Maryland: Rowman & Littlefield, 1996), 138

Ibn Kathīr, Abū l-Fidā Ismā'īl ibn 'Umar, *Tafsīr al-Quran al-'aẓīm*, on-line English version: http://www.quranwebsite.com/tafsir%20ibn%20kathir/tafsir_ibn_kathir.html

Ibn Rushd, Abu Al-Walid M. Ibn Ahmad, *Tahafut-al-Tahafut* : Averroes' The Incoherence of the Incoherence, trans. with intr. and notes by Simon Van den Bergh (Oxford: Luzac,1954)

Izutsu, Toshihiko, *Ethico Religious Concepts in the Quran* (McGill-Queen's University Press: 2007), 3

Izutsu, Toshihiko, *God and Man in the Koran: Studies of the Qur'anic Weltanschauung* (Tokyo: Keio Institute of Cultural and Linguistic Studies, 1964) 11

Jayyusi-Lehn, Ghada, 'The Epistle of Ya'qu'b ībn Isha'q al-Kīndī: On The Device for Dispelling Sorrows' in *British Journal of Middle Eastern Studies*, 29, 2 (2002), 121-135

Joseph, Stephen, 'Agents of Control', *The British Psychological Society* (July 2007), 20, 429-431

Jurji, Edward, Jabra, *Illumination in Islamic Mysticism* (Princeton: Princeton University Press, 1938), 14

Karaca, Faruk, *Modern Thanatological Researches and Ibn Sina (Avicenna)*, Conference paper, downloaded on 24 July 2014, www.interdisciplinary.net/ptb/mso/dd/dd3/karaca%20paper.pd

Kassem, Hammond and Crim, Elias., '*The Ideas of Justice in Islamic Philosophy*' (September 1972), on-line version downloaded 25 August 2014, http://dio.sagepub.com/content/20/79/81.citation

Keeler, Annabel, 'Joseph: In Qur'ānīc Exegesis', *Encyclopaedia Iranica* (2009), 15, 1, 34-41

Kobeisy, Ahmed Nezar, 'Faith-Based Practice: An Introduction', *Journal of Muslim Mental Health* (2006), 1, 57-63

Koenig, G. Harold, *Faith and Mental Health Religious Resources for Healing* (Philadelphia and London: Templeton Foundation Press, 2005), 43-81

Kuşpinar, Bilal, '*Nursi's Evaluation of Sufism*'. Paper delivered at the Third International Symposium of Bediuzzaman Said Nursi. Paper downloaded on 6 November 2015, http://www.iikv.org/academy/index.php/sympeng/article/view/902/1229

Leaman, Oliver, 'Al-Balkhi, Abu Zayd', *The Biographical Encyclopedia of Islamic Philosophy* (London: Bloomsbury Publishing PLC, 2006), 48-49

Leaman, Oliver, *The Quran: An Encyclopedia*, ed. by Oliver Leaman, (Routledge: London, 2006)

Long, A.A., *Hellenistic Philosophy: Stoics, Epicureans, Sceptics* (University of California Press: Berkeley, 1986), 107-152

Mardin, Şerif, *Religion and Social Change in Modern Turkey: The Case of Bediuzzaman Said Nursi* (Albany: State University of New York Press, 1989), 23

Martelli, Anna Maria, *Islamic Images and Ideas: Essays on Sacred Symbolism* (North Carolina: McFarland & Company, 2014), 70

Mawdūdī , Sayyid Abul A'lā, 'Towards Understanding the Quran', ed. by Jane Dammen McAuliffe, *Encyclopedia of the Quran* (Boston 2002), 2

Mawdūdī , Sayyid Abul A'lā, 'Towards Understanding the Qur'ān: abridge version of *Tafhīm al-Qur'ān*, ed. and trans. by Zafar Ishaq Ansari (Leicester: Markfield Islamic Foundation, 2006)

McAuliffe, Jane Dammen ed., *The Cambridge Companion to the Qur'ān* (New York: Cambridge University Press, 2006) 32-33

McMahon, M. Darrin, 'What Does the Ideal of Happiness Mean?' *Social Research*, 77, 2 (2010), 469-490

Mir Valiuddin, Mu'tazilīsm, in 'A History of Muslim Philosophy', ed. by M.M. Sharif, 1,Book Three, Chapter Ten, *Islamic Philosophy on-line* (2004), accessed 9 May 2015 http://www.muslimphilosophy.com/hmp/index.html

Miskawayh, Ahmad ibn-Muḥammad, *The Refinement of Character*, trans. by Constantine K. Zurayk (Beirut: Heidelber Press, 1968)

Mohaghegh, Mehdi, 'Notes on the Spiritual Physic of Al-Rāzī', in *Studia Islamica,* 26 (1967), 6

Mohamed, Y., 'Greek Thought in Arab Ethics: Miskawayh's Theory of Justice', in *Phronimon*, 2 (2000), 242

Murray, J.L. Christopher and Lopez, D. Alan, 'Evidence-Based Health Policy Lessons from the Global Burden of Disease Study', *Science* (1996), 274, 740-743

Mutahhari, Murtadā, 'Understanding the Uniqueness of the Quran', trans. By Mahliqa Qara'i, *Al-Tawhid*, 1 (*Muharram – Rajab* 1404 AH), http://www.alseraj.net/maktaba/kotob/english/women/Womenin/al-tawhid/default.htm accessed 29 October 2013

Nakamura, Kojiro, 'Imām Ghazālī's Cosmology Reconsidered with Special Reference to the Concept of "Jabarūt"' in *Studia Islamica*, 80 (1994), 32

Nasr, Seyyed Hossein and Leaman, Oliver, *History of Islamic Philosophy* (London: Routledge, 1996), 254

Nicholson, A. Reynold, *The Mystics of Islam* (London: Arkana, 1989), 36-39

Nursi, Bediuzzaman Said, *Letters*, trans. by Şükran Vahide (Istanbul: Sözler Neşriyat, 1994)

Nursi, Bediuzzaman Said, *The Reasonings: A Key to Understanding the Qur'an's Eloquence*, trans. by Hūseyin Akarsu (New Jersey: Tughra Books, 2008), 4

Nursi, Bediuzzaman Said, *The Damascus Sermon* (Istanbul: Sozler Publications, 1996), 26-27

Nursi, Bediuzzaman Said, *The Rays Collection*, trans. by Şükran Vahide (Istanbul: Sözler Neşriyat, 1998)

Nursi, Bediuzzaman Said, *The Words: On the Nature and Purposes of Man, Life and All Things*, trans. by Şükran Vahide (Istanbul: Sözler Neşriyat, 2008)

Nursi, Bediuzzaman Said, *The Flashes Collection*, trans. by Şükran Vahide (Istanbul: Sözler Neşriyat, 1995)

Nursi, Bediuzzaman Said, *Signs of Miraculousness*, trans. by Şükran Vahide (Istanbul: Sözler Publications, 2007)

Omar 'Abdul Mannān, *Dictionary of The Holy Qur'ān* (United States: Noor Foundation, 2005)

Ormsby, Erin Linn, *Theodicy in Islamic Thought: Dispute over Al-Ghazali's "Best of All Possible Worlds"* (New Jersey: Princeton Legacy Library, 1984)

Pavlin, James, 'Sunni kalām and theological controversies' in *History of Islamic Philosophy,* ed. by Seyyed Hossein Nasr and Oliver Leaman,108-109

Plato, *The Apology*, trans. by Benjamin Jowett, accessed on 16 December 2013, http://www2.hn.psu.edu/faculty/jmanis/plato/apology.pdf

Powers, S. David, 'On the Abrogation of the Bequest Verses', *Arabica,* 29, 3 (September,1982), 246-295, URL:http://www.jstor.org/stable/4056186, accessed 14 September 2013

Rahman, Fazlur, *Avicenna's Psychology* (London: Oxford University Press, 1952)

Rahman, Fazlur, *Major Themes of the Quran* (Chicago & London: The University of Chicago Press, 1980), 1-12

Rahman, Fazlur, 'Review of Izutsu's book: God and Man in the Koran', in *Islamic Studies* (June, 1966) 5, 2, 221-224

Robinson, Neal, *Discovering the Quran: A Contemporary Approach to a Veiled Text* (London: SCM Press, 2003), 62

Rouzati, Nasrin, *Trial and Tribulation in the Quran: A Mystical Theodicy* (Berlin: Gerlach Press, 2015)

Russell, Bertrand, *The History of Western Philosophy* (Abingdon and New York: Routledge, 2004), 241-256

Saeed, Abdullah, *Interpreting the Quran, towards a contemporary approach* (New York: Routledge, 2006), 1

Saeedimehr, Mohammad, 'The Infallibility of Prophets from the Viewpoint of Fakhr Al-Din Al-Razi', *Philosophical Investigations* (2010), 6, 17, 125-143

Salkever, G. Stephen, *Rousseau and the Concept of Happiness*, Polity, 11, 1 (1978), 27-45

Scott, S.M. Mark, 'Suffering and Soul-Making: Rethinking John Hick's Theodicy', *The Journal of Religion,* 90, 3 (July 2010), 313-334

Shuman, Joel James and Meador, G. Keith, *Heal Thyself: Spirituality, Medicine, and the Distortion of Christianity* (New York: Oxford University Press, 2003), 34

Stanford Encyclopaedia of Philosophy, 'Epictetus', URL: http://plato.stanford.edu/entries/epictetus/ Accessed 20 December 2013

Still, Arthur & Dryden, Windy. 'Ellis and Epictetus: Dialogue VS. Method In in *Journal of Rational-Emotive & Cognitive-Behaviour Therapy*, 21, 1 (2003), 43-44

Suhrawardi, Shihabuddin Yahya, *The Mystical and Visionary Treatises of Shihabuddin Yahya Suhrawardi,* introduction and trans. by W.M. Thackston (London: The Octagon Press, 1982), 5

Ṭabāṭabā'ī, Muḥammad Ḥusayn, *al-Mizān fī l-tafsīr al-Quran*, 20 vols. (Beirut: Mu'assasat al-A'lamī lil- Maṭbū'āt, 1974)

Tayob, Abdulkader, 'An analytical survey of al-Tabari's exegesis of the cultural symbolic contstruct of Fitna', in *Approaches to the Qur'an,* ed. by G.R. Hawting and Abdul-Kader A. Shareef (New York: Routledge, 2002), 158-59

Topper, Charles, *Spirituality in Pastoral Counseling and the Community Helping Professionals* (New York: Haworth Press, 2003), 9

Trethowan, Illtyd, 'Dr. Hick and the Problem of Evil', *Journal of Theological Studies,* N.S. XVIII, 2 (October, 1967), 407-416

Turner, Colin ed. *The Koran, Critical Concepts in Islamic Studies,* IV (Oxon: Routledge, 2004)

Turner, Colin ed. *Islam the basics* (Oxon: Routledge, 2011), 21

Turner, Colin ed. *The Qur'an Revealed: A Critical Analysis of Said Nursi's Epistles of Light* (Berlin: Gerlach Press, 2013), 4

Turner, Colin ed. 'Wealth as an Immortality Symbol in the Quran: A Reconstruction of the *māl/ amwāl* Verses', *Journal of Quranic Studies* (2006) 8, 2, 58-83

Turner, Colin and Horkuç Hasan, *Said Nursi* (Oxford University Press: Oxford, 2009), 23.

Ullmann, Stephen, *Semantics: an Introduction to the Science of Meaning* (New York: Barnes and Noble, 1962) 7

Vahide, Şūkran, *Islam in Modern Turkey: An Intellectual Biography of Bediuzzaman Said Nursi* (State University of New York Press: Albany, 2005) 71-72

Vahide, Şūkran, *The Author of the Rīsale-ī Nur: Bediuzzaman Said Nursi* (Istanbul: Sőzler Neşriyat, 2000) 33-37

Wadud, Amina, 'Towards a Quranic hermeneutics of Social Justice: Race, Class and Gender', *The Journal of Law and Religion,* 12, 1 (1995-1996), 37-50

Wakefield, C. Jerome, 'The Concept of Mental Disorder: Diagnostic Implications of the Harmful Dysfunction', *World Psychiatry* (2007), 6, 153

Walker, E. Paul, 'The Political implications of Al-Razi's Philosophy' in *The Political Aspects of Islamic Philosophy,* ed. by E.C. Butterworth, 86-87

Waltzer, Richard, *Greek into Arabic: Essays on Islamic Philosophy,* ed. by S.M. Stern and R. Walzer (Cambridge, Massachusetts: Harvard University Press, 1962), 232

Watt, Montgomery, 'Review of God and Man in the Koran and the concept of belief in Islamic theology', *Journal of Semitic Studies* 12, 1 (Spring 1967), 155-57

William Lane dictionary on-line: http://www.tyndalearchive.com/tabs/lane/

Woodward, James and Pattison, Stephen, *The Blackwell Reader in Pastoral and Practical Theology,* (USA: Blackwell, 2000), 5.

Wyman, E. Walter, Jr., 'Rethinking the Christian Doctrine of Sin: Friedrich Schleiermacher and Hick's "Irenaean Type"', *The Journal of Religion,* 74, 2 (1994), 199-217

Zakaria, Idris, 'Ibn Sina on Pleasure and Happiness' in *Advances in Natural and Applied Sciences,* 6, 8 (2012), 1285

Zarrinkub, Abd Al-Husayn, *Sir Nay: A Critical Analysis and Commentary of Masnavi* (Tehran, IR: Ettellat, 1388)

Ziadeh, Farhat J and Winder R Bayly, *An Introduction to Modern Arabic* (New York: Dover Publications, 2003), 21

Zurcher, J. Erik, *Turkey: A Modern History* (London: I.B. Tauris, 1998), 103-104

Printed and bound by CPI Group (UK) Ltd, Croydon, CR0 4YY
09/06/2026
02133011-0001